The Library of Orthodox Theology

No. 4

INTRODUCTION TO LITURGICAL
THEOLOGY

The Library of Orthodox Theology

Published under the direction of
B. Bobrinskoy, O. Clément, B. Fize, J. Meyendorff
and N. Struve

INTRODUCTION TO LITURGICAL THEOLOGY

BY

ALEXANDER SCHMEMANN

TRANSLATED BY ASHELEIGH E. MOORHOUSE

'. . . and thou shalt not cease to do all things until thou hast raised us up to heaven, and hast endowed us with thy kingdom which is to come.' *(Liturgy of St. John Chrysostom)*

THE FAITH PRESS LTD

7 TUFTON STREET LONDON SWI

THE AMERICAN ORTHODOX PRESS
PORTLAND, MAINE

FIRST PUBLISHED IN ENGLISH IN 1966

This translation © Asheleigh Moorhouse, 1966
Translated from the Russian

PRINTED IN GREAT BRITAIN
in 10pt. Garamond type
BY THE FAITH PRESS LTD
LEIGHTON BUZZARD

DEDICATED TO
THE MEMORY OF
ARCHIMANDRITE KIPRIAN
FEBRUARY 10, 1960

CONTENTS

THE TASK AND METHOD OF LITURGICAL THEOLOGY

I

THE study of liturgics, understood as liturgical theology, has appeared comparatively recently within the system of theological disciplines. What was called liturgics in the religious schools was usually a more or less detailed practical study of ecclesiastical rites, combined with certain symbolical explanations of ceremonies and ornaments. Liturgical study of this kind, known in the West as the study of 'rubrics,' answers the question how : how worship is to be carried out according to the rules, i.e. in accordance with the prescriptions of the rubrics and canons. But it does not answer the question what : what is done in worship. It does not set forth the meaning of worship either as a whole or in its separate parts. It does not define the place of liturgical tradition in the life of the Church and her members. In more developed courses of Orthodox liturgics the systematic description of worship is often preceded by brief theological and historical introductions (concerning the institution of the Sacrament by Christ, the development of worship and hymnody, etc.). The theological and historical elements of liturgics are usually disposed of by just such introductions as these. Up to quite recent times, therefore, liturgics has belonged to the category of 'supplementary' or 'practical' disciplines.

This neglect of liturgics, its acceptance as an applied science of interest for the most part to the clergy, but not to theologians, has been hardly accidental. It corresponded perfectly to that form of theology which is now called 'school' theology, which in fact the Orthodox Church borrowed from the West. Enough has been written about the merits and short-comings of this theology.[1] At this point it is only necessary to emphasize that in appropriating the structure and method of the West our theology has for a long time been cut off from one of its most vital, most natural roots—from the liturgical tradition.[2] In the West the rupture between theological study and liturgical experience was already a chronic disease. In the view of one Catholic author, 'theology did not know how to embrace the whole wealth of tradition, and to the present day worship is studied in school either as a part of canon law, or in connection with the history of ecclesiastical institutions.'[3] It is not surprising therefore that the authors of our own 'school' dogmatics in the nineteenth century—Metropolitan

Makary, Bishop Sylvester and others—somehow overlooked the liturgical witness of the Church. Of course they did not deny explicitly the significance of this witness, and occasionally in their works one comes across references to this or that liturgical text, but the whole spirit of their system and method excluded a living interest in liturgics, in a search for those elements in the Church's liturgy which could operate as an independent and indeed theological 'standard of measurement' in the task of expounding the Church's Faith.

What broke through this indifference for the first time was the revival of historical interest in worship. In the old applied liturgics 'historical genesis,' in the words of Professor Glubokovsky, 'was either flatly rejected or just barely tolerated to illustrate in special cases what had hardened into stereotyped inviolability. It was natural that without an explanation of its historical development there could be no objective understanding of the real nature of worship, and without this there could be no thought of correct comprehension or true interpretation. The latter were replaced in fact by scholastic symbolism.' [4] But beginning with the middle of the last century and in connection with the rise of Russian theology of the 'historical school,' [5] a new interest was awakened in the development of worship. The names of N. F. Krasnoseltsev and A. A. Dimitrievsky have a recognized position in the broad field of learning, the latter's name having even something of the glory of a 'Russian Goar.' But these are only two of the best known representatives of a whole brilliant generation of Russian liturgiologists. As stars of no less magnitude we must also mention I. D. Mansvetov, M. N. Skaballanovich, A. I. Karabinov, A. P. Golubtsov, Bishop Porfiry Uspensky and others. All these scholars, in the words of one of them, were inspired by a lofty desire to 'raise our reverent but rather subconscious admiration of the Church's ceremony to the level of historical understanding and conscious appreciation.' [6] It must be admitted that as a result of their work not only did Russian liturgical study win a recognized and glorious position in the realm of scholarship, but also a solid foundation was laid without which it would be impossible to speak of liturgical theology in any real sense of the term. In the West this historical and archeological interest in worship arose before this : as early as the seventeenth century Isaac Hubert (Ἀρχιερατικόν, *Liber pontificalis Ecclesiae Graecae*, 1647) and Jacques Goar (Εὐχολόγιον, *Sive Rituale Graecorum*, 1647) were laying a foundation for historical liturgics upon which the whole edifice was later to be built. [7] Since that time the historical study of worship has continued in the West, supplying scholars with more and more editions of texts, monographs, dictionaries and other aids. Finally a similar revival of historical interest in worship took place also in the Greek and Russian Orthodox Churches.[8]

As we have said, the contributions of this historical phase in the development of liturgics were enormous. But still this was only clearing the way for a genuine liturgical theology or, more accurately, for the growth of liturgics into a genuinely theological discipline. It is characteristic that some of the most eminent founders of historical liturgics did not feel the need for a theological completion of their work. Thus in 1907, for example, in summing up the results of the work accomplished, the renowned French liturgiologist F. Cabrol wrote: 'Liturgics is no longer a young science. It is possible for us to say now that its basic structure has been roughed in and that the various parts of the building are almost complete. The work that remains is not the easiest or the most interesting.' [9] In his opinion this work consisted simply in a constant improvement of that same technical side of liturgics (the edition and criticism of texts, etc.), with the final goal a synthesis in which the whole development of worship would be set forth as a single and organic process. Evidently in the theological categories of the nineteenth century something was concealing the significance of the liturgical tradition and blocking its growth into theological consciousness. Surely one of the reasons for this insensitivity to liturgics as theology must be sought in the similar but even deeper insensitivity of scholastic theology to the theme of ecclesiology, to any real apprehension of the doctrine of the Church. In this respect the fate of liturgics is not only similar to that of ecclesiology in dogmatic theology, but is also directly bound up with it. In order to sense worship as something more than a 'public cult' it is necessary to see and sense the Church as something more than a 'society of believers.' In the meantime, as contemporary theologians have pointed out more than once, the theme of the Church—of her divine-human nature, of her life as the Body of Christ—is almost completely absent in post-patristic theology.[10] The revival of a liturgical consciousness, of a new and in fact theological interest in the liturgical tradition, has therefore accompanied the revival of ecclesiology, that genuine return to the Church which has marked the last few decades.

This liturgical revival or movement, which in the last analysis has led also to the rise of liturgical theology, began almost simultaneously in different parts of the Christian world in the years following the First World War. There is no need here to describe the basic stages of this movement. It had different forms and colourings in each of the Christian confessions it touched, and within these confessions it developed in a variety of ways in various countries. It has its own special history in

Orthodoxy, Catholicism and Protestantism, and already a special literature exists on this subject.[11] What is important for us here is its substance. And its substance lies in the genuine discovery of worship as
the life of the Church, the public act which eternally actualizes the
nature of the Church as the Body of Christ, an act, moreover, that is
not partial, having reference only to one function of the Church (her
'corporate prayer') or expressing only one of her aspects, but which
embraces, expresses, inspires and defines the whole Church, her whole
essential nature, her whole life. 'The Christian religion is not only a
doctrine . . . it is a public action or deed.' [12] It is a return from the
pietistic and individualistic understanding of worship to worship once
more conceived as the eternal self-revelation of the Church. It is a
return through worship to the Church and through the Church to
worship. Once more the catholic view of worship was discovered as the
public service of the spirit-filled people of God, as the 'fulfilment' of
the Church in her divine-human plenitude. It is true that many still
do not understand the real nature of the liturgical movement. Everything is still fettered by the categories of 'school theology.' It is
thought that this is nothing more than a new awakening of an
aesthetically religious, psychological enthusiasm for cultus, for its
ceremonial and ritual, for its external aspects; a sort of new liturgical
pietism. The best answer to this is the fact that the liturgical movement
has appeared everywhere closely bound up with a theological, missionary and spiritual revival. It has been the source of a greater realization
by Christians of their responsibility in the world. It has been a revival
of the Church herself.

The liturgical movement is now leading us directly to the question
of liturgical theology. It should be said that the movement itself—with
the exception of the Benedictine centre at Maria Laach, connected
especially with the name of Dom Odo Casel [13]—was not theological in
the sense of being a systematic and indeed theological elucidation and
interpretation of the liturgical tradition. Its main efforts were directed
toward the practical revival of Church life, by giving worship its real
place and meaning. But in the first place it created the necessary conditions for liturgical theology by its focus on worship, by its experience of worship as the centre of the whole life of the Church. And
second, in its inner development, it finally pointed up the need for
a strictly theological analysis of the data of the liturgical experience and
tradition of the Church. It became clear that without such theological
'reflection' the liturgical revival was threatened either by an excessive
submission to the 'demands of the day,' to the radical nature of certain
'missionary' and 'pastoral' movements quite prepared to drop old forms

without a second thought or, on the other hand, by a peculiar archeologism which considers the restoration of worship in its 'primitive purity' as the panacea for all contemporary ills.[14]

It should be added here that even though the liturgical revival as an organized movement arose and developed for the most part among non-Orthodox people in the West, it has nevertheless a deep internal bond with the Church in the East, and is therefore of special interest to Orthodox theologians. From a certain point of view and with a critical appraisal of each of its achievements, it can be regarded as a kind of 'Orthodox' movement in a non-Orthodox context, since this is the restoration in the thought and life of the Church of those emphases and categories which were in some measure lost by the Christian West. The leaders and founders of this movement have repeatedly declared that in their eyes Orthodox worship bears witness to the 'great liturgical prayer' of the early Church. 'The Orthodox Church,' writes a Catholic historian of the liturgical movement, 'has preserved the liturgical spirit of the early Church and continues to live by it and to draw life from its source.' [15] Hence the special interest in the West in the liturgical tradition of Orthodoxy, the natural sympathy for Orthodoxy. This means that for the Orthodox theologian the material and experience accumulated by the liturgical movement in the West is not something foreign but, on the contrary, one of the most valuable aids to his own work. However paradoxical this may sound, it is very often just the western interest in liturgical tradition, the efforts of just these western scholars, which can help us overcome the defects and limitations of our own scholastic theology. This does not mean that we must blindly accept all that has been done or is being done in this field in the West, nor does it mean the purely mechanical appraisal of western works in the light of the abstract criteria of 'Orthodoxy.' In the western liturgical revival we must know how to discern first of all the question which is being addressed to Orthodoxy, which can be answered properly only within the wholeness of the Orthodox perspective. Since only the 'inner memory of the Church brings fully to life the silent evidence of the texts." [16] Thus the uninterruptedness of the liturgical tradition in the Orthodox Church on the one hand, and the intense liturgical interest and research of the West on the other, form a twofold basis for the creative shaping of Orthodox liturgical theology.

2

In the light of what has been said we may now proceed to a definition of the nature of liturgical theology, of its place in the general structure of theological disciplines, and of its method. Let us begin with a definition.

As its name indicates, liturgical theology is the elucidation of the meaning of worship. Of course liturgics has always had as its goal the explanation of worship, but, as we have just been saying, this explanation was very often content with an elementary and in many superficial and arbitrary symbolism. Even the concept of symbolism was taken in its simplest and most popular sense : as the 'representation' of something. The Little Entrance of the Liturgy was seen as the symbolic representation of Christ going out to preach, the Great Entrance as the representation of His burial, and so on. But in all this it was forgotten that before using this symbolic explanation it is necessary to define the nature and essence of the liturgical symbol and its place in worship. There is also another concept which liturgics has frequently used without clarifying its theological content : liturgical commemoration. It is not hard to say that such and such a ceremony 'symbolizes' something, or that on such and such a day we celebrate the commemoration of something. But in popular usage both these concepts are so vague that their precise meaning must be clarified prior to their use in any explanation of worship.

The examples mentioned are enough to show what the explanation of worship ought to be : it ought to be the elucidation of its theological meaning. Theology is above all explanation, 'the search for words appropriate to the nature of God' ($\theta\epsilon o\pi\rho\epsilon\eta\epsilon\tilde{\iota}$ $\lambda\acute{o}\gamma o\iota$), i.e. for a system of concepts corresponding as much as possible to the faith and experience of the Church. Therefore the task of liturgical theology consists in giving a theological basis to the explanation of worship and the whole liturgical tradition of the Church. This means, first, to find and define the concepts and categories which are capable of expressing as fully as possible the essential nature of the liturgical experience of the Church; second, to connect these ideas with that system of concepts which theology uses to expound the faith and doctrine of the Church; and third, to present the separate data of liturgical experience as a connected whole, as, in the last analysis, the 'rule of prayer' dwelling within the Church and determining her 'rule of faith.'

If liturgical theology stems from an understanding of worship as the public act of the Church, then its final goal will be to clarify and explain the connection between this act and the Church, i.e. to explain how the Church expresses and fulfils herself in this act.

The accepted doctrine of the Church sees in 'the tradition of sacraments and sacred rites' [17] an inviolable element of Tradition, and thus also one of the sources which theology must utilize if it seeks to expound fully the faith and life of the Church. The neglect of this source in scholastic theology is explained by a narrowing down of the concepts both of Tradition and of the Church.[18] But the early Church firmly confessed the principle *lex orandi lex est credendi.* Therefore the science of liturgics cannot fail to be a theological science by its very character and purpose; and theology as a whole cannot do without the science of liturgics.

All that has been said thus far points to the place liturgical theology must occupy in the system of theological disciplines. Of course each of the classifications is conditioned by its own nature.[19] In the last analysis they all have the same goal : the setting forth and explanation of the doctrine of the Church. But some division is necessary, since the one truth preserved by the Church is discovered from different angles and, what is most important, if it is to be discovered at all various methods or means of apprehension are required. In the accepted classification dogmatic theology is the discipline which unites the conclusions of all others and brings them together into a balanced and convincing whole. But that it may be a crowning synthesis there must be an independent 'order' for each of the disciplines which lead into it. If Holy Tradition and Holy Scripture are the sources of dogmatics, neither can be drawn simply from 'texts' and 'proofs'—whether biblical, liturgical, patristic, etc. By using its sources in such an over-simplified way dogmatics frequently overlooks the essential part of the Word of God and Tradition and falls into the error of one-sidedness. In order to use them properly, dogmatics must accept the evidence of Scripture and Tradition not in the form of 'texts,' but in the fullness and interrelatedness of their theological significance. Thus, between Scripture as a 'text' and its use in dogmatics there stands biblical theology, and between worship as a fact and its use in dogmatics there stands liturgical theology. In order to be 'useful' to dogmatics, liturgics must first of all be the independent and complete setting forth of the liturgical tradition. We say 'complete,' because under the old concept of liturgics, its relationship with dogmatics suffered one major weakness : liturgics had to do with worship, while dogmatics used only liturgical texts or separate rites. In the meantime, as has been said above, worship simply cannot be equated either with texts or with forms of worship. It is a whole, within which everything, the words of prayer, lections, chanting, ceremonies, the relationship of all these things in a 'sequence' or 'order' and, finally, what can be defined as the 'liturgical coefficient' of each of these elements (i.e. that significance which, apart from its own immediate content, each acquires as a result of its place in the general sequence or order of worship), only all this together defines the meaning of the whole and is therefore the proper subject of study and theological evaluation. To the extent that this study must have its own method, in many respects distinct from the method of other theological disciplines, it is only right that liturgical theology should occupy a special, independent place in the general system of theological disciplines. For without an appropriate theological systematization and interpretation, the liturgical tradition does not 'arrive' at dogmatic consciousness, and there is a danger either of its complete neglect, or of its haphazard and improper use.

Liturgical theology is therefore an independent theological discipline, with its own special subject—the liturgical tradition of the Church, and requiring its own corresponding and special method, distinct from the methods of other theological disciplines. Without liturgical theology our understanding of the Church's faith and doctrine is bound to be incomplete.

3

The question of the method of liturgical theology deserves special attention because the lack of clear methodological principles opens the door to arbitrariness in the theological use of liturgical material. Not a few examples of such arbitrariness could be cited. First of all, we might ask if everything in the immense liturgical tradition which has come down to us is of equal value. Does it all have the same significance? Can it all be equated with 'Tradition' in the theological sense of this word? We know of course that worship has passed through a long and complicated development, and that the contemporary uniformity of liturgical norms in Orthodoxy is a comparatively late phenomenon. The Church has never believed that complete uniformity in ceremonies and prayers is an obligatory condition of her unity, nor has she ever finally identified her *lex orandi* with any particular 'historical' type of worship. Even now, in spite of the virtual monopoly of the Byzantine type of worship, there exists between the various Orthodox Churches a quite significant variation in rubrics and liturgical practice. And it is characteristic of the Church's view that the *Typicon*, the basic rule book for her worship, is in its two basic variants (the Greek and the Slavonic) not called the 'Typicon of the Orthodox Church,' but is referred to in terms of its place of origin : *The Ordo of St. Savva Monastery*, or *The Ordo of the Great Church of Constantinople*.

Liturgical life has developed, it has changed its forms. It would not be difficult to show that it is changing still. The absence of development would be the sign of a fatal sclerosis. But then it is very important to know, first, whether all these changes express the Church's 'rule of prayer' in equal measure, and second, whether it is possible to find in liturgical development itself some law, something which in fact makes it a development of the age-old and immutable *lex orandi* and not just a series of more or less accidental metamorphoses. It is evident that liturgical theology must begin with the historical study of worship. Archbishop Filaret of Chernigov, one of the pioneers of Russian liturgical study, demonstrated the necessity of this approach in the middle of the nineteenth century. 'The historical investigations of worship are important,' he wrote, 'and of value to the holy Church in that they bring to light the inadequacy of the convictions of the Avvakums.[20] For such people the rubrics which they know so well are a set of age-old and unchangeable regulations. Why? Because they are quite ignorant of the history of the Church's life, and in addition because they are preoccupied with their own way of doing things and prize this way above all others. As a result of historical research it is clear and beyond doubt that the Holy Church has acted with reasonable freedom in regard to the ceremonies of worship. She has adopted new orders of services for their beneficial effect upon the people, and has replaced these by others when she saw that they were not altogether helpful or necessary. A theory of worship in the Church which does not rest on historical data is in itself false, and is also harmful in its consequences.' [21]

In contrast to the old historical liturgics which we have been speaking about, the history of worship no longer appears as an end in itself. It is precisely the theory of the worship of the Church which remains as the ultimate problem to resolve. History is needed only to the extent that this theory has from the very beginning expressed itself in facts, has become concrete and has been revealed in facts, and also in these facts has been exploded or distorted. In our liturgical practice there are things which to many people seem to be the age-old tradition of the Church, but which in fact distort this tradition. It is impossible to discern them outside their historical perspective, without comparing facts, just as it is impossible to define the basic path of liturgical development and its general meaning outside a similar perspective. But after historical analysis there must come a theological synthesis—and this is the second and major part of liturgical theology. The theological synthesis is the elucidation of the rule of prayer as the rule of faith, it is the theological interpretation of the rule of prayer. Here the work of the liturgiologist is extremely varied, and it is impossible to give in advance a detailed definition of its approach. However it should be emphasized once again that both historically and theologically the liturgiologist is above all dealing with the basic structures of worship. These structures can be defined as worship as a whole, i.e. the interrelatedness of all the individual services and of each liturgical unit in particular. So then the liturgical cycle of the week could develop, become more complex and find ever newer expressions in hymnody and ceremony, but its basic kernel—the rhythm of the 'Lord's Day' as the day of the Eucharistic commemoration of the death and resurrection of Christ—is integral to the liturgical tradition itself, and in this sense appears as its original and basic structure. The same also with the order of the Eucharist; no matter how it has developed and changed its form in history, it has from the beginning been defined by a certain basic structure ('shape' in the words of G. Dix) and it is precisely this shape which appears as the starting point for the discovery of the meaning of the Eucharist and its development. The concept of 'structure' must be applied also to the offices of the daily and yearly cycles, to the rites of other sacraments, and so on. Historical liturgics establishes the structures and their development, liturgical theology discovers their meaning : such is the general methodological principle of the task. The significance of these basic structures is that only in them is there any full expression of the general design of worship, both as a whole, and taken in its separate elements. They fix the 'liturgical coefficient' of each element and point to its significance in the whole, giving to worship a consistent theological interpretation and freeing it from arbitrary symbolic interpretations. Thus when we compare rubrics which have long been accepted as mere 'rubrical details' and establish their position in their respective liturgical structures, they sometimes reveal their theological meaning and the tradition is as it were 'decoded.' In the light of the discernible general 'structure' of liturgical action the 'details' of the Ordo can reveal something which was at one time expressed by the Church in the language of worship but which we have forgotten how to apprehend directly. Taken by itself the omission of the chanting of the first prayer ('O Heavenly King') during Pentecost is nothing more than a 'rubric,' but if taken in connection with other exceptions to the rule, it reveals the exact meaning of these fifty days in the Church's year, and this in turn clarifies one of the marks of that eschatology which is inseparable from the Orthodox doctrine of the Church. On the other hand, in the rubrics dealing with the 'hours and days' of worship (which seem to every one so secondary that they are constantly broken) the whole theology of time—which is essential for an understanding of Orthodox ecclesiology—lies 'in code.' It would be possible to cite many such examples; at this point they interest us not so much in themselves. They serve, rather, as illustrations of the method used by liturgical theology. From the establishment and interpretation of the basic structures of worship to an explanation of every possible element, and then to an orderly theological synthesis of all this data—such is the method which liturgical theology uses to carry out its task, to translate what is expressed by the language of worship —its structures, its ceremonies, its texts and its whole 'spirit'—into the language of theology, to make the liturgical experience of the Church again one of the life-giving sources of the knowledge of God. What is needed more than anything else is an entrance into the life of worship, into life in the rhythm of worship. What is needed is not so much the intellectual apprehension of worship as its apprehension through experience and prayer.

The question of the plan and subdivisions of liturgical theology would not present any special interest if there were not already signs of the inadequacy and evil effects of scholastic theology. Under its influence, for example, a distinction has arisen in the minds of believers between 'corporate' worship and 'private' worship designed to meet some need. The Sacraments of Baptism, Chrismation, Marriage, not to speak of requiems, funeral services, etc., have fallen into the category of requested ceremonies or 'private' offices.[22] In the meantime this distinction between 'corporate' and 'private' worship is a contradiction of the basic and ancient concept of Christian worship as the public act of the Church, in which there is nothing private at all, nor can there be, since this would destroy the very nature of the Church. Under this same scholastic influence liturgics began to regard the Eucharist as just one among a number of offices or sacraments of the Church, in this way distorting the whole perspective of the liturgical tradition, which has always regarded the Eucharist as the centre and source of the whole life of the Church. Old fashioned liturgics was unable to view critically that realm of the Church's life in which worship had long since in fact been accepted on the one hand as the 'public cult of the Church,' and on the other hand as a 'meeting of needs' governed by the 'demands' of believers. The venom poisoning our ecclesiastical life was as it were 'legitimized' by liturgics which, instead of having as its goal the theological comprehension of worship, thought of itself first of all as an applied science, called only to meet 'practical needs.'

Hence the necessity of reviewing the plan of liturgical theology, of bringing it into a proper relationship with the object of its study and with the method of its investigation.

As we have said, the division in principle between 'corporate' and 'private' worship must be discarded. The purpose of worship is to constitute the Church, precisely to bring what is 'private' into the new life, to transform it into what belongs to the Church, i.e. shared with all in Christ. In addition its purpose is always to express the Church as the unity of that Body whose Head is Christ. And, finally, its purpose is that we should always 'with one mouth and one heart' serve God, since it was only such worship which God commanded the Church to offer. In the same way it is impossible to justify the division of the Sacraments into separate liturgical departments, with the Eucharist regarded simply as 'one among several.' The Eucharist is *the* Sacrament of the Church, i.e. her eternal actualization as the Body of Christ, united in Christ by the Holy Spirit. Therefore the Eucharist is not only the 'most important' of all the offices, it is also source and goal of the entire liturgical life of the Church. Any liturgical theology not having the Eucharist as the foundation of its whole structure is basically defective.[23]

The general plan of liturgical theology proposed here is, of course, not the only one possible. But it does seem to take into account those fundamental conditions related to the subject which we have attempted to identify in the preceding pages.

A study of ecclesiastical rubrics, understood not simply as the expounding of the rules governing the Church's liturgical life but as the general and basic structure of this life, must necessarily be a preliminary step in the study of worship. Before examining the separate parts of the building we must not only sense that we are dealing with a building, but also see it as a whole, having a certain overall design or architectural plan, in which all its elements are set in a mutually dependent relationship. The task of this introduction is to sketch in this whole, to discover this design.[24]

Furthermore, while the Eucharist must unquestionably be placed in the centre of the first part of liturgical theology, the essential nature of the Church being actualized in the Eucharist as the Sacrament of the Church's life, it is also true that the sacraments of entrance into the Church (Baptism and Chrismation) lead us into this life and unite us with this essential nature. They lead into the Church and into the Eucharist, and it is appropriate to relate their theological and liturgical explanation to the study of the celebration of the Eucharist itself.

That form of worship which we shall henceforth call the liturgy of time, which is by its very nature connected with 'hours and days' and is expressed in three cycles, daily, weekly and yearly, forms another clear pole in the liturgical life of the Church. The structure for these cycles, their significance in the Church's 'rule of prayer' and their relationship to the Eucharist—these are questions which must be answered in the second part of our liturgical theology.

Finally, that worship whose object is not the whole Church but rather her individual members will be the third area of liturgical theology. We say 'object,' since the 'subject' is always the Church herself, and the fact that a given form of worship is conditioned by the needs of individual members of the Church does not turn it into a 'private' liturgy. What is accomplished in them is accomplished in the Church, and has significance for the Church; it is its initial cause which lies in the need of the individual Christian. Such worship is connected especially with the Christian's life—it includes all those rites of a non-sacramental nature which are associated with birth (the prayers of the mother and child on the first, eighth and fortieth days); the Sacrament of Marriage; the Sacraments of Penitence and Healing and the whole liturgy connected with death. Up to now liturgical scholarship has scarcely touched this whole area, and yet it occupies a prominent place in the real Church and requires therefore its own theological and liturgical evaluation and explanation.

The plan of liturgical theology may therefore be presented schematically as follows :

Introduction : the Church's Ordo.
1. The Sacraments of Baptism and Chrismation.
2. The Eucharist (and all that is directly connected with it).
3. The Liturgy of Time.
4. The Liturgy of the Sanctification of Life.

Again let us say that this is not presented as the only possible or correct scheme. It seems to us, however, that it answers the purpose of liturgical theology better than former plans. Its intent is not to break down the Church's worship into parts, but to demonstrate it in its wholeness, as an elucidation of the rule of prayer which is always and in all places the same. It can be 'justified' only *post factum*. At present we propose it only as a kind of guide line in the difficult task of reading and apprehending the liturgical tradition of the Church.

4

To conclude these general remarks on the task and method of liturgical theology, a few more words must be said about the 'liturgical situation' of contemporary Orthodoxy which will be the object of consideration in the present work. Without equivocation and with a full awareness of the significance of my words, I define this situation as a profound liturgical crisis. Such an assertion will undoubtedly cause surprise and even indignation among many people. How can this be? Surely everything is as it should be in our worship . . . such is the way the majority of Orthodox people think, and even non-Slavic experts on Orthodoxy are inclined to agree. 'She (the Orthodox Church) has no need to enter the liturgical movement,' writes Dom Rousseau, 'since she has never wavered in devotion to her liturgy, has always remained faithful to it in every way. . . .' [25] And indeed at first glance everything can appear to be just as it should be. Our Church remains a liturgical Church *par excellence* not only in the sense of the uninterruptedness of her ancient tradition of worship, but also because of the place which worship occupies in the life of the faithful, because of the special love the faithful have for the church building and its services. It can be said that in our time the life of the Church has become almost exclusively liturgical, has been reduced to worship and worship alone. 'Love for the Church' (*tserkovnost*) has become a synonym for love of the church building and its worship. The church building, the care of the church and the maintenance of the services, love of worship, of its beauty and reverence . . . such is the main content of *tserkovnost*. Several variations can be distinguished in this liturgical piety. But its general and basic element is always the same : the obvious concentration on worship (in the restricted sense) in the life of the Church and in personal religious experience. Need we be disturbed by this?

But really the question is : Does this contemporary Orthodox 'liturgism' constitute a happy state of affairs? Does it correspond to the Church's everlasting 'rule of prayer'? Is it a realization of that 'worship in Spirit and in Truth' which was given to the Church by the commandment of Christ?

We shall not dwell here on the many rather alarming faults and defects of contemporary liturgical practice, although there are enough of them to make us doubt the complete liturgical soundness of Orthodoxy. They have been dealt with more than once in specialized literature. It is not in these defects, taken by themselves, that we find the essence of what we have called the liturgical crisis. The crisis is connected with something at a far deeper level, and only in relation to this—as its symptom or manifestation—do all the individual shortcomings of our worship life acquire their true significance.

The liturgical crisis consists, first of all, in the mistaken concept of the function and place of worship in the Church, in the profound metamorphosis in the understanding of worship in the mind of the Church. Let us emphasize the fact that we are speaking here about something much more important than the misunderstanding of the texts, ceremonies and language of divine service. We are speaking here about the whole approach to worship and its 'experience.' Worship— its structure, its form and content—remain what they were before and essentially what they have always been. In this sense it is right to speak of Orthodoxy's faithfulness to its liturgy. But to understand it and to use it are two different things. A discrepancy has appeared between the basic purpose of worship and the way it is understood, while the membership of the Church has simply not noticed this discrepancy, and the 'key' which supposedly leads to an understanding of the Church's worship actually excludes the possibility of this understanding. No matter how paradoxical it may sound, what obscures the meaning of worship is that it has become for the faithful an object of love, indeed almost the sole content of Church life.

Just what is this new 'key' and how does it fail to correspond to the nature of worship? The fact is that worship has ceased to be understood as a function of the Church. On the contrary, the Church herself has come to be understood as a function of worship. Christian worship, by its nature, structure and content, is the revelation and realization by the Church of her own real nature. And this nature is the new life in Christ—union in Christ with God the Holy Spirit, knowledge of the Truth, unity, love, grace, peace, salvation. . . . In this sense the Church cannot be equated or merged with 'cult'; it is not the Church which exists for the 'cult,' but the cult for the Church, for her welfare, for her growth into the full measure of the 'stature of Christ' (Eph. 4:13). Christ did not establish a society for the observance of worship, a 'cultic society,' but rather the Church as the way of salvation, as the new life of re-created mankind. This does not mean that worship is secondary to the Church. On the contrary, it is inseparable from the Church and without it there is no Church. But this is because its purpose is to express, form, or realize the Church—to be the source of that grace which always makes the Church the Church, the people of God, the Body of Christ, 'a chosen race and a royal priesthood' (1 Peter 2:9). In fact, to the extent that the Church exists not only *in statu viae* but also *in statu patriae,* she embodies in worship her participation in God's Kingdom, gives us a glimpse of the mystery of the age to come, expresses her love to the Lord who dwells within her, and her communion with the Holy Spirit. In this sense worship is the purpose of the Church, but the purpose precisely of the Church, as the highest and fullest expression and fulfilment of her nature : of her unity and love; of her knowledge of and communion with God. But in the contemporary approach to worship there is the characteristic absence of an understanding of it as the expression of the Church, as the creation of the Church and as the fulfilment of the Church. The Church has been merged with worship, has come to be understood as a sacramentally hierarchical institution existing for the performance of divine

23

worship seen as a sacred, supra-temporal, immutable mystery. The Church is that which guarantees the objective character of this 'sacred action,' its reality, so to speak, and in this sense the Church in her sacramentally hierarchical structure is the instrument of this mystery and is subordinated to it. The Church cannot express, create and fulfil herself in it, because outside the mystery itself there is no Church. There are separate believers, to a greater or lesser extent living individually by sacred contact with it, by the sanctification or nourishment received from it; there is also the 'parish,' i.e. an essentially lay organization, bound together by concern for the presence of this 'sacred something'—for the church building and for the provision of the priesthood that it needs. But the individual believer, entering the church, does not feel he is a participant and celebrant of worship, does not know that in this act of worship he, along with the others who together with him are constituting the Church, is called to express the Church as new life and to be transformed again into a member of the Church. He has become an 'object' of worship, it is celebrated for his 'nourishment,' so that he may as an individual satisfy his 'religious needs.' In the same way the parish does not know that worship, as an expression of the parish, transforms it into the Church, gives it those 'dimensions' which it does not and cannot have naturally. It remains a limited human and only human community, living not as the Church but by its own necessarily limited human interests. Having been turned into something 'sacred in itself,' worship has is it were 'profaned' everything else in the Church : her government becomes juridical and administrative in our eyes; her 'material' life is strictly separated from its spiritual content; and the hierarchy (having become the celebrants of the sacraments only, in which nobody sees the expression, creation and fulfilment of the Church) are naturally pushed out of the sphere of Church administration, finances and even teaching, since all these spheres have become profane and unsanctified.[26] Now the sole content of the Church's life, worship has ceased to be understood in its own real content, which is to be the expression, creation and fulfilment of the Church. The overwhelming majority of Orthodox people have no interest in the meaning of worship. It is accepted and experienced in mystical and aesthetic but never 'logical' categories. It moves the soul of the believer by its sacredness, by its mysteriousness, by its 'otherworldliness.' And everything that happens to fall within its orbit becomes overgrown with complicated symbolic explanations. It is characteristic that in this symbolism there is no symbolism of the Church. Thus, people love to explain the Divine Liturgy as the depiction of the life of Christ. But who explains it as the expression of the life of the Church, as the action by which she is eternally realized?

THE TASK AND METHOD OF LITURGICAL THEOLOGY

Who ever sees that in this action she is not depicting the life of Christ before the congregation, but is manifesting, creating and fulfilling herself as the Body of Christ? The believer loves the ceremonies, symbols, the whole atmosphere of the church building, this familiar and precious nourishment for his soul, but this love does not long for understanding, because the purpose of the cult is thought of precisely as the bestowal of a spiritual experience, spiritual food. For the membership of the Church worship has ceased to be the Church's self-evidencing.

And finally, having become a 'cultic society,' existing in and for the sake of the cult, the membership of the Church has become unable to understand that worship—as the expression, creation and fulfilment of the Church—places the Church before the face of the world, manifests her purpose in the world, the purpose of the people of God, set in the world with a Gospel and a mission. Having ceased to be the expression of the Church, worship has also ceased to be the expression of the Church in relation to the world. It is no longer seen as the leaven which raises the loaf, as the love of God directed toward the world, as a witness to the Kingdom of God, as the good news of salvation, as new life. On the contrary, worship is experienced as a departure out of the world for a little while, as a 'vent' or break in earthly existence, opened up for the inlet of grace.

Our task is not to trace all the reasons for this liturgical crisis. This would require a long digression into the field of religious psychology and sociology. Let us say simply that this metamorphosis in the understanding of worship, this transformation of the Church into a 'cultic society' can in some sense be accepted as natural. Only the question remains : Is it natural for Christianity, for the religion of the New Testament? Does our 'liturgicalness' correspond to the meaning, spirit and purpose of the Liturgy? In order to answer these questions, it is necessary once more to consider the Church's everlasting 'rule of prayer,' and to hear and understand in it the 'rule of faith.' This is the task of liturgical theology.

FOOTNOTES TO THE INTRODUCTION

[1] cf. the appraisal of 'school theology' in Archpriest G. Florovsky's study *Puti russkogo bogosloviya* (Ways of Russian Theology), Paris 1937, Chapter 4, pp. 82–127.

[2] 'The very institution of the schools was a definite sign of progress. However, this transfer of the Latin school onto Russian soil marked a rupture in ecclesiastical consciousness, a rupture between theological "scholarship" and ecclesiastical experience. . . . Prayers were still said in Slavonic, but theology was now studied in Latin. . . . Theology was constructed along western lines.' Florovsky, op. cit., p. 101.

[3] J. M. Dalmais, o.p., 'Le Mystère. Introduction à la Théologie de la Liturgie,' *Maison-Dieu*, 14, 1948, p. 67.

[4] N. N. Glubokovsky, *Russkaya bogosloskaya nauka v ee istoricheskom razvitii i noveishem sostoyanii* (Russian Theological Science in its Historical Development and Present Condition), Warsaw, 1928, pp. 63–4.

[5] Concerning this 'historical school' in Russian theology, cf. Florovsky, op. cit., pp. 322ff.

[6] Quoted from Glubokovsky by Florovsky, op. cit., p. 65. For further listing of names and works of Russian liturgical scholars see Lazar Mirkovich, *Pravoslavnaya liturgika* (Orthodox Liturgics), Sremski Karlovtzy, 1918, pp. 38–45.

[7] Concerning the history of liturgical studies in the West see Dom F. Cabrol, 'Introduction aux études liturgiques,' in *Compte Rendu du IVm Congrès Scientifique International des Sciences Réligieuses Catholiques*, Fribourg, 1898, pp. 299–315; K. Mohlberg, *Ziehle und Aufgaben der Liturgie*, Munster, 1919, pp. 1–36; C. Callwaert, *Liturgicae Institutiones*, I. de Sacra Liturgia Universim., 3rd ed., Brugis, 1933, pp. 56–211; L. Eisenhofer, *Handbuch der Katolischen Liturgik*, Freiburg in Bayern, 1932, pp. 118–41; P. Oppenheim, *Introductio Historica in Litteras Liturgicas*, 2nd ed., Torino, 1945.

[8] cf. L. Mirkovich, op. cit., pp. 35ff.

[9] Dom F. Cabrol, op. cit., pp. 128–30.

[10] cf. Y. M. Congar, 'Bulletin d'Ecclesiologie 1939–1946' in *Révue des Sciences Philosophiques et Théologiques*, XXXI, 1947, pp. 77–96; also his *Jalons pour une Théologie du Laicat*, Paris, Les Editions du Cerf, 1953, pp.65ff.

[11] For a general history and analysis of the liturgical movement: Dom O. Rousseau, *Histoire du Mouvement Liturgique*, Paris, Les Editions du Cerf, 1945; J. H. Srawley, *The Liturgical Movement*, London, A. R. Mowbray, 1954; L. Bouyer, *La Vie de la Liturgie*, Paris, Les Editions du Cerf, 1956; and a special number of the journal *Maison-Dieu*: 25, 1951, 'Avenir et risques du renouveau liturgique.'

[12] L. Bouyer, *Le Mystère Pascal*, Paris, Les Editions du Cerf, 1947, p. 9.

[13] Concerning the Maria Laach movement and Casel's theory of the liturgical mystery, cf. T. Filthaut, *La Théologie des Mystères*, Fr. trans., Paris, Desclée, 1945; also a special number of *Maison-Dieu*, 14, 1948: 'Dom Odo Casel: La doctrine du mystère chrétien.' This also contains a major bibliography. The organ of the movement was the annual *Jahrbuch fur Liturgiewissenschaft*, Vols. 1–15, 1921ff.

[14] On this subject see especially L. Bouyer, 'Ou en est le mouvement liturgique?' in *Maison-Dieu*, 25, 1951, pp. 49ff.

[15] Dom Olivier Rousseau, op. cit., p. 188.

[16] Florovsky, op. cit., p. 516.

[17] 'The term "Sacred Tradition" refers to the fact that those who truly believe in and honour God transmit by word and deed, to one another and as ancestors to descendants, the doctrine of the faith, the law of God, the Sacraments and sacred rites.' (*Catechism*: 'Concerning Sacred Tradition.')

[18] Thus, for example, the author of the well known Catholic survey of Orthodox theology, M. Jugie, hardly mentions worship in his definition of Tradition according to Russian and Greek theologians; cf. *Theologia Dogmatica Christianorum Orientalium ab Ecclesia Catholica Dissidentium*, I, Paris, 1926; II, Paris, 1933; cf. also F. Gavin, *Some Aspects of Contemporary Greek Orthodox Thought*, Milwaukee, Morehouse, 1923, pp. 27ff.

[19] cf. Y. M. Congar, 'Théologie' in *Dictionaire de Théol. Cath.*, 15, col. 492ff, and J. M. Dalmais, 'Théologie et Liturgie' in *Initiation Théologique*, Vol. 1, Paris, Editions du Cerf, 1952, pp. 102ff.

[20] Archpriest Avvakum was one of the leaders of the 'Schism of the Old Believers' which split the Russian Church in the seventeenth century. The schism was centred on questions of ritual.

[21] Filaret, Archbishop of Chernigov, *Istorichesky obzor pesnopisstzev i pes-*

nopenii Grecheskoy Tserkvi (Historical Survey of Hymnographers and Hymns of the Greek Church), Chernigov, 1864, p. 5.

[22] cf. K. Nikolsky, *Posobie k izucheniu ustava* (An Aid to the Study of the Typicon), St. Petersburg, Synodal Typograph, 1907, pp. 6 and 656. Also L. Mirkovich, op. cit., pp. 22–3.

[23] cf. Archimandrite Kiprian, *Evkharistiya* (The Eucharist), Paris, Y.M.C.A. Press, 1947, pp. 25ff.: 'If in our time Eucharistic life is weakened to the point that we have almost completely lost the proper Eucharistic consciousness, and regard the Divine Liturgy being celebrated in our churches as just one of the ceremonies, considering secondary devotional services as no less important in worship, then in the times of genuine ecclesiastical life it was not so. The Eucharist was the basis and culmination of all liturgical life. But gradually everything that was concentrated around the Eucharist as the centre of liturgical life—the Sacraments, prayers, orders of service . . . were turned in the consciousness of Christians into private rites, became the private business of each individual person or family, having (apparently) nothing to do with the concept of the gathered community.' Concerning the relationship of the Sacraments to the Church see Fr. N. Afanassiev, 'Sacramenta et Sacramentalia' in *Pravoslavnaya Mysl* (Orthodox Thought), Vol. 8, Paris, 1951, 1.

[24] Concerning the concept of liturgical 'structures' cf. A. Baumstark, *Liturgie Comparée,* Monastère d'Amay à Chevetogne, 1939, pp. 32ff.; J. Pascher, *L'Evolution des Rites Sacramentels,* Paris, Editions du Cerf, 1952.

[25] Dom O. Rousseau, *Histoire du Mouvement Liturgique,* Paris, Editions du Cerf, 1945, p. 188.

[26] See the development of this thought in Fr. N. Afanassiev *Sluzhenie miryan v Tserkvi* (The Ministry of the Laity in the Church), Paris, 1955.

CHAPTER ONE

THE PROBLEM OF THE ORDO

I

THE worship of the Orthodox Church is conducted according to Ordo, that is, according to definite regulations, according to an order or rite established once and for all. Our Church knows no worship which is not according to Ordo. Moreover the concept of Ordo applies not only to the Church's life of worship as a whole but also, with equal force, to each separate 'cycle' and service. Thus the word Ordo, taken in its basic and general sense, is defined by what we have called the shape or structure of worship. For this reason the elucidation of the content of the Ordo and its place in the liturgical tradition of the Church constitutes the primary task of liturgical theology.

At first glance the notion of Ordo seems so simple that the definition of its nature and function would not seem to present any difficulties. The Ordo is the collection of rules and prescriptions ('rubrics' in the language of western liturgics) which regulate the Church's worship and which are set forth in the *Typicon* and various other books of rites and ceremonies. Thus to know the Ordo is to know the content of the *Typicon* and its 'rubrics'; to fulfil the Ordo is to observe its prescriptions in liturgical practice. But in fact the simplicity of such a definition is deceiving, and it would not be hard to show that a problem has been brewing for a long time in connection with the Ordo, a problem which is not made less urgent by the fact that the majority of the Church's members are either unable or do not wish to notice it. The problem has several aspects or dimensions which must be formulated before we proceed further.

First, the exact scope of the Ordo is problematical. More than half of our liturgical rules are not drawn from the official and written Ordo, the *Typicon*. In the words of Archpriest K. Nikolsky: 'the numerous and varied rules which touch on a single service, and sometimes even on a single prayer, are for a variety of reasons expounded in different ways in different liturgical books, or in different places in the same book.' [1] But even if all these rubrics were to be gathered together and systematized (which is being done in works such as that of Fr. Nikolsky), the plain fact remains that there is a profound lack of correspondence between this written Ordo and our liturgical practice, and here the question of the scope of the Ordo is opened up in all its significance. It can be stated confidently not only that the

Ordo is not being observed in full, but also that such observance is impossible. When an attempt was made at the beginning of this century, in the Kiev Religious Academy, to conduct an 'ideal' Great Vespers—i.e. one in which all the prescriptions of the Ordo would be observed in full—the preparations for this service took more than a year and involved a tremendous amount of historical and liturgical research.[2] This one example is enough to show, first, the extent to which our Ordo is not 'self-sufficient' but requires supplementary instructions for its understanding and proper use, and second, how far our liturgical practice has departed from the prescriptions of the Ordo. It is not just a matter here of 'weakness' or 'laziness.' The fact that many of the *Typicon's* prescriptions cannot be fulfilled is explained, first of all, by the very nature of the book. Later on we shall dwell in more detail on the history of its early development. But even a rapid survey of its contents is enough to convince us that its compilers were making no claim either to a full presentation of the whole Ordo or to the provision of a kind of eternal and immutable norm. Thus the Slavonic Ordo is still called *The Form of the Church's Ritual in the Holy Monastery in Jerusalem,* while the Greek, in spite of the fact that it is called *The Ordo of the Great Church,* is the slightly modified Ordo of the Studite Monastery in Constantinople. In other words the written Ordos were originally the exposition of local rules, the description of how the Church's liturgical tradition was observed under given conditions in a given period. Hence the abundance of prescriptions having a historical and archeological significance, by their very nature temporary and incapable of claiming to be an eternal liturgical norm. Over and above this consideration the *Typicon* elucidates the Ordo of *monastic* worship, i.e. indicates how a liturgical norm is to be fulfilled in specifically monastic conditions of life. As we shall see, the monastic Ordos in ancient times differed from one another, and even now the two Ordos accepted in the Orthodox Church arise from two different types of monastic worship: the Jerusalem and the Studite traditions. In both places general rules were interspersed with rules which would be impossible to fulfil in conditions other than those for which they were established. And finally it would not be difficult to show, and in fact it will be shown in the treatment of the history of the development of the Ordo, that our present *Typicon* represents an amalgam of local rules not infrequently marked by contradictions and obscurities. We come to the conclusion, therefore, that the Ordo is problematical both in scope and content, and that selectivity and judgment are required in its use; i.e., the application of criteria and premises which are not found within it in explicit form.

Not only must the vagueness of the scope of the Ordo be recognized as a characteristic and striking aspect of the 'problem of the Ordo,' but even more the clear-cut divergence between the Ordo and the Church's liturgical life. This divergence touches not just certain disputed or obviously temporary rules, but precisely those which can be accepted as fully defined and capable of execution. We may point, for example, to the attitude of liturgical custom to the times and hours of worship appointed by the Ordo. The *Typicon* prescribes the celebration of the Liturgy in the evening on certain days, after Vespers. We can hardly place this rule in the category of local or temporary rules, since we find evidence for it in all the variants of the Ordo which have come down to us.[3] Yet in fact this rule is not only not observed, its fulfilment would undoubtedly provoke a real schism in the Church, so firmly entrenched is the conviction that the Liturgy must be celebrated in the morning and in the morning only. This conviction is so established that on the days when the Liturgy is prescribed for evening the Vespers is transferred to the morning, but this obvious misinterpretation of the Ordo disturbs nobody, just so long as the rule concerning the morning celebration of the Liturgy is observed. The office most widely attended and frequently conducted in the Russian Church—the short memorial service for the departed (*panikhida*)—is for the most part not even mentioned in the Ordo, and the celebration of numerous 'private' memorials at any time, especially on the day of the Sunday Eucharist, contradicts the entire spirit of the Ordo.[4] And yet this service appeared and is in use. Again, nowhere in the Ordo is there sanction for, rather there is a clear prohibition of the reading of the so-called 'prayer of absolution' apart from the Sacrament of Repentance; and yet this is a widespread practice, and no one seems to have any misgivings about it. Many other examples could be cited. Quite evidently liturgical practice follows its own 'logic,' which does not always coincide with the logic of the Ordo, and in many ways clearly contradicts it. It is hardly possible to explain all this by laziness, indifference, or an accommodation to human weakness. Behind the problem of the scope and content of the Ordo there appears therefore the problem of its meaning, the problem of its 'inner logic,' which, having been misunderstood, has been replaced by another and indeed alien logic.

It is all the more necessary to recognize these problems now, since two approaches to the Ordo are becoming ever more clearly established in the Church as a result of the situation just described, both of which should be recognized as not only false but also definitely harmful. For some people everything that is printed in the *Typicon* or in any 'rubric' is an absolute and immutable law, and to touch or change this material in any way whatever is tantamount to the subversion of Orthodoxy. For such people everything that has at any time or for any chance reason fallen into our liturgical books constitutes, by this fact alone, an unchangeable part of the Tradition, and must be preserved at all costs. The question of a review of the Ordo or of the immense amount of liturgical material contained in the Monthly Service Book (*Menaion*) and the *Oktoichos* is denounced as heresy and modernism by the partisans of this view. To the extent that it is impossible (as pointed out above) to carry out the Ordo in full, it turns out that in the last analysis the deciding factors are taste, local tradition and custom; in other words, accidental factors. What is sometimes called a service 'according to the Ordo' is in fact full of striking absurdities. As a typical example of this legalistic and formal approach to the Ordo we may point to the 'Orders of Service' so often seen in our churches. In such 'Orders' not one of the parts of the liturgy is preserved in its complete form, each is simply 'denoted.' Thus the reading of the appointed psalms (*kathisma*) is reduced to a few verses taken from each psalm, to 'denote' the division of each *kathisma* into three parts. The chanting of the *canon* is reduced to two or three hymns (*troparia*) taken from different *canons,* in order to 'denote' the rules of their composition. All this is done with the general intention of 'reading through' (or 'singing through') as much as possible in the time available, even at the expense of the intelligibility of the chanting and reading.

The second approach, which is even more widespread than the first, may be described as essentially indifference to the Ordo or structure of worship as such. The Ordo is not denied in principle. But it remains simply as a kind of background, allowing the most 'popular' moments of worship to stand out and be performed with maximum effect. But these very moments gradually lose their connection with the structure of the service and become, as it were, ends in themselves. It is just here that the obvious crisis in Church singing can be traced with special accuracy. Once a most important element of the liturgical structure, it is being torn away more and more from the overall scheme of worship, from its structure, and in ceasing to be the expression of this structure it very often becomes the expression only of 'what is human . . . all too human.'

It is precisely in these two approaches, to the same degree although in different ways witnessing to the loss of an understanding of the Ordo and of any interest in its meaning and intent, that the problem of the Ordo is revealed in its spiritual and theological significance. Little by little the belief has been created within the Church that the

Ordo does not even require understanding. It has come to be a dead letter which either must be followed blindly, or may be ignored just because of its lifelessness, with the selection from it of that which pleases or can make an impression on the congregation. Now the question must be asked: Does this view of the Ordo—as a Law, as an incomprehensible Rule, or finally as Custom—does this view correspond to the worship 'in Spirit and Truth' which is to be offered to God by the Church as the People of God, a royal priesthood, a chosen people, the Body of Christ? This is the real and fundamental problem of the Ordo. On the one hand the whole liturgical tradition of the Church witnesses to the fact that the Ordo is an essential part of the Church and that ideas of 'rite,' order and structure are contained in the very idea of worship. Even the violations of the Ordo, as we have seen, strive to become in themselves a 'rule' or norm. It can hardly be doubted that in spite of the vagueness of the scope and content of the Ordo, the Church's worship continues to be defined by a certain general norm or structure which remains always unchanged; the adaptation or violation of written rubrics does not violate this structure to the extent that it cannot be recognized. On the other hand, the Ordo cannot be unrelated to the very nature of Christian worship as worship 'in Spirit and Truth,' as a 'reasonable service' (λογικὴ λατρεία), a service of Logos and Meaning. It cannot be unrelated to the essence of the Church as the new people of God and the Body of Christ, living not by the law but by grace. It can be neither a law requiring blind submission to the letter and nothing more, nor a good and ancient custom to be fulfilled only insofar as it corresponds to the 'demands of the times' or to the taste of those who are praying. On the contrary the meaning of the Church's liturgical life must be contained within the Ordo, insofar as it defines the general structure or 'rite' of her worship. Torn away from this meaning, the Ordo becomes a lifeless and meaningless 'law.' And if it is torn away from liturgical practice, the latter is surrendered to the mercy of the customs, tastes and whims of this or that epoch, making liturgical practice the expression of these customs and tastes but not of the Church in her spiritual and eternal vocation.

To find the Ordo behind the 'rubrics,' regulations and rules—to find the unchanging principle, the living norm or 'logos' of worship as a whole, within what is accidental and temporary: this is the primary task which faces those who regard liturgical theology not as the collecting of accidental and arbitrary explanations of services but as the systematic study of the *lex orandi* of the Church. This is nothing but the search for or identification of that element of the *Typicon* which is presupposed by its whole content, rather than contained by it, in short, its general 'philosophy.' It is the elucidation of those principles and premises upon which all the regulations contained within it are founded. It is not hard to explain the absence of this general element in the *Typicon* itself : the written Ordo arose after worship, and arose not as the elucidation of its theory, or as the outline of a liturgical rite for given conditions, or even as an aid for deciding disputed questions of liturgical practice.[5] The relationship of the written rubrics to worship itself is analogous to the relationship of the canons to the structure of the Church. The canons did not create the Church or determine her structure; they arose for the defence, clarification and definition of that structure which already existed and is essential to the very nature of the Church. The written Ordo does not so much determine the law of worship as it adapts this law to this or that need. And this means that it presupposes the existence of this law or 'general element.' The search for, elucidation and explanation of, this basic principle constitutes the problem of the Ordo.

Methodologically this problem falls naturally under three headings. First the question must be raised as to the nature of the basic structure of worship presupposed, revealed and established by our present rubrics, by the whole collection of rules which regulate the liturgical life of the Church today. In order to be true to its calling, liturgical theology must always draw its conclusions from the concrete data of the living tradition of worship, from the liturgical facts. On more than one occasion we have been made aware of the way in which a theory of worship formed *a priori,* without sufficient attention being paid to liturgical reality in all its variety and complexity, can lead along false paths. It can even be said that this rupture between theory and fact is the central drama in the history of worship. Therefore, before attempting to clarify the Ordo as the τύπος of worship, we must define its basic outlines, discover the form or structure of worship which it presupposes. The second point to be considered is the question of the origin and development of this structure, of the history of the Ordo. We have already indicated why the historical moment in liturgical theology occupies such an important place. Later we shall see that the question of origin and development has a quite special significance with regard to the Ordo. Finally, the third question which we must try to answer concerns the meaning of the Ordo, its theological content as the *lex orandi* of the Church, as something inseparable from this *lex orandi.*

2

One would think that even a superficial acquaintance with the Ordo would be enough to convince the reader that it is based on the com-

C

bination of two fundamental elements : the Eucharist (with which all the other Sacraments are connected in some way), and that form of worship which in the language of western liturgics is called *officium divinum,* connected above all with the three cycles of time : daily, weekly and yearly.[6]

It need hardly be demonstrated that both these elements are essential in the present day Ordo. The centrality of the Eucharist in the liturgical life of the Church is self-evident. The weekly and yearly cycles also do not raise any difficulties. The daily cycle, however, has practically fallen out of use in the majority of parish churches. Its neglect obviously does not correspond to the spirit and letter of the Ordo. On the contrary, according to the Ordo it is the indispensable and necessary framework for the whole liturgical life of the Church. According to the Ordo there are days when the celebration of the Liturgy is not permitted, or when one 'commemoration' or 'feast' replaces another, but there are no days when Vespers and Matins are not to be said. And all the feasts and commemorations are always combined with the constant, unchanging material of the daily cycle.

It is evident that the Eucharist and the 'liturgy of time' are separate and distinct elements in the liturgical tradition. While the dogmatist may be content to express this distinction in categories of 'sacramental' and 'non-sacramental' worship, such a definition is inadequate from the standpoint of liturgical theology. It does not indicate the principle of the relationship of these two elements in the common structure of the Church's worship. It does not show how they are both elements of the Ordo. In the meantime, from a study of this Ordo, it is quite apparent that the Eucharist (the 'sacramental' element) and the 'liturgy of time' (the 'non-sacramental' element) do not simply 'co-exist' in the liturgical life of the Church, but are connected in such a way that this connection actually constitutes the Ordo in its general and basic form. What then is the nature of this connection?

On the level of simple description and analysis we can assert that the relationship of these two elements of the Ordo to time is the principle both of their relatedness and their differentiation. The question of time, as we shall try to show, has an outstanding importance for liturgical theology. But even without raising the question here in its theological context, it is easy to show how the connection of these two elements of worship with time sets them off as two distinct areas in the Church's liturgical life, and at the same time defines the method of connecting them with one another in the Ordo, the method of their 'structural inter-relation.'

The worship of the Church has at its real centre the constant renewal and repetition in time of the one unchanging Sacrament; unchanging, that is, in its meaning, content and purpose. But the whole significance of this repetition is in the fact that something unrepeatable is being recalled and actualized. The Eucharist is the actualization of one, single, unrepeatable event, and the essence of the Sacrament consists first of all in the possibility of the conquest of time, i.e. the manifestation and realization (within this Sacrament) of a past event in all its supra-temporal, eternal reality and effectiveness. No matter when the Liturgy is celebrated, on Sunday, a Feast Day, or on any day, in the daytime or at night, it is essentially independent of the day or hour; it is not determined or restricted by them. From this standpoint the time of its celebration is unimportant, since what is being accomplished in the service introduces and incorporates us into a reality which is in no way subject to time; 'O Son of God, receive me this day as a partaker of thy Mystical Supper. . . .' All theological theories of the Sacrament agree that its meaning lies in the fact that while it is performed as a repetition in time, it manifests an unrepeatable and supra-temporal reality.

On the other hand the second liturgical 'area' of the Church may be given the name 'liturgy of time' because here time is not only the external and natural framework, but in a sense also the very object of worship, the principle defining its content. This is most clearly seen in the liturgy of the daily cycle. If only by their names—Matins, Vespers, Hours, etc.—the services of this cycle point to their temporal 'colouring,' to their inseparability from time. But also in the other cycles the connection with fixed times and hours and periods is not only a natural and irremovable condition, it also, in an important way, defines their content. It was no accident that the development of the yearly cycle began with disputes over the time of the celebration of Easter, or that in the history of the Nativity cycle the significance of the dates of December 25th and January 6th have primary importance. It may be concluded that the relationship between the Church year and the 'natural' year, this intentional and obvious connection of worship with time, constitutes one of the characteristic elements of the Church's liturgical life. The same can be said about the weekly cycle, which is still based on the age-old celebration in the Church of the 'Lord's Day,' which in turn presupposes a whole 'theology of the week.'

But if the relationship of worship to time is thus a principle of differentiation, it is also true that time is a principle binding both the above-mentioned liturgical areas into a single unified structure or Ordo. If on the one hand the Ordo emphasizes the fact that the

35

Eucharist is not essentially connected with any definite time (in the Eucharistic canon there is almost no mention of particular festivals or days, and there are morning, evening as well as night-time Liturgies specified in the Ordo), still, on the other hand, all references to the celebration of the Eucharist are inseparably connected with the liturgy of time, are placed in some relation to time. Thus in the scheme of the daily cycle the Eucharist can occupy various places : before Vespers, after Vespers, etc., but these variations are not accidental, they are fixed precisely according to the Ordo. The celebration of the Eucharist is placed within the framework of the liturgy of time, so that being neither bound essentially to time nor determined by it, it is a 'correlative' of time. This is seen even more clearly in the weekly cycle, where the Eucharist has its own day—the Lord's Day or Sunday. As we shall see later, however, its connection with this day or unit of time is not at all like the connection of non-sacramental worship with time. As for the position of the Eucharist in the worship of the yearly cycle, this is indicated by the connection of the Eucharist with feast days, a relationship which requires further clarification by liturgical theology, but which in any case definitely testifies to the link which exists between the Eucharist and the liturgy of 'times and seasons.'

Thus the most superficial and preliminary analysis of the Ordo, as it has come down to us and as it governs the liturgical life of the Church to-day, shows that this connection between the Eucharist and the liturgy of time contains a clue to the understanding of the Ordo. Only with reference to the Eucharist and within it can the other principles of the Ordo be understood and explained in their true light. If this fundamental connection or structure exists, then clearly it must be the first object of any historical and theological study of the Ordo. If this connection is at the basis of our contemporary Ordo, does it correspond to an original norm? And if so, then what is its theological significance? What does it represent and express in our liturgical tradition?

3

In concluding this chapter a few words must be said about that new spiritual and theological perspective which the modern liturgical movement is creating for the study of the problem of the Ordo. Our day is marked by an unmistakable Eucharistic revival, expressed especially in preaching missions and in the practice of more frequent communion. This revival must be welcomed, of course, as a most happy event in the life of the Church, a genuine sign of her spiritual renewal.

But, as with every revival, there is a danger of falling into extremes. Both in the theological theories which have been evolved and in the life of the Church herself there is an increasing tendency to reduce the whole of her liturgical life to the Eucharist alone, to regard it not as the summit, or centre, or source of this life, but in fact as its sole content. It has happened that in joyfully discovering the possibility of a fuller Eucharistic life and more frequent communion, believers are somehow losing interest in the other elements of worship and in the Church's life as a whole. The receiving of communion is becoming for them the 'one thing needful,' the self-sufficient goal and content of all their churchly life. Without even mentioning the fact that such a situation contradicts the Ordo as we have just now described it, it can be asked whether this view corresponds to the nature and purpose of the Eucharist itself, and therefore whether this Eucharist revival is altogether right and sound. Only a fuller definition and explanation of the place of the Eucharist in the general system of the Church's worship can help us answer this question.

On the other hand, within the liturgical movement, more and more attention is being paid to the liturgy of time—the daily cycle; the feast days; the seasons of the Church Year; their origins and theological meaning. But here another extreme is possible and is also making itself felt to some degree : the tendency to fail to differentiate clearly between the various expressions or 'modes' of the Church's worship. The liturgical theology which goes under the name of *Mysterienlehre* and which is connected with the name of Dom Odo Casel and the Benedictine liturgical centre of Maria Laach may be taken as a typical example of this second tendency. The contributions of this centre in the work of liturgical renewal in the West are enormous and should be welcomed by all. But having placed the concept of μυστήριον in the centre of his whole theory of worship, Dom Odo Casel failed to define it in such a way as to draw a clear line between sacramental and non-sacramental worship. On the contrary he seems to merge everything in a general mysteriological terminology. All worship appears as the manifestation and expression of μυστήριον. Though it may be valuable and helpful for liturgical theology, this concept leads to a dangerous theological ambiguity and deprives the Sacrament (in the strict sense of this word) of its 'uniqueness' in the liturgical life of the Church. On the one hand we have the danger of reducing the whole liturgical tradition to a single Sacrament with a corresponding neglect of its other elements. On the other hand we have the widening of the concept of Sacrament to include all worship. In both cases an error in spiritual and theological perspective threatens a serious distortion not only of the

INTRODUCTION TO LITURGICAL THEOLOGY

lex orandi of the Church, but also of her *lex credendi,* as it is expressed, inspired and nourished in worship.

All this makes the problem of the Ordo—the problem of the origin, development and above all of the 'logos' of the basic structures of worship—more than ever the basic problem of liturgical theology.

FOOTNOTES TO CHAPTER ONE

[1] K. Nikolsky, *Posobiya k izucheniyu ustava,* p. 6.

[2] For a description of this 'ideal' Great Vespers cf. M. Skaballanovich, *Tolkovy Typikon* (Analytical Typicon), Kiev, 1915, appendix.

[3] Nikolsky, op. cit., pp. 155–9.

[4] cf. Archimandrite Kiprian, *Evkharistiya,* pp. 25–6.

[5] cf. I. Mansvetov, *Tserkovny Ustav* (Typicon), Moscow, 1885: 'The Church's Ordo, as the systematic rule for the order of services of the daily cycle as well as of the *triodion* and the monthly calendar, is one of the latest of the Church's liturgical books and was composed in the epoch when these three orders had already been formed and taken on a definite shape' (p. 1).

[6] For those who are not familiar with the worship of the Orthodox Church it might be helpful to give a description, if only schematic, of the liturgy of time in its present form.

As we have indicated, this worship is divided into hours, days, weeks and months. The daily cycle, consisting of the following offices—Vespers, Compline, Nocturne, Matins and the Hours (First, Third, Sixth and Ninth, together with the so-called Inter-hours)—forms the basis of this worship. The Ordo for these services is set forth in the *Typicon:* Chapter 1—Rite of Little Vespers; Chapter 2—Great Vespers, with Matins, i.e. the so-called All-night Vigil; Chapter 7—Great Vespers, All-night Vigil and Matins for Sunday; Chapter 9—Vespers and Matins for ordinary days. It is also found in the *Book of Hours (Horologion).* The common material for these offices (i.e. what is repeated each day) is found in the *Liturgical Psalter.* It is taken almost entirely from the Holy Scriptures and includes psalms, biblical canticles and individual verses from the Old and New Testament (cf. the verses sung before the biblical readings—called *prokeimena*). It should also be noted that according to the Ordo the Church day begins in the evening and the first office of the daily cycle is Vespers (cf. Nikolsky, op. cit., pp. 142–354).

After the daily cycle, and completing it, comes the weekly cycle. It does not have its own separate offices, but its material is inserted into certain parts of the daily offices, depending on the day of the week. This material is entirely hymnographical and non-biblical. Each day of the week has its own liturgical theme and this is expressed in a series of canticles. These canticles are called *stikhiras, troparia, kondakia,* depending on their form and purpose (cf. E. Wellecz, *A History of Byzantine Music and Hymnography,* Oxford, Clarendon Press, 1949). They are all divided into eight basic melodies or tones and printed in the book called the *Octoichos.* Each week has its own tone, and so the whole *Octoichosis* is divided into eight parts, according to tone, and each tone is divided into seven days. The weekly liturgy is composed of cycles of eight weeks, which are repeated throughout the course of the entire year, beginning with the first Sunday after Pentecost. Finally there is the third cycle in the liturgy of time, the yearly cycle, which is the most complex in its structure. It includes:

(a) the liturgy of the *Menaion* (Month)—the fixed feasts, fasts and commemorations of saints. The material is found in the twelve books of the *Menaion* and is divided according to dates, beginning with September 1st.

(b) the liturgy of the cycle of the Great Fast (Lent), including the three pre-Lenten weeks, the six weeks of Lent and Passion Week. This material is found in the *Lenten Triodion.*

(c) the liturgy of the Paschal cycle, consisting of the services of Easter, Easter Week, and the whole period between Easter and Pentecost. The *Pentecostarion* is the liturgical book for this cycle.

The liturgy of the yearly cycle includes both biblical and hymnographical material and once again this liturgy does not consist of independent services, but of material inserted into the structure of the daily cycle.

CHAPTER TWO

THE PROBLEM OF THE ORIGIN
OF THE ORDO

I

IF we are correct in seeing the basic structure or 'form' of the Ordo in the connection of the Eucharist with the liturgy of time, then the first question which we must attempt to answer is the question of the origin of this form. Contemporary liturgical scholarship does not give a simple and unanimous answer. The genesis of what we have called the 'liturgy of time' presents the main difficulty. Some historians simply deny its primitiveness in the liturgical tradition of the Church. They even deny the presence of the daily cycle in this tradition. The early Christian cult, in their opinion, was limited to the Eucharistic assembly, and all its other 'expressions' (preaching, Baptism, the Laying on of Hands) were simply bound up with the Eucharist as its indispensable elements. 'The early Church,' writes O. Cullman, 'knows only the following two forms of cult: the common meal, after which there follows always the preaching of the Gospel and Baptism.' [1] G. Dix is even more radical. In his opinion even the night vigils, whose existence in the pre-Nicene Church was never before open to any special doubt, are nothing but the 'invention of liturgical textbooks.' [2] Duchesne [3] and Battifol [4] also deny the presence of the daily cycle in the early Church.

How then did this liturgy of time arise and how did it become the all-embracing framework of the Church's prayer? The historians mentioned above connect its beginning with the rise of monasticism in the second century, which is described as nothing less than a 'liturgical revolution.' [5] No one, of course, has denied the existence of prayer connected with fixed hours of the day, as a kind of distant forerunner of the daily cycle, in the early period of Christianity. The evidence for it among pre-Nicene authors is too clear. But before the fourth century, according to Duchesne, these were exclusively private prayers. The significance of the 'liturgical revolution' of the fourth century lies precisely in the fact that through monasticism these private prayers were incorporated in the official cult of the Church. From the prayers of separate individuals or groups in the Church they became the prayer of the Church. 'Once sanctioned in the Church, private prayer,' writes Duchesne, 'will never again depart out of her life.' [6] The early pre-Nicene worship is thus contrasted with that which begins to take shape after Constantine. The development and proliferation of the other cycles of the liturgy of time is also connected with this same epoch. This means that the Ordo in its present form is not just something which did not exist in the early years of the Church's life, it is in fact the product of a profound transformation, a genuine metamorphosis of the liturgical tradition.

This theory has a two-fold foundation. Such 'pillars' of liturgical scholarship as Duchesne and Battifol were limited by the fact that in their day the study of early Christian worship was in its very earliest stages. The absence of sound and reliable evidence of the liturgy of time in the memorials of that period seemed a sufficient argument for its denial. G. Dix bases his views on entirely different grounds. He believes that the early Church did not and could not have any 'liturgy of time' because by its very nature her cult was eschatological and consequently incompatible with that acceptance and sanctification of the natural 'times and hours' which is characteristic of the worship of a later epoch. 'The worship of pre-Nicene Christians,' writes Dix, 'in its official and organized form—the synaxis and the Eucharist—was an overwhelmingly world-renouncing cult, which deliberately and firmly rejected the whole idea of sanctifying or relating to God the life of human society in general, in the way that catholic worship after Constantine set itself to do.' [7] There could be no liturgy rooted in time, having reference to the times and hours of human life, because the Church herself regarded herself as a departure out of time, as the renunciation of that world which lives wholly in time and is subordinated to it and measured by it. At the basis of Dix's theory there is therefore the affirmation of the purely eschatological nature of the Church and the Eucharist. Indeed her eschatology is equated with world renunciation, with the rejection of any attempt whatever to 'Christianize' the world. Dix explains the development of worship after Constantine, therefore, as primarily a departure from eschatology. He believes that the eschatological experience of the Eucharist was so profoundly modified in this epoch that it is even possible to speak of its 'collapse.' [8] Constantine's world gave birth to a new idea in the Church, the idea of the *sanctification of time,* something completely alien to the early Church. The rise of the liturgy of time and its gradual transformation into the norm of the Church's liturgical life was tied up with this change in outlook.

But the theory which denies that the liturgy of time existed in the Church from the beginning is now contradicted by another theory which traces it back to the very origin of the Church. The English liturgiologist, P. Freeman, defended this thesis as early as the last century, in a now-forgotten book entitled *The Principles of the Divine Office*.[9] In our own time it has received full treatment in C. W. Dugmore's book *The Influence of the Synagogue on the Divine Office*.[10] The theory may be summarized as follows : the structure of Christian worship originates in the worship of Judaism, primarily in its synagogue variation. Hebrew worship can be definitely characterized as a liturgy of time; it is set up in relation to the daily, weekly and yearly cycles. It is only natural therefore to assume the same structure in the worship of the early Christians. Reviewing in the light of this hypothesis all that is known to us now about the earliest stratum of Christian worship, Dugmore comes to the conclusion that all three of the contemporary cycles of the liturgy of time may be traced ultimately to the apostolic period and constitute an organic part of the unchanging *lex orandi* of the Church. 'From the very beginning,' writes Dugmore, 'the daily services, modelled on the synagogue ritual, were common to both East and West, although in certain areas there could also be deviations from the general custom of the Church.' [11]

This is where we now stand in the question of the rise of the liturgy of time, i.e. in the problem of the origin of the Ordo. Must we accept one or other of these theories unconditionally? It seems to us that in spite of the tremendous value of the work of Dix and Dugmore, both of the theories which they have advanced are still really only hypotheses, requiring much further study. In the first place, is Dix right in equating early Christian eschatology with 'world renunciation,' and drawing the conclusion that the liturgy of time was impossible in the early Church? Or that it was incompatible with the eschatological nature of the Eucharist? Does not the whole distinctiveness and uniqueness of the cult lie precisely in the fact that within it various 'affirmations' which seem incompatible and contradictory are actually transformed in a cultic synthesis which removes and resolves these contradictions? And is it not just this synthesis which a genuine liturgical theology is seeking, as the goal of all its efforts to understand and explain worship? So then that eschatology which Dix rightly considers to be inherent in early Christian worship must itself be defined in the light of all the elements of this worship, is itself something yet to be discovered, yet to be found; and then not by way of denying *a priori* those elements which do not happen to come under one possible definition of eschatology. But at least in Dix there is a clear presentation of a basic principle which determined the merging of the Hebrew into the Christian cult, which made the old new, marking the beginning of the already independent development of the new. This principle Dix rightly sees in the exclusive and central place of the Eucharist in the life of the early Church, in the Sacrament which from the beginning Christians regarded as the expression of the whole fullness of their faith. Dugmore, who of course does not deny the importance of the Eucharist, does not make clear the connection between the Eucharist and the worship inherited from the synagogue. Behind the facts in the early Church Dix sees a definite liturgical theology which would explain these facts. With Dugmore, however, there is no clear presentation of a liturgical theology as the unifying principle of the structure and development of early Christian worship. One may therefore ask : Are these two theories really as contradictory as it might seem at first glance? Is it really impossible, after having tested the truth in each of them, to reconcile these truths in such a way that, taken together, they will give us a more complete answer to the question of the origin of the Ordo?

2

No matter what disagreement may exist between the historians of the Christian cult, they all agree on the acceptance of a genetical link between this cult and the liturgical tradition of Judaism as it existed in that period. The study and evaluation of this link has been hindered for a long time by a myth which has been central in liberal theology, the myth of the rebirth of the Church under the influence of the Hellenistic world. According to this myth, the organized catholic Church, as we see her from the middle of the second century on, with her doctrine, worship and discipline, was separated by a deep gulf from her Hebrew beginnings, and was the fruit of the Hellenistic metamorphosis which the original teaching of Christ underwent, it is said, some time prior to the Church's emergence as an organized structure. And it is precisely in the area of worship, above all in the area of 'sacramentalism' (as if this were something completely alien to the Hebrew consciousness), where the major symptom of this Hellenistic metamorphosis is to be seen. As for more traditional and confessional liturgical study, we have already pointed out that here the question concerning the beginnings or early sources of Christian worship was not even posed. As strange as it may seem, the problem of the liturgical connection between the Church and Judaism has for a long time been simply unnoticed.

To-day we may assume that this Hellenistic myth in its pure form has finally been laid to rest. There is no need for us to dwell here on that careful re-examination to which the hitherto generally accepted theories about early Christianity have been subjected over the past several decades. It is enough to point out the general significance and chief results of this re-examination. There has been a restoration to its proper place of the fundamental principle of Judaism in the Church, the *interpretatio judaica,* and its acceptance as a decisive factor in the historical 'formulation' of Christianity. The question of the Hebrew origins of Christian worship has been raised once again in historical liturgics in connection with this general reappraisal. The works of Oesterley,[12] Jeremias,[13] Dix,[14] Gavin,[15] Baumstark,[16] Dugmore,[17] and after them the study of the new material discovered at Qumran,[18] have all shown clearly the general dependence of Christian prayer and cult on the cult of the synagogue, and this in turn has begun more and more to attract the attention of Hebrew liturgiologists.[19] This comparative study of early Christian worship and the liturgical forms of Judaism, although it is by no means finished, leaves no doubt about the formal dependence of the former upon the latter, 'No one studying the pre-Christian forms of Hebrew worship and the prayer of the Church,' writes Oesterley, 'can fail to notice the similarity of atmosphere or fail to see that both are cast in the same form. . . . In spite of all the differences they are undoubtedly one and the same type of worship.'[20] It is impossible to cite all the material which has been gathered and studied thus far. We shall only emphasize the fact that this dependence is by no means restricted to that biblical terminology or to those biblical linguistic forms and constructions which are common to both Hebrew and Christian worship. We are dealing here, above all, with a structural dependence, a similarity in plan of whole services, with what Baumstark has called 'great liturgical units'; in other words, with those basic elements which in both cases determine the formation of the liturgy, its content and general movement. Thus, for example, if such things as the blessing of the name of God, praise, confession of sins, intercession and finally the glorifying of God for His work in history—as elements set in a definite order and relationship—if these constitute the normal structure of the prayer of the synagogue,[21] it is to be noted that the same elements, in the same order and relationship, make up the structure of early Christian prayer. We have here a dependency of order, not simply a similarity of separate elements, but an identity of sequence and of the relative subordination of one part to another, which defines from within the liturgical significance of each part. Let us repeat that this comparative study has really only just begun; and yet what has been discovered so far fully confirms Oesterley's conclusion. 'The early Christian communities,' he wrote, 'continued and preserved the traditional form of synagogue worship to which the people who made up these communities were

44

accustomed. . . . So that when the time came for the creation of an independent Christian worship it was only natural that it should be influenced—both in form and spirit—by that traditional worship which was so close to the first Christians.' [22]

It should be noted here in passing that the confirmation of this structural dependence of Christian upon Hebrew worship destroys the argument of those who are inclined to deny the existence of any 'order' whatever in the early Church. The opinion has been held that early Christian worship was 'charismatic' by nature, and had a sort of ecstatic, fluid character which excluded the possibility of any fixed structure, of any unchangeable liturgical Ordo. This worship has been described as an inspired, 'prophetic' manifestation, which only later, in the era of a diminishing of charismatic gifts, was cast in fixed and established forms. There is a religious philosophy which considers every rule a symptom of the weakening of the spirit. But it is just here that the comparative study of liturgical forms has led to the conclusion that the charismatic gifts did not exclude 'rule' and that an Ordo, in the sense of a general structure, was indeed adopted by Christianity from Judaism.

This is especially clear in the case of the Eucharistic assembly. There was a time when the Christian Sacraments in general, and the Eucharist in particular, were considered to be the direct product of the pagan mysteries, of that Hellenistic metamorphosis which has already been discussed. But, as the famous Swedish liturgiologist Brillioth has written, 'the attempts to derive the Sacraments directly from the pagan mysteries are now regarded as one of the distortions of historical scholarship, a symptom of a childhood illness which is common to all youthful sciences.' [23] We now know that no matter how much was absolutely new in the content of the Eucharist, and no matter how much the charismatic manifestations of early Christianity were connected with it in the beginning, still, in its general structure, it derived from a Judaistic prototype, and this prototype determined the whole future development of the Eucharistic 'rite.'

Summarizing the results of this work which has been going on now for many years, Dugmore writes : 'We can and must conclude that from the days of the Apostles the synagogue worship was the norm for Christian worship.' [24]

3

But we must go further and ask : How should this norm be understood? Or, better : What meaning did the Christians of that time attach to it? Research has firmly established the connection between the Hebrew and Christian liturgical traditions. But the establishment of a connection is not yet the explanation of its significance. Surely we fail to take sufficient account of the sense of the absolute newness of life and faith which marked Christianity from the beginning (even in its Judeo-Christian form) if we simply say—with certain historians—that since all early Christians were Jews they naturally and in a sense automatically preserved the structure and spirit of their old worship. 'The old has passed away, now all things are become new' (2 Cor. 5:17). These words of the Apostle Paul express the sense that a profound break had occurred with the coming of Christ. It can hardly be doubted that even before Paul, in the first Jerusalem community, Christians were fully aware of this newness. If in spite of this newness Christians continued to regard Jewish worship as a norm even after the rupture with Judaism, we also have evidence to show that this norm did not contradict the newness of Christianity, but on the contrary had to include this newness within itself in some way, had to find its 'level' within this newness.

From the Gospels and the Acts of the Apostles there is no doubt that Christ Himself and His disciples not only did not reject the Temple and the synagogue, but took part regularly in the traditional worship. It is no accident that the one 'harsh' action in the life of Christ—the whipping and eviction of the merchants—is connected precisely with His zeal for the Temple. Christ observed the religious prescriptions of the Law, accepted the divinely instituted priesthood, the sabbath, the feast days. The Book of the Acts also emphasizes the faithfulness of the Jerusalem Christians to the traditional Hebrew cult. Before the persecution stirred up against them by the Sanhedrin, the Apostles and all who 'continued in their teaching' did not cease also to pray in the Temple (2:46), to observe the fixed hours of prayer (3:1), and the feasts (20:16). Their faithfulness to the Jewish cult, maintained in Jerusalem up to the catastrophe of the year A.D. 66, was so evident that they could call themselves 'zealots of the Law' (21:20), and considering the hostility expressed toward them by the official leaders of Judaism, it is remarkable that there is no mention in the charges brought against them of their infringement of the cultic law.

But another motif runs just as clearly through the whole of the New Testament. Over against the old traditional cult Christ set up a new one—'in Spirit and in Truth' (John 4:23-4). The religious community which He formed in His disciples was not only united by His teaching, but also had its own 'rule of prayer' (Luke 11:1) and its own cultic assemblies. There is evidence also in the Book of the Acts that

Christians already had their own exclusively Christian worship alongside their participation in the traditional Hebrew worship. This included Baptism, the Eucharistic breaking of bread, and common prayer. In fact it was precisely this worship which distinguished them outwardly from other Hebrews. The Christian community could be entered only by way of the Baptismal washing; one could be a member only by participating in the Eucharistic assembly and in the common prayers of the brethren. Although in its outward forms this independent Christian worship clearly derives from specifically Hebrew 'prototypes,' no one would deny its newness in relation to the cult of the Temple and the synagogue.

The history of Christian worship does not begin as the simple continuation of the traditional cult with the inclusion of a few new elements. It begins rather with a situation which can best be described as a liturgical dualism. It is a participation in the old cult and at the same time the presence—from the very beginning—of the cult of the new. Let us stress again that the newness of this new cult comes not from non-Hebrew sources (it is Hebrew both in form and spirit) but consists rather in its new relationship to the old traditional cult.

'In the Temple and from house to house. . . .' It is just this liturgical dualism which constitutes the original basis for Christian worship, its first 'norm.' The study of the early Christian *lex orandi* must begin with the discovery of its meaning; and of course its meaning must be sought in the faith of the first Christians. At the centre of the Judeo-Christian view stands the faith in the long-awaited and now accomplished coming of the Messiah, the faith that Christians belong to the Messianic society. There is no need to dwell here on all the various aspects of this messianic consciousness, which in recent years has been subjected to exhaustive study. For our purpose it is sufficient to recall that from the point of view of this messianic consciousness the 'logic' of the faith of early Christians was the opposite of our own. The modern Christian accepts the Old Testament because he believes in the New. But they believed in the New because they had seen, experienced and perceived the fulfilment of the Old. Jesus was the Christ; the Messiah; the One in whom all the promises and prophecies of the Old Testament were fulfilled. They experienced Christianity as the beginning of the 'Lord's Day,' toward which the whole history of the chosen people was moving. 'So then let the whole house of Israel know for certain that God has made this Jesus Lord and Messiah' (Acts 2:36). But this means that Christianity was for them—as 'Hebrews after the flesh'—not a new religion to which they were converted through a rejection of the old (as pagans were converted later on) but the fulfilment and ultimate

47

perfection of the one true religion, of that one sacred history of the Covenant between God and His people. That newness in Christianity which the early Christians felt so keenly was for them (as Hebrews) not something new in the sense of something completely unexpected, but precisely the fulfilment of what had been promised, the coming of what was expected. Everything was contained in the words 'Jesus is the Christ,' 'Jesus is the Messiah.' But for this reason also the newness of Christianity could not be felt and experienced in any other way than in relation to the old, to that which it was fulfilling and consummating, to that which it was renewing. The Church is the New Israel, Judaism renewed in the Messiah and spread through all mankind; it is the renewed Covenant of God with His people. How well Dix puts this when he writes: 'Christianity appeared in the world not as a clergy performing rites without a doctrine for the benefit of any one they could attract, like the eastern cults . . . not as a digest of intellectual assertions for discussion, like Greek philosophy, but as the Israel of God, renewed in Jesus. Above all as a life (a 'way'), a life determined by God in all its aspects: religious, moral and social; a life which could really be lived only in the 'Covenant' with God and, therefore, in the society instituted through this Covenant by God Himself.' [25]

All this is well known. But it had to be mentioned once more since only in the light of this fundamental messianic standard of early Christian faith and consciousness is it possible to explain correctly the liturgical dualism referred to above. The Messiah came not to destroy the Law, but to fulfil it; to consummate it; to fill it with ultimate meaning. He came to make it effective, to make it Law in the deepest sense of the word; the Law established by God to bring people to an acceptance of the Messiah. Only in Him, only in the Messiah, therefore, do all the ordinances of the Old Testament acquire their true significance. 'Search the Scriptures, for they testify of me' (John 5:39). We may apply this principle also to worship, since the whole divinely-instituted life of Israel is given meaning by its fulfilment and renewal in the Messiah. The Jewish Christians did not simply continue to take part in a cult which had become unnecessary and outmoded for them, they kept this cult as their own, in exactly the same way as when they read the Old Testament they understood it as Scripture about Christ. 'The Scriptures of the Old Testament,' writes Dix, 'remained the Scriptures of the New, because they contained that revelation which He, the Messiah, had proclaimed as His own and which He had fulfilled. Without them not only the Messiah but also the Church herself and all her life would be incomprehensible. In other respects too the Jewish Christians preserved the Law of Moses. . . . As He fulfilled it they too lived the life of God's people, since they were Jews just as He was. What distinguished them from the Jews after the flesh was the fact that in Jesus the Messiah they were now, in Him, the New Covenant with God, while the Old Israel was not . . . [26]

In the light of this Judeo-Christian faith the attitude of Christ Himself to the official cult, as reflected in the Gospels, also becomes understandable. His acceptance of it on the one hand, and on the other hand His insistence on its limited nature, its inadequacy and, most important, His condemnation of that legalistic, external, ritualistic interpretation of the cult which had spread out in the traditions, regulations and explanations of the rabbinical *haggada*. The whole point of Christ's condemnation was that such explanations of the cult obscure and distort the meaning of the cult, turn it into an end in itself, while its true purpose was that through it people might be able to recognize and accept the Christ. The cult must be subordinated to the common destiny and purpose of the Law and the Old Israel. Outside this destiny and purpose it becomes a stumbling block and even a sin. Only by taking all this into account can we understand the meaning of that new cult which from the very beginning constituted the central liturgical act of the Christian community and was the line which divides the Church from the Israel 'after the flesh.'

Where is the essential difference between this new cult and the old? We have already said that from a purely formal point of view the new cult—Baptism and the Eucharist—was derived from the Jewish tradition. It is not in form that we must seek its absolute newness. This newness is found rather in its content : in the fact that these liturgical acts were connected wholly and exclusively with the fact of the coming of the Messiah and the events of His messianic ministry : His preaching, death and resurrection. We have just said that in the light of their faith in the accomplished coming of the Messiah Christians experienced the 'old' cult in a new way, saw in it a meaning which was hidden from the rest of the Jews. But even looking at it in this new way the old cult could only be a prophecy of the Messiah, a figure of the Messiah, an affirmation of the need for His coming; it could not be a witness to the Messiah as having already come, or a manifestation of the messianic Kingdom now coming into being. By its very nature and purpose this old cult revealed and proclaimed a doctrine of God, the world and man which in a way provided all the 'conditions' of the messianic faith, all the 'premises' for the coming of the Messiah. One thing only it could not give—the affirmation that what had been announced in the past had now become a fact. Just as the Scriptures of the Old Testament found their 'key' in the apostolic preaching of

49

D

the Word, in the *kerygma* of the messianic community so the 'old' cult needed to be fulfilled in the new, and only in and through it did it receive its true significance, a significance hidden from those who thought they were preserving and expounding it.

We need not examine here all the countless theories which have been and are still being advanced as explanations for the appearance of the new Christian worship, i.e. Baptism and the Eucharist. Studies of this sort may be found in every textbook on liturgics. Whether the Eucharist can be traced to the simple *kiddush* or passover supper; whether in this connection it is possible to regard the society of Christ's disciples as a *shabburoth* or religious brotherhood, which were quite common at the time and within whose life a shared sacred meal occupied an especially important place; how and when the early Church adopted the rite of Baptism? . . . the answers to these and many other similar questions (upon which the recently discovered Qumran documents are shedding new light) do not alter the basic meaning of this new cult. Its significance was the affirmation and 'actualization' of the coming of the Messiah as an accomplished fact— the actualization of the beginning—in Him—of salvation and new life. There can be no doubt that the new cult has its historical foundation in that 'private' cult which united Christ and the little group of disciples whom He had chosen, in the prayer, the meal and the communion which He had with them. But precisely because Jesus was not just one of many teachers or prophets, but the Messiah Himself, this private cult becomes the cult of the messianic community, its central and so to speak 'constitutive' act. In addition, because Christ Himself instituted this cult as a remembrance of Himself—'Do this in remembrance of me'—it has no content other than Himself, His coming, the work which He accomplished. The disciples understood this cult as the *parousia,* the presence of Christ. In it they 'proclaimed the death of the Lord and confessed His resurrection.' Outside the faith in Christ as Messiah, outside the faith in His *parousia* in the Church, it has no meaning. For this reason also it is inevitably a secret cult, the worship only of those who are already in the Messiah, who are through Him 'in the Spirit and the Truth,' of those who through faith in Him and unity with Him have already entered into the New Covenant with God, and as sharers in the 'aeon of the Kingdom' have received and actually possess the new life.

We come therefore to an explanation of the liturgical dualism of the early Christian community. This is not just a co-existence of the 'old' and the 'new,' to be explained by an incomplete understanding of their faith on the part of the first Christians, as something which will soon change as the 'old' dies out and they become more fully aware of the 'new.' It is rather the inevitable liturgical expression of that relationship between the Old and New Covenants outside of which the preaching of the Christ-Messiah is impossible. Just as the New Testament does not replace the Old, but fulfils and completes it, so also the new cult, if it is to be the cult of the New Covenant, does not replace or abolish the old, but appears as its necessary fulfilment. The permanent revelation of the Old Testament concerning God, creation, man, sin and salvation, lives in all fullness within the New, and it is impossible to understand the work of Christ outside this revelation. Everything to which the old cult bears witness is presupposed by the new. For this reason the new has meaning only on condition that the old is preserved. Only in relation to the old is it both revealed and actualized as something eternally new. We must see the liturgical dualism of Judeo-Christianity not as the accidental phenomenon of a passing era, but as the primary and fundamental expression of the Christian *lex orandi*.

4

Was this *lex orandi* preserved when the Church finally broke away from Judaism, when the Judeo-Christian period in her history came to an end? And if it was preserved, then in what form? The rest of our study will be an attempt to answer these questions. The centuries immediately following the apostolic age deserve our special attention. While not denying the 'liturgical-dualism' in Judeo-Christianity, Dix flatly denies its existence in that period when the Church broke all direct ties with the Temple and the synagogue. According to the theory which he and others have defended, everything that the Church inherited from her Hebrew origins entered into the 'new' cult, above all into the Eucharistic assembly, which then became the only form of regular Christian worship. The liturgical dualism found its expression in the two-fold structure of the Eucharistic assembly—in the conjunction of the synaxis and the Eucharist in the real sense of the word. The synaxis—according to the generally accepted theory—preserved the structure of the synagogue assembly, in which the reading of Scripture and its explanation in preaching occupied the main position. The Eucharistic part preserved the form and order of the *kiddush*. In this way the liturgical dualism was transposed into a unified Christian cult, and the determining principle of this unity was the content of the new cult, the cult of the messianic community of the New Covenant.

This is the hypothesis which can be found in almost every textbook on the history of the liturgy. In its positive assertion, that is, in what it says about the relationship of the synaxis to the Eucharist, this theory is undoubtedly right. But does it really answer the whole question of the 'liturgical dualism' in the Gentile Church which took the place of Judeo-Christianity? Does it answer the question of the origin of the liturgy of time (as distinct from the Eucharist) which later on occupied such a large place in the Church's liturgical tradition? We may begin testing this theory by indicating just one of its obviously weak points. Any one familiar with the history of the Eucharistic rite knows that the question of how the conjunction of the synaxis (the 'liturgy of the catechumens' in our terminology) and the Eucharist came about still represents, for liturgiologists, a kind of *crux interpretum.* 'How and why did they become a single liturgy?' asks the respected English liturgiologist Srawley. His answer : 'It just happened.' [27] It is hardly possible to accept this as a scientifically satisfactory answer. Dix, on the other hand, having insisted so much on the absence in the early Church of any form of worship other than that which was sacramentally eschatological, admits that before their combination into a single organic whole—a process which he considers was not completed until the fourth century—the synaxis and the Eucharist could be and indeed frequently were celebrated separately. But does this not mean that besides the Eucharist in the early pre-Constantine Church there existed at least one service which was not of a 'sacramental' character? And if so, it could then be asked : When and why was it celebrated, what did it signify and express in the liturgical tradition of that era? We shall not dwell on this question here, since we shall be returning to it later on. At this point we need only emphasize, first, the obviously synagogical character of that part of the Eucharist called the pre-anaphora, still evident to-day and acknowledged by all liturgiologists. Here is one indication of the preservation in the 'Gentile' Church of a direct link (at least in one point) with the pre-Christian Hebrew cult. And second, it should be noted that the place of the synaxis in Christian worship is not fully explained by its conjunction with the Eucharist. After all, the synaxis also existed apart from the Eucharist. The early Christian 'synaxis' is really the first and most important evidence for the preservation by the Church—even after the break with Judaism—of a liturgical dualism, if only in its basic form, or the preservation of elements of the old and the new within a kind of biform liturgical structure.

But here again the real meaning of this preservation of a liturgical dualism in the post-apostolic period can be understood only by way of a more general appraisal of the relationship between the Judeo-Christian period and that which followed just after. What is the major

difference between the two? As we have already said, modern studies
are showing more and more clearly that in spite of all its uniqueness
Judeo-Christianity was not a prolonged 'misunderstanding,' but rather
a genuine and basic principle of the Church which she has never
renounced. The one essential difference between the Judeo-Christian
Church and the 'Gentile' Church lay in the fact that the Judeo-Christians did not break away from their people and believed in the possibility of the conversion of all Israel to its Messiah. They thought of
themselves as the forerunners of this conversion, the nucleus of the
New Israel, called first to renew the Israel 'after the flesh.' The Jerusalem community believed in this way, and so did Paul, who has been
regarded as a rebel against Judeo-Christianity only as the result of
some incomprehensible misunderstanding. 'His epistles show that he
remained a Jew who preached a "Hebrew" Gospel to the Greeks based
on purely Hebrew presuppositions.' [28] Paul's dispute with his opponents over circumcision was a dispute within Judeo-Christianity, within
a certain general agreement of principles. Nobody denied the world-
wide mission of the New Israel nor the necessity of preaching to
the Gentiles. The disagreement touched only on the place of the Law
within the Church, which was the New Israel for the Gentiles too. In
defending the Gentiles' exception from the law of circumcision, Paul
was defending not the independence of Christianity from the Jewish
Law, but the true nature of the New Israel, the New Covenant in the
Messiah and, therefore, the true meaning of the Law. Circumcision
was not obligatory because it was a sign of the Old Covenant, while
Baptism was now the sign of its renewal, in which the separation of
the Gentiles and the Hebrews 'after the flesh' was being broken down,
in which all could be one in the New Israel. Later on we find a
similar argument in the Epistle to the Hebrews, on the question of
sacrifices. Here again we find not a rejection of sacrifices altogether
but a reminder that after the Sacrifice of Christ they have become
unnecessary, since they were the prophetic forerunners of this complete and perfect sacrifice. This was not the negation of the 'old' cult
as a whole, but simply of those elements in it which were overcome
and fulfilled in the new cult, in the life of the New Israel. There was
nothing essentially false or mistaken in the Christians' faith in the
possibility of the conversion of Israel. Indeed very many were converted, and the first century was marked by the rapid expansion of
Christianity within the sphere of Judaism. But this faith was not
destined to be justified by events. The Old Israel, as a whole, 'hardened
its heart' and rejected Christianity. In Romans 11:28 Paul accepts this
as an accomplished fact: 'As concerning the good news they (the

Jews) are enemies. . . .' But this change in the mind of Jews changed nothing in the essence of the Church, even at the moment when it took place. Even with the comparatively rapid disappearance from the Church of Jews after the flesh, the Church was and remained the New Israel, the sole inheritor—in the eyes of believers—of the calling of and promises to the Old Israel. 'The transfer of the Church into the hands of the Gentile Christians,' Dix writes, 'can be considered as completed by the end of the '60s. But it was completed only when it became clear that the Gentile Church was flesh of the flesh and bone of the bone of the Church of the Circumcision, that her faith was the same faith, her life was that life which had been promised in the Old Testament, and that all her members were children of Abraham, "who is the Father of us all" (Rom. 4:16) and the "inheritor of the world" ' (Rom. 4:13–16).[29]

But if this general position is true, is it not reasonable to suppose that it should be demonstrated in the development of the liturgical life of the Gentile Church, that it should find expression in her cult? If the 'rule of prayer' of Judeo-Christianity expressed the essence of the Church, her faith and her life, then certainly it must have defined the formation and development of Christian worship when the Israel after the flesh withdrew from the Messiah and locked the doors of the synagogues and the Temple against the Christians. The first clear proof that this was indeed the case is seen in the preservation by Gentile Christians of the synagogue assembly, which by its combination with the Eucharist maintained the 'liturgical dualism' of Judeo-Christianity. But is this all? Could the whole meaning, the whole content of this original *lex orandi* be expressed and embodied in this combination? Or could all the rest of the wealth of Christian worship have grown out of some other foreign, alien root? The whole problem of the origin of the Ordo demands some answer to this last question.

Here we must return to the theme of the eschatological character of early Christian worship. The whole theory which denies the existence of any special liturgy of time in the early Church is based on the supposed impossibility of the combination of such a liturgy with the eschatological content of the Eucharist. In the meantime there can be no doubt that the 'old' Hebrew cult in its combination with the Eucharist represents a basic feature of the Judeo-Christian *lex orandi*, and must be defined in fact as a liturgy of time. It is not only divided up into hours, days, weeks and months, a great part of it is also devoted to prescriptions connected with time, and its very content can be defined as a kind of liturgical expression and sanctification of time. It is just this 'organic' bond between liturgy and time which the

Judeo-Christians accepted, to the extent that they adopted Jewish worship as their own. This bond entered into the original Christian liturgical tradition. But then its absence or denial in the following period could only be the result of a profound change in this tradition, its actual 'metamorphosis.' Indeed if the 'liturgical dualism' which constituted a characteristic feature of the liturgical life of the first Christian community was retained after this only within the Eucharistic assembly, while the Eucharist, in turn, was by its 'eschatological' nature the negation of any connection between the Church and the natural cycles of time, then in order to explain this change we shall have to admit a new beginning of liturgical tradition at the time when the Church passed into the hands of Gentile Christians, an actual exchange of one liturgical theology for another. This is the dilemma which confronts any one who follows Dix in his understanding of the liturgy of time as being opposed to the eschatological nature of the Eucharist and the 'sacramental' cult in general. This question, as we shall soon see, is not limited to the early Church, but cuts like a knife right down through the whole history of worship and is certainly one of the basic questions not just of liturgical history but also of the theology of liturgy.

Within the limits of the history of early Christian worship the question can be posed in the following terms : Is what has been defined as the 'eschatology' of the early Church (and therefore the eschatology of the Eucharist) really compatible with the idea of the sanctification of time, as it was expressed, first of all, in Hebrew worship? To answer this question we must first make a more careful analysis of the two concepts involved : 'eschatology' and 'the sanctification of time.'

Quite recently O. Cullman has dealt with the biblical concept or theology of time in his well-known book *Christ and Time*.[30] In it he very clearly presents the fundamental distinction between the linear Hebrew understanding of time and the cyclical Hellenistic concept. Without entering here into a detailed analysis of the Hebrew conception, it is important to emphasize that within it eschatology does not signify a renunciation of time as something corrupt, nor a victory over time, nor an exit out of it. On the contrary, within this conception time itself can be described as eschatological, in the sense that in it those events develop and happen by means of which time is given its meaning, which make it a process or history, and which direct it toward an ἔσχατον and not just toward an ending or precipice—not toward that which would render it meaningless but toward its consummation in a final event revealing its whole meaning : ἔσχατον is therefore not simply an ending, but the fulfilment of that which has developed in time, that to which time has been inwardly subordinated as means is to end, that which fills it with meaning. The cycles of time (of 'natural' time) are not self-sufficient for the Jew, since they are wholly subordinated to Yahweh, to a personal God. They always constitute the revelation of the living God who has created the world and who 'holds all things in His hand.' Time in this sense is defined by its movement toward the fulfilment of God's plan or design for the world, which will come about in and through time, by its movement in the direction of the 'Lord's Day.' The 'liturgy of time' in Judaism is the expression of this biblical and in fact 'eschatological' theology of time. It begins with the blessing of the Kingdom of Yahweh, toward which time it is directed; it is entirely a cult of the God of history, the God of salvation. It 'sanctions' human life in all its aspects, gives it a religious sanction, again not as something self-sufficient but always connecting it with the ἔσχατον—comprehending it in the light of the ultimate truth about the world, man and history. Morning, evening, day, the sabbath, feast days—all these have an 'eschatological' significance, as reminders of the ultimate and great 'Day of the Lord' which is coming in time. This is the liturgy of time; but not natural or cyclical time, not that time which is, so to speak, 'immanent' in the world, determining and containing it within its own self-sufficient, cyclical rhythm. It is time that is eschatologically transparent, time within which and over which the living God of Abraham, Isaac and Jacob is constantly acting, and which discovers its real meaning in the Kingdom of Yahweh, 'the Kingdom of all ages.'

But this same understanding of time, as Cullman demonstrated very well, lies also at the basis of the Christian New Testament concept, and without it it is impossible to understand either early Christian eschatology or what we call the eschatology of the early Christian cult. 'Repent, for the Kingdom of God is at hand.' The centre of the Christian *kerygma* is this, that the Messiah has come. That event has been accomplished toward which the whole history of Israel (and in the light of this history—in relation to it—the history also of the whole world) was directed. The difference between Christianity and Judaism is not in their understanding or theology of time, but in their conception of the events by which this time is spiritually measured. Judaistic time is eschatological in the sense that it is still directed toward the coming of the Messiah and the messianic Kingdom. In Christian time the Messiah has already come, is already revealed, the Kingdom of Yahweh is at hand. If eschatology is to be understood only in the futuristic sense, then, as Cullman says, 'the unconditional affirmation of the eschatology of early Christianity' is wrong—'the norm is not something which is still coming in the future, but that One who has already come . . .' [31] The new element in Christianity is not its conception of time or of the world living in time, but in the fact that the event which even in the old Judaistic conception constituted the 'centre' of time, and which defined its meaning, has already begun. And this event, in turn, is eschatological, since in it is revealed and defined the ultimate meaning of all things—creation, history, salvation.

The advent of the 'Lord's Day' signifies therefore neither the ending, nor the rendering absurd, nor the emptying of time. Indeed the whole meaning, the whole point and uniqueness of early Christian eschatology is just this, that in the light of the coming of the Messiah and the 'drawing near' of the messianic Kingdom, in the light of its manifestation in the world, time becomes truly real, acquires a new and special intensity. It becomes the time of the Church : the time in which the salvation given by the Messiah is now accomplished.

It is in the light of this eschatology (as not simply identical with 'world renunciation') that we must understand the eschatological character of the new Christian cult and, above all, the Eucharist. The event which is 'actualized' in the Eucharist is an event of the past when viewed within the categories of time, but by virtue of its eschatological, determining, completing significance it is also an event which is taking place eternally. The coming of the Messiah is a single event of the past, but in His coming, in His life, death and resurrection, His Kingdom has entered into the world, becoming the new life in the Spirit given by Him as life within Himself. This messianic Kingdom or life in the new aeon is 'actualized'—becomes real—in the assembly of the Church, in the ἐκκλησία, when believers come together to have communion in the Lord's body. The Eucharist is therefore the manifestation of the Church as the new aeon ; it is participation in the Kingdom as the *parousia,* as the presence of the Resurrected and Resurrecting Lord. It is not the 'repetition' of His advent or coming into the world, but the lifting up of the Church into His *parousia,* the Church's participation in His heavenly glory. Later Christian thought will begin to interpret the nature of the Sacrament—of this repetition of the unrepeatable—in concepts borrowed from Greek philosophy. It would be wrong to ascribe such a theological interpretation in its full form to Judeo-Christianity and the early Church. But there can be no doubt that even at that time, and perhaps more strongly and clearly then than at any time after, all the elements of this future theological development were alive in the faith and experience of the Church. The Church belongs to the new aeon, to the Kingdom of the Messiah, which in relation to this world is the Kingdom of the age to come.

It is therefore not of this world; and yet the Church does exist in this world, in this aeon. In Christ the Kingdom has entered this world and exists in it in the Church. From the perspective of this world it is something in the future; in God it is eternal and actual, as well as future. Christians live wholly by the life of this world, they are flesh of its flesh and bone of its bone, yet at the same time their life as new beings is 'hid with Christ in God' and will be manifested in glory in the second coming of Christ, that is, when the dualism of these two aeons is concluded and 'this world' comes to an end. The Eucharist or Lord's Supper is also the actualization of the new aeon within the old, the presence and manifestation in this age of the Kingdom of the Age to Come. The Eucharist is the *parousia,* the presence and manifestation of Christ, who is 'the same to-day, yesterday and forever' (Heb. 13 :8). By participating in His Supper Christians receive into themselves His life and His Kingdom, i.e. the New Life and the New Aeon. In other words the eschatology of the Eucharist is not 'world renouncing,' not a turning away from time, but above all the affirmation of the reality, the certainty and the presence of the Kingdom of Christ which is 'within,' which is already here within the Church, but which will be manifest in all glory only at the end of 'this world.' This is a conquest of time not in the sense of rendering it empty and valueless, but rather in the sense of creating the possibility of being made partakers of or participants in the 'coming aeon,' in the fullness, joy and peace that is found in the Holy Spirit, while still living in 'this world.' [32]

So we come to the final meaning and 'justification' of the liturgical dualism of early Christianity. We have said that the new cult, being by nature a witness to the already accomplished coming and manifestation of the Messiah as the fulfilment of the images and promises of the Old Testament, thereby postulated the existence of the old cult, without which it could not in fact be new—new eternally, and by its very nature not just something new in the chronological sense. We may now go further. We can say that it is precisely the eschatology of the new cult which in turn postulates the old cult as the liturgy of time. Since this eschatology is itself in relation to time, and only in relation to time can it be ultimately and truly an eschatology, i.e. a manifestation and actualization (ἔσκατον).

The Church is set in the world in order to save it by her eschatological fullness, by the *parousia* of Christ, by His coming and presence, by the waiting for Him to illumine, judge and give meaning to its life and time. If the Church were a salvation from the world, then her new cult would be sufficient; moreover, it would be the sole content

and goal of the whole life of the Church. A so-called 'world renouncing' eschatology has perhaps been held by individual Christians
(cf. 'let thy Kingdom come and let this world pass away . . .' in the
Didache). But even these not so much eschatological as apocalyptic
expressions have not extinguished among Christians the consciousness
that the Church is set in this world with a mission, and that it is
precisely to this mission 'to proclaim the Lord's death and confess His
resurrection' that the Sacrament of the Church bears witness. This
Sacrament 'consecrates' Christians to this mission, and it is within the
Church that this mission is actualized as the manifestation of the new
aeon, the new life in the *parousia* of the Lord. 'This world' will pass
away, the Lord will reign in glory. The Church is expecting this fulfilment of time, is directed toward this ultimate victory. But this
expectation is not a passive state, it is a responsible service—it is to
'be as He was in this world.' This is the time of the Church. Only
now, as we see it coming to an end on the one hand, and on the
other hand as we see it penetrated by the light and power of the
Kingdom, does time acquire its full significance. Only thus does the
world, 'whose image is passing away,' cease to be reduced to a meaningless disappearance into the stream of non-existence. Just as the Church,
although she is 'not of this world,' exists within the world and for its
sake, so too the Sacrament (in which the oneness of the Church with
the New Aeon is eternally created and actualized) does not abolish or
strip time of meaning. While it is by nature a victory over time and a
departure out of it, it is also performed within time, and it fills it with
new meaning.

The liturgy of time (now recognized as the old Jewish cult preserved
by the Church) was therefore preserved in a way by necessity—as the
completion of the Eucharist, without which the application of the
Eucharist to time or any real sanctification of the life of this world
would be incomplete. The Eucharist does not replace the liturgy of
time, since by nature it is the manifestation in this aeon of another
Aeon, it is the communication of the faithful in eternal life, in the
Kingdom of God already 'come in power.' It cannot abolish the liturgy
of time, because then time would be really emptied and deprived of
meaning, would be nothing but 'intervals' between celebrations of the
Eucharist. Thus the new cult, an eschatological cult in the deepest
sense of the word, required for its real fulfilment inclusion in the
rhythm of time, and its combination within this rhythm with the
liturgy of time, as the affirmation of the reality of the world which
Christ came to save. But, it can be objected, all this is simply theological 'interpretation.' Is it possible to find support for what has been
said in the facts of the early Christian liturgical tradition?

We must first see how well grounded is the idea of the liturgy of time on which we have based our notion of the structure of the early Christian 'rule of prayer.' We find support in the obvious link between the Eucharist and time expressed from the very first days of the Church in the Christian celebration of the Lord's Day. This was the day of Jesus' resurrection from the dead, His manifestation of the new life, and this day became in the Church the day of the Eucharist. For an understanding of the place of the 'Lord's Day' in the liturgical life of the early Church it is important to clarify its relationship to the Hebrew sabbath. Christian thought has so ignored this relationship that the whole week has been simply 'advanced,' and the day of resurrection (the first day of the week, the *prima sabbati*) has gradually become another sabbath. All the Old Testament prescriptions and definitions touching the seventh day were little by little transferred to Sunday, and the seventh day has been converted into a kind of 'proto- type' of the Christian day of rest. This displacement of the week became especially apparent when the emperor Constantine gave the 'day of the sun' an official state sanction, and made it a generally obligatory day of rest. But even before the end of the fourth century the memory still lived in the mind of the Church of the original rela- tionship of the 'Lord's Day' with the sabbath and the whole Old Testament week. It is still possible to find evidence of this, although in a rather unclear form, in our contemporary Ordo.

For the early Church the Lord's Day was not a substitute for the sabbath; it was not (so to speak) its Christian equivalent. On the contrary the real nature and significance of this new day was defined in relation to the sabbath and to the concept of time connected with it. The key position of the sabbath (and all its related prescriptions) in the Old Testament law and Hebrew piety is well known. From what- ever source the weekly cycle of time may have been acquired by Israel its religious interpretation and experience was rooted in a specifically biblical theology of time. The Seventh Day, the day of complete rest, is a commemoration of the creation of the world, a participation in the rest of God after creation. This rest signifies and expresses the fullness, the completion, the 'goodness' of the world, it is the eternal actualiza- tion of the word spoken about the world by God from the beginning : 'it is very good.' The sabbath sanctions the whole natural life of the world unfolding through the cycles of time, because it is the divinely instituted sign of the correspondence of the world to God's will and purpose. On this day the Law prescribes joy : 'thou shalt eat and drink and give thanks to Him who created all things,' since 'He who created all things honoured and sanctified the sabbath day and commanded that it should be so' (2 Macc. 15 : 2–4). Faithfulness to the sabbath was bound up with the ultimate mystical depths of the people of Israel, and only by understanding it as something for which men were prepared to die is it possible to comprehend the significance of the *new* day introduced by the Church.

The appearance of this new day is rooted in the expectation of salvation, in that striving toward the future and in those messianic hopes which were just as characteristic of the theology of the Old Covenant as the cult of the Law. If in the sabbath the Hebrew honours the Creator of the universe and His perfect Law, he knows too that within this world created by God hostile forces are rebelling against Him, that this world is spoiled by sin. The Law has been broken, man is sick, life is poisoned by sin. The time which is included in the weekly cycle is not only the time of a blessed and God-pleasing life, but also the time of a struggle between light and darkness, between God and all that has rebelled against Him. This is the time of the history of salvation which is founded in an eschatological realization—the Day of the Messiah. And again, no matter what may have been the original content and genesis of Hebrew Messianism and the apocalypticism connected with it, the important thing for us is that the time of the manifestation of Christianity coincided with the ultimate limit of intensity of these expectations, with their growth into a universal eschatological outlook. It was precisely in connection with or as a result of this eschatology that there arose the idea of the Lord's Day, the day of Messianic fulfilment, as the Eighth Day, 'overcoming' the week and leading outside of its boundaries.[33] In the eschatological perspective of the struggle of God with 'the prince of this world' and the expectation of the new aeon, the week and its final unit—the sabbath—appear as signs of this fallen world, of the old aeon, of that which must be overcome with the advent of the Lord's Day. The Eighth Day is the day beyond the limits of the cycle outlined by the week and punctuated by the sabbath—this is the first day of the New Aeon, the figure of the time of the Messiah. 'And I have also established the eighth day,' we read in the book of Enoch, a characteristic example of late Hebrew apocalypticism, 'that the eighth day be the first after my creation, that in the beginning of the eighth (millennium) there be time without reckoning, everlasting, without years, months, weeks, days or hours.' The concept of the eighth day is connected with another idea characteristic of Jewish apocalypticism : the cosmic week of seven thousand years. Each week is thus a figure of all time, and all time, that is the whole of 'this age,' is one week. So then the eighth day and the eighth millennium are the beginning of the New Aeon not to be reckoned in time. This eighth day (coming after and standing outside the week) is also, therefore, the first day, the beginning of the world which has been saved and restored.

Christ rose not on the sabbath, but on the first day of the week (μία σαββάτων). The sabbath was the day of His rest, His 'en-sabbathment' in the tomb, the day which completed His task within the limits of the 'old aeon.' But the new life, the life which had begun to 'shine out of the tomb,' began on the first day of the week. This was the first day, the beginning of the risen life over which 'death has no dominion.' This day also became the day of the Eucharist as the 'confession of His resurrection,' the day of the communication to the Church of this risen life.[34] And here it is quite remarkable that in early Christianity, up to and including the time of Basil the Great, this day was often called in fact 'the eighth day.' This means that the symbolism of Hebrew apocalypticism was adopted by Christians and became one of the theological 'keys' to their liturgical consciousness. There is no need to dwell especially on the first epistle of Peter, in which there seems to be a hint of the significance of the number eight (3:20-1). In the Gospel according to John, undoubtedly the most 'liturgical' of all the Gospels, the risen Christ appears after eight days (John 20:26). Later the 'mystery' of the eighth day is explained by Christian authors in application to the Eucharistic Day of the Lord, which points to a clear tradition. These numerous texts on the eighth day have been collected by J. Daniélou.[35] Their meaning is clear: Christ rose on the first day, i.e. on the day of the beginning of creation, because He restores creation after sin. But this day which concludes the history of salvation, the day of victory over the forces of evil, is also the eighth day, since it is the beginning of the New Aeon. 'So the day which was first,' writes St. Augustine, 'will be also the eighth, so that the first life might not be done away, but rather made eternal.'[36] And even more clearly St. Basil the Great writes: 'The Lord's Day is great and glorious. The Scripture knows this day without evening, having no other day, a day without end; the psalmist called it the eighth day, since it is outside of time measured in weeks. Whether you call it a day or an age, it is all the same. If you call it an aeon, it is one, and not a part of a whole. . . . '[37] In this way the eighth day 'is defined in opposition to the week,' writes J. Daniélou. 'The week is related to time. The eighth day is outside time. The week stands within the sequence of days, the eighth day has nothing coming after it, it is the 'last one.' The week involves multiplicity; the eighth day is one. . . .'[38]

In the Church this first-eighth day (the Lord's Day: κριακὴ ἡμέρα) is the day of the Eucharist. The early Christian tradition bears uniform witness to this fact. The Eucharist has its day, Christians gather together on a *statu die* [39]—on an established day. We know that the 'Day of the Sun' was not a holy day of rest in either the Jewish or the Roman calendars. Nonetheless the Eucharist 'became so firmly connected with this day that nothing has ever been able or will be able to undermine this connection.' [40] But then this is the whole point: though the Eucharist is celebrated on a *statu die*, though it has its own day and thus reveals a connection with and is set in the framework of time, still this day is not simply 'one out of many.' Everything that has been said above about the first and eighth day shows that this connection of the Eucharist with time emphasizes the eschatological nature of the Eucharist, the manifestation in it of the Lord's Day, the New Aeon. The Eucharist is the Sacrament of the Church. It is the *parousia*, the presence of the Risen and Glorified Lord in the midst of 'His own,' those who in Him constitute the Church and are already 'not of this world' but partakers of the new life of the New Aeon. The day of the Eucharist is the day of the 'actualization' or manifestation in time of the Day of the Lord as the Kingdom of Christ. The early Church did not connect either the idea of repose or the idea of a natural cycle of work and rest with the Eucharistic Day of the Lord. Constantine established this connection with his sanction of the Christian Sunday. For the Church the Lord's Day is the joyful day of the Kingdom. The Lord's Day signifies for her not the substitution of one form of reckoning time by another, the replacement of Saturday by Sunday, but a break into the 'New Aeon,' a participation in a time that is by nature totally different.

In this connection of the Eucharist with the Lord's Day, so well supported by evidence from the liturgical tradition of the early Church, we have therefore a confirmation of that eschatological theology of time of which we have been speaking. The eschatology of the new Christian cult does not mean the renunciation of time. There would have been no need for a fixed day (*statu die*) in a 'wholly world-renouncing' cult, it could be celebrated on any day and at any hour. Nor does this eschatology become related to time through the sanctification of one of the days of the week, like the sabbath in the Old Testament law. The 'Lord's Day' actualized in the Eucharist was not 'one of the ordinary sequence of days.' Just as the Church herself while existing in 'this world' manifests a life which is 'not of this world,' so also the 'Lord's Day,' while it is actualized within time on a given day, manifests within this sequence that which is above time and belongs

63

to another aeon. Just as the Church though 'not of this world' is present in this world for its salvation, so also the Sacrament of the Lord's Day, the Sacrament of the new aeon is joined with time in order that time itself might become the time of the Church, the time of salvation. It is precisely this fulfilment of time by the 'Eschaton,' by that which overcomes time and is above it and bears witness to its finitude and limitedness, which constitutes the sanctification of time.

But if the connection of the Eucharist with a 'fixed day' and the nature of this day as the 'Lord's Day' point to a definite theology of time, and if they confirm our first hypothesis concerning the early Christian rule of prayer, they do not yet prove the existence in the early Church of what we have defined as the liturgy of time, i.e. of a form of worship distinct from the Sunday Eucharistic assembly and immediately connected with the natural cycles of time. We have already said that the opinions of historians differ as to the origin of this form of worship, which will occupy such a large place in the liturgical life of the Church in the following epoch. We have also expressed our conviction that to the extent that the 'liturgical dualism' of Judeo-Christianity represented something essential and basic in the Church's faith, it had to be preserved in one form or another after Christianity's final break with Judaism. Are we now able to point out the facts which support this hypothesis?

Let us note first of all that the disagreements of historians on this point are to be explained frequently by an inadequate grasp of the question itself. Until quite recently the attention of liturgiologists has been concentrated almost exclusively on questions connected with the history of the sacramental Christian cult—the Eucharist and Baptism. The other aspects of the liturgical life of the early Church have been left in shadow. Their study is only just beginning: 'too many problems remain unresolved, too many hypotheses unproved.' [41] From the purely historical point of view, therefore, every unconditional 'yes' or 'no' in this matter of the early existence of a Christian liturgy of time must be regarded as premature. Yet even on the basis of the material which has been gathered and studied so far the inadequacy of the hypothesis which insists on the late and specifically monastic origin of the liturgy of the daily cycle is becoming more and more evident. As we shall see shortly, the opinion concerning the post-Constantine origin of the idea of the 'yearly cycle' is also untenable.

We must be able to furnish unanimous evidence from pre-Nicene tests for the hours of prayer, for the connection of prayer with definite times of day. And in fact in the Epistle of Clement of Rome to the Corinthians we read: 'We must do all things in order . . . at fixed times . . . not haphazardly and not without order, but at definite times and hours.'[42] Three hours of prayer are indicated in the *Didache*,[43] by Tertullian,[44] by Cyprian of Carthage,[45] by Origen,[46] in the *Apostolic Tradition* of Hippolytus.[47] 'We should pray in the early morning,' writes Cyprian, 'that by means of our morning prayer the resurrection of the Lord might be recalled; also at the setting of the sun and in the evening we should pray again. . . .' The tradition of hours and times of prayer can certainly be accepted as a tradition common to the whole of the early Church. We know that some historians of worship explain this tradition as referring to private prayer rather than to prayer in the Church. But even this would indicate a definite interest in prayer within time, an understanding of time as the necessary 'framework' of prayer. Quite early we find a reference (in the *Apostolic Tradition* of Hippolytus) to the theological significance of these hours and times. Therefore if we have nothing more in the tradition of the pre-Nicene Church than these prescriptions to say prayers at fixed hours, this would be enough to infer the subsequent development of the daily cycle of worship. Nor would this be a 'liturgical revolution,' but simply the development and ordering of the early tradition.

In fact we can go further. First, the texts which are usually used to defend the exclusively private nature of the prayer of hours and times very plainly show that this prayer could and actually did have an ecclesiological character, was offered in the assemblies of the community. Thus, in the *Apostolic Tradition*, immediately following the prescriptions to pray each morning, it is said: 'but if there is instruction by the word (*catecizacio*) let every one prefer to attend that, since when he has said prayer in the assembly, he will be able to avoid the evil of the day. . . .'[48] We do not know whether these assemblies with 'instruction by the word' and prayer were daily occurrences. But if we take into account the whole spirit and 'ethos' of the early Church, this prayer will have to be defined as 'ecclesio-centric,' having its basis in the experience of the assembly or communion of the *ecclesia* and at the same time being directed to this end.[49] 'Strive to be together as often as possible,' writes St. Ignatius of Antioch[50]; and St. Cyprian of Carthage echoes his words: 'The Lord of unity did not command that prayer be offered to Him individually and in private.'[51] Origen,[52] Tertullian,[53] and others[54] insist on the value of being 'together as often as possible,' in the assembly of common prayer and fellowship. We repeat that it is impossible to make categorical assertions about a regular daily worship on the basis of these texts alone. But they do point, first of all, to a firm tradition of times of prayer in the early

E

Church, and second, to the existence of assemblies (although perhaps not in all places) devoted to prayer and sermons. Finally, they point to the acceptance of this prayer of the Church as something necessary, and indeed superior to private prayer. They point therefore to the inclusion of this form of worship in the *lex orandi* of the Church.

Comparative liturgics, whose principles and method were developed so brilliantly by Baumstark, has delivered an even more serious blow to the hypothesis of the monastic origin of the daily cycle. This study has shown that the epoch of the development of the daily cycle after Constantine was marked by a rivalry and even conflict between two types of daily service: 'corporate' and 'monastic' in Baumstark's terminology. We will have occasion to dwell on this rivalry in greater detail in the following chapter. Here it is sufficient to say that this fact clearly demonstrates the preservation in the Church of daily services and a daily cycle which were not only distinct from their monastic types, but even appeared before the rise of monasticism. But what is still more important, there can be no doubt about the connection between the daily services of the 'corporate' type with synagogue worship, about their structural dependency on Jewish daily worship. C. W. Dugmore devoted a special work to the study of this dependency, and has demonstrated the synagogical structure of the two basic services of the daily cycle—Vespers and Matins. On the days when the Eucharist was celebrated the daily service (on the pattern of the synagogue worship) preceded the Eucharist, as its first part (*missa catechumenorum*), while on other days it constituted an independent service, assigned usually to definite hours of the day.[55] In the third century, as is evident even from the very partial texts which reflect this epoch, Vespers and Matins 'already occupied their present honoured position in the cycle of daily services.'[56] The existence of these daily services, devoted (according to Tertullian) 'to common prayer . . . to the reading of Divine Scripture, to exhortations and instructions,' explains the cause and manner of combining the synagogue 'synaxis' with the Eucharist. Srawley's answer—'it just happened'—acquires greater significance.

In any case the universal acceptance in all Ordos of the cycle of Vespers and Matins as liturgical services, i.e. as presupposing an assembly of the Church (cf. the participation in these services of the bishop, the presbyters and deacons, in the *Apostolic Constitution*), and consequently as existing apart from the purely monastic services (Compline, etc.), confirms the theory that they belong to the Church's liturgical tradition, to the Church's *lex orandi*. The clearly synagogical elements which have been preserved in them even down to the present day—in spite of extensive monastic reworking—also point to their early inclusion in this *lex orandi*.

So then the liturgy of time which we saw already embodied and expressed in the liturgical dualism of Judeo-Christianity, and later in the cycle of the eschatological 'Day of the Lord,' is also confirmed by the preservation by the 'Gentile Church' of the worship of the daily cycle. From the very beginning the Church's liturgical tradition included the idea of the day as a liturgical unit, in which definite hours and times—evening, morning and night—should be devoted to prayer; and not just to private prayer, but also to prayer in the Church. It may be supposed that not all believers had the opportunity to gather twice each day, and that from the beginning it was a minority which participated in these services. Tertullian's distinction between *coetus* and *congregationes* is possibly a reference to this situation; also the exhortations to attend these assemblies which we find, for example, in the *Apostolic Constitutions* and in the *Order*. But this does not alter the ecclesiological, liturgical character of these services. The Church is praying 'in order to surround God with common prayers as with an army, gathered together in a single place. . . .'[57] This idea of the praying Church, *ecclesia orans*, clearly corresponds to the whole spirit of early Christian ecclesiology, to the liturgical piety of the pre-Nicene Church.

6

Finally, we must also trace the basic principle of the Church year back to the apostolic beginnings of the Church. We see this basic principle in the preservation by the early Christian *lex orandi* of Passover and Pentecost.[58] The Church's adoption of these two basic Hebrew festivals is evidenced not only by the New Testament epistles but also by other early Christian writings. Not long ago an attempt was made to discover the Christian 'adoption' of a third great Hebrew festival connected with the Old Testament *heilsgeschichte*—the Feast of Tabernacles. This attempt is still so much in the realm of hypothesis that we will not dwell on it here. There are no doubts, however, about Passover and Pentecost. The Church preserved these feasts not out of any 'inertia' but because they represented the necessary biblical-liturgical premise of the Church's faith. Christ died as 'our Passover,' while in the 'last and great day' of Pentecost, which had already acquired an eschatological character in late Judaism, the descent of the Holy Spirit was accomplished. This was the actualization of the Church, marking the beginning of the time of the Church. We need not enter here into a review of the complicated problems connected with the New Testament texts concerning the Passover celebrated by Christ on the eve of His death, or with the 'Paschal controversies' of the second century. The various solutions to these problems do not disturb the one fact which is important for us at this point : the presence in the early Christian liturgical tradition of two annual festivals dedicated to the commemoration (μνῆμα in Origen's works) of Redemption and Salvation. This fact demonstrates the preservation by the Church of the idea of the year as a liturgical unit, and it is perhaps here more than anywhere else that the connection between the Christian and Jewish *lex orandi* is made plain, since the liturgical year would seem to stem least of all from the nature of the liturgical life of the Church. Everything that we know about the way Christians at that time experienced the Eucharist and the Lord's Day points to a constant Paschal theme, just as Baptism with the laying on of hands was felt by them to be a continuing Pentecost, the constant outpouring of the Holy Spirit and His gifts. There was apparently no need for them to separate the commemoration of the death and resurrection of Christ on the one hand—or the descent of the Holy Spirit on the other—into isolated and special 'feasts.' The mystery of death and resurrection and the experience of the new life in the Holy Spirit are dominant themes in the whole life of the early Church. These feasts were neither special historical commemorations (since each Eucharist was a 'recollection of His death and a confession of His resurrection' and each Baptism was the actualization of Pentecost) nor were they a casting of the dogmatic significance of these events into special liturgical forms. If the Church preserved these two festivals of the old Israel, even when the idea of their consummation in Christ saturated the whole of her life, then this was because she preserved that theology of time of which they were the expression. Within this time or history the coming of the Messiah and His Passover, the descent of the Holy Spirit and in Him the manifestation of the 'New Aeon' in the world represent a decisive crisis, in the literal sense of this world. But time and the history of salvation continue. In the Messiah they acquire their whole meaning, and also a new goal : the ultimate cosmic victory of the Kingdom is already manifested in the Messiah. For this reason the Christian Passover is the same Passover of the chosen people of God, the Passover of the Exodus and of deliverance from bondage, the Passover of the desert, the Passover of the coming into a promised land. To this Passover as a series of events there was added yet one more meaning, the final one, including all the others : 'Christ our Passover has been sacrificed for us.' This final event established the Christian Passover as a sign of the new period of the history of salvation, directed toward the consummation of the Passover in the 'unending day of the Kingdom of God.'

No matter what the original liturgical expression of Pentecost may have been, its preservation in the Church—as the fifty day period following Easter—points once again to the Christian 'adoption' of a definite understanding of the year, of time, of the natural cycles, as having a relation to the eschatological reality of the Kingdom. As an ancient agricultural feast, Pentecost was, in the words of Kohler, 'transformed in rabbinical Judaism into a historical festival, a commemoration of the Decalogue given on Sinai.' [59] 'If this transformation was completed in the period of the Gospels,' notes McArthur, 'it is remarkable that the Holy Spirit in His dynamic power was received by the disciples precisely on that day. Just as the Old Covenant established in the Exodus and remembered at Passover was fulfilled on Sinai, so the New Covenant established in the events remembered by the Christian Passover was fulfilled on Pentecost. The Christian Pentecost became the birthday of the Church as the New Israel of God.' [60] Once again there is the characteristic affirmation, on the one hand, that Christians live as it were in a continuing Pentecost (cf. Origen : 'he who can truly say that we are risen with Christ and that "God has glorified us and in Christ has set us at His right hand in heaven" lives always in the time of the Pentecost' [61]), and on the other hand the setting apart of Pentecost as a special festival celebrated at a special time of year. 'We celebrate also,' writes St. Athanasius, 'the holy days of Pentecost, looking to the age to come.' 'And so let us add the seven holy weeks of Pentecost, rejoicing in and praising God for the fact that He has in these last days manifested to us the joy and eternal rest prepared in heaven for us and all those who truly believe in Christ Jesus our Lord. . . .' [62] Again eschatology, the experience of the Church as the New Aeon and an anticipation of the 'Kingdom of the age to come,' is related to the affirmation of time as a history within which this Kingdom must grow and 'be fulfilled' in the faith and practice of men.

If this were not so it would be impossible to understand and explain the whole subsequent development of the liturgical cycle of Easter and Pentecost. Since even in its final Byzantine version it preserved a clear connection with the original biblical theology of time out of which it had grown, the connection of the redemptive Sacrifice of the Messiah with the Hebrew Passover, the connection of the descent of the Holy Spirit with Pentecost, the 'last and great day' of that Passover.

Although it is impossible to affirm the universal acceptance of a developed liturgy of time in the early pre-Constantine Church, it is both necessary and possible to trace its general principle and therefore its historical beginning back to the original, apostolic, Judeo-Christian *lex orandi.* We are brought to this conclusion not only by an examination of the theology of time which existed in the early Church and which constituted the distinctive feature of her eschatology, but also by all that we know about the form, structures and content of her worship. The hypothesis concerning the late post-Constantine appearance of the idea of a liturgy of time, and thus also of a 'liturgical revolution' marking the end of the early Christian period of the history of worship, must be regarded as completely unfounded.

There is good reason to regard the principle of the Ordo, i.e. of that co-relation and conjunction of the Eucharist with the liturgy of time in which we recognize the fundamental structure of the Church's prayer, as having existed from the very beginning in her 'rule of prayer,' as the real principle of this rule.

FOOTNOTES TO CHAPTER TWO

[1] O. Culmann, *Le Culte dans l'Eglise primitive,* Neuchâtel and Paris, Delachaux, 1944, p. 30.

[2] G. Dix, *The Shape of the Liturgy,* Westminster, Dacre Press, 1945, p. 325; cf. p. 319f.

[3] L. Duchesne, *Origines du culte chrètien,* Paris, E. de Boccard, 1925, p. 469.

[4] P. Batiffol, *Histoire du Bréviare Romain,* Paris, Gabalda, 1895, pp. 28ff.

[5] Batiffol, op. cit., p. 29; cf. Dix, op. cit., pp. 317ff.

[6] L. Duchesne, op. cit., p. 472.

[7] Dix, op. cit., p. 326.

[8] ibid., p. 265.

[9] P. Freeman, *The Principles of the Divine Office,* Vol. 1, 'Morning and Evening Prayer,' London, James Parker, 1893.

[10] C. W. Dugmore, *The Influence of the Synagogue on the Divine Office,* Oxford University Press, 1944; cf. I. Dalmais, 'Origine et constitution de l'Office,' *Maison-Dieu,* 21, pp. 21–39; J. M. Hanssens, 'Nature et Genèse de l'Office des Matines,' in *Analecta Gregoriana,* Vol. LVII, Rome, 1952.

[11] Dugmore, op. cit., p. 57.

[12] W. O. E. Oesterley, *The Jewish Background of the Christian Liturgy,* Oxford University Press, 1925.

[13] J. Jeremias, *The Eucharistic Words of Jesus,* Oxford, Blackwell, 1955.

[14] G. Dix, *The Jew and the Greek: A Study in the Primitive Church,* Westminster, Dacre Press, 1953.

[15] F. Gavin, *The Jewish Antecedents of the Christian Sacraments,* London, S.P.C.K., 1928.

[16] Baumstark, *Liturgie Comparée.*

[17] Dugmore, *The Influence of the Synagogue on the Divine Office.*

[18] *The Dead Sea Scrolls of St. Mark's Monastery,* M. Burrows, ed., Vols. I and II, The American School of Oriental Research, New Haven, 1950–1.

[19] cf. F. C. Grant, 'Modern Study of Jewish Liturgy' in *Zeitschrift f. altest. Wissensch.,* 65 B, 1953, 1/2, pp. 59–77; J. Shirman, 'Hebrew Liturgical Poetry and Christian Hymnology,' *Jewish Quarterly Review,* October 1953, 2, pp. 123–61.

[20] Oesterley, op. cit., p. 125.

[21] ibid., pp. 52ff.

[22] ibid., p. 90.

THE PROBLEM OF THE ORIGIN OF THE ORDO

[23] Y. Brillioth, *Eucharistic Faith and Practice*, London, S.P.C.K., 1930, p. 50.

[24] Dugmore, op. cit., p. 50.

[25] Dix, *The Jew and the Greek*, p. 28.

[26] ibid., p. 29.

[27] J. H. Srawley, *The Early History of the Liturgy*, Cambridge University Press, 2nd edition, 1949, p. 14

[28] Dix, *The Jew and the Greek*, p. 32.

[29] ibid., p. 61.

[30] O. Culmann, *Le Christ et le Temps*, Paris, Delachaux et Nestlé, 1947 (English trans. Philadelphia, Westminster, 1951).

[31] ibid., p. 108.

[32] cf. essays collected in *Le Jour du Seigneur*, Paris, R. Laffont, 1948.

[33] cf. J. Daniélou, 'La Théologie du dimanche' in *Le Jour du Seigneur* pp. 120ff.

[34] cf. H. Chirat, 'Le Dimanche dans l'antiquité chrétienne' in *Etudes de Pastorale Liturgique*, Paris, Cerf, 1944, pp. 127–48; H. Callewaert, 'La synaxe eucharistique à Jerusalem, berceau du dimanche' in *Ephemerides Theolog. Lovansienses*, 15, 1938, pp. 34–73; Dom H. Dumaine, art. 'Dimanche' in *Dict. Archeol. Lit. Chrét.*, 4, 1, 858–994.

[35] Daniélou, 'La Théologie du dimanche,' pp. 120ff., and also a special issue of *Vie Spirituelle* ('Le Huitieme Jour'), April 1947.

[36] Epist. 55 : 17.

[37] Migne, *Patr. Graec.*, 29, 49.

[38] Daniélou, 'La Théologie du dimanche,' p. 126.

[39] Pliny, Epist. 10 : 96.

[40] Daniélou, op. cit., p. 113.

[41] Dalmais, 'Origine et constitution de l'Office,' p. 21.

[42] *Epistle to the Corinthians*, 60.

[43] *Didache*, 8.

[44] *De Oratione*, 15.

[45] *De Oratione*, 35.

[46] *In Rom.*, 9, 1.

[47] *Apost. Trad.*, 35, 1, 2.

[48] ibid.

[49] cf. H. Chirat, *L'Assemblée chrétienne à l'Age apostolique*, Paris, Cerf, 1949, pp. 15ff.; G. Bardy, *La Théologie de l'Eglise de St. Clément de Rome à St. Irenée*, Paris, Cerf, 1945, pp. 19ff.; N. Afanassiev, *Trapeza Gospodnya* (The Lord's Table), Paris, 1952.

[50] *Eph.*, 3.

[51] *De Oratione*, P.L. 4, 541.

[52] cf. J. Daniélou, *Origine*, Paris, La Table Ronde, 1948, pp. 41ff.

[53] *Apol.*, 1, 39.

[54] Bardy, op. cit., pp. 19–53.

[55] Dugmore, op. cit., p. 57.

[56] M. Skaballanovich, *Tolkovy Typikon*, p. 87.

[57] Tertullian, *Apol.*, 1, 39.

[58] cf. Allan McArthur, *The Evolution of the Christian Year*, London, S.C.M., 1953; Baumstark, *Liturgie Comparée*, pp. 174ff.; Dom B. Botte, 'La Question Pascale' in *Maison-Dieu*, 41, 1955, pp. 88–95.

[59] K. Kohler, *Jewish Theology*, New York, 1918, p. 463.

[60] McArthur, op. cit., p. 143.

[61] *Contra Celsum*, 8, 22.

[62] *Paschal Epis.*, 4 : 5 and 19 : 10.

CHAPTER THREE

THE PROBLEM OF THE DEVELOPMENT
OF THE ORDO

I

AT the beginning of this work we indicated that the majority of historians consider the era of Constantine, when the Church and Empire came to terms with one another, as a moment of crisis in the history of the development of worship. But the opinions of the historians vary greatly when it comes to evaluating this crisis. One of the reasons for this variation is of course that it is 'confessional' historians who are usually concerned with the history of worship, and consciously or unconsciously these historians transfer their own dogmatic and apologetic premises to the material they are studying. For historians of 'Protestant' persuasion the luxurious growth and complication of the cult after Constantine—the extraordinary development of the veneration of saints, Mariology, ritual, etc.—is nothing but a tarnishing of the original Christian worship, a process of corruption by alien and harmful accretions which gradually turned Christianity into a sacramental cultic religion. For historians of the 'Catholic' party this whole liturgical growth was only a manifestation of what was contained in the Church's worship from the very beginning. What was it in fact: a natural development or a metamorphosis? As we can see, the primary question which one brings to a study of liturgical development, and so also the basic problem of such a development, depends on one's point of view. Must we choose between these alternatives? Not necessarily. We do not claim to rise above 'confessional premises.' It seems to us, however, that the very state of the scientific knowledge now available concerning the development of worship excludes the above mentioned alternatives, or in any case requires their fundamental reexamination. We can now say that the problem of the development of worship is no longer a choice between a 'positive' and a 'negative' approach, but of seeing this development as a complex and critical process involving both positive and negative factors—principles of natural development as well as of crisis. Orthodox writers are usually inclined to 'absolutize' the history of worship, to consider the whole of it as divinely established and Providential. Archbishop Filaret of Chernigov was one of the first among our liturgiologists to object to this absolutization, and indeed it scarcely corresponds to the traditional Orthodox approach to worship. In any case it is a major obstacle in the

72

path of a genuine liturgical theology and a properly understood liturgical revival. It is time to realize that both the history of the Church herself as well as the history of her worship contain elements of tragedy—declines as well as revivals, the human element as well as the divine. The historian of worship is called upon to comprehend this history, not justify or condemn it in a wholesale fashion.

The history of worship, beginning with the conversion of the Emperor Constantine, can be reduced to the following basic processes: (1) the development and complication of the external ceremonial of worship, related at first to the building of churches; (2) the increasing complication of liturgical 'cycles'—the Church Year, the week and the day; the appearance of new feasts or whole festal cycles, new liturgical days and new services; (3) the rapid growth of hymnody, which gradually became the main element of worship; and finally (4) the extraordinary development of the Sanctoral—the reverencing of the tombs of the saints, relics, etc. Following Mansvetov and Skaballanovich, it is possible to divide the history of all these processes into the following periods: (1) the fourth and fifth centuries—as the epoch of unchecked liturgical 'flowering,' and all the profound changes in the Church's life connected with this growth; (2) the sixth to eighth centuries—as the epoch of the gradual stabilization of new cult forms; and (3) beginning with the ninth century—the epoch of the final completion of the Byzantine 'type' of worship, when it acquired its present form. Each of the processes listed requires special study and has already been divided into a special field of liturgics or Church history. In the present work, dedicated as it is specifically to the rise and development of the Ordo and thus only of the basic structures of worship, we are unable to consider each of these individual processes in detail. But to the extent that each of them has influenced the history of the Ordo in one way or another, we must characterize—if only in the most general terms —the significance and basic tendencies of this liturgical 'flowering.'

First of all, if we carefully study and consider each of the indicated lines of liturgical development, we will see that none of them had its 'absolute' beginning in the epoch of Constantine. They were all prepared in one way or another in the Church's life in the preceding epoch. Beyond any doubt the peace of Constantine gave a new impetus to these processes of growth, hastened them, and (as we shall see) frequently gave them a new direction. But it would be a gross mistake to assert that one type of worship was simply exchanged for another, or that this change was the result of a liturgical revolution. The construction of churches, for example, although central to Constantine's work in the Church and something which exercised a tremendous influence on the development of worship in the whole of the following epoch, cannot be traced back simply to the days of Constantine. We know that Christians already had churches in the third century, and the destruction of churches was one of the chief measures taken in all subsequent persecutions of the Church. The development of the ritual and ceremonial side of worship can be judged in the light of the 'Apostolic Constitutions,' a document dating at least partially from the second half of the third century. Furthermore, while we can reasonably regard the rapid growth of the Church Year—the appearance of new feast days and liturgical cycles—as one of the most characteristic features of the post-Constantine period, once again this growth was undoubtedly prepared in the evolution of the Church's liturgical life before Constantine. We may point to the appearance and establishment of the cycle of the Manifestation of God (Christmas and the Epiphany in our present terminology), which represent 'une histoire singulierement compliqée' in the words of Dom Botte, one of the best students of this cycle.[1] Even if we reject the hypothesis advanced by McArthur which dates this cycle from the first century, the fact remains that the feasts of Christmas and Epiphany have a 'pre-history' which dates back to the pre-Constantine period. Daniélou has recently proposed a hypothesis which connects the feast of our Lord's entrance into Jerusalem with the Hebrew feast of Tabernacles—one of the three great soteriological festivals of the Jewish year. All this shows that contemporary study of the calendar is not inclined to see any 'revolution' or radical change in the structure of the Church Year in the fourth century. The same can be said for the other lines of liturgical development mentioned above. The appearance of new services in the daily cycle (primarily in the monasteries) and the liturgical evolution of special days of the week did not destroy the basic structures of the daily or weekly cycles as they were formed prior to the fourth century. And finally, the cult of the saints, which was indeed growing to tremendous proportions in the Byzantine period, was rooted directly in the *natalia* of the martyrs, and these are evidenced in texts from the second century.[2]

In studying the liturgical changes which took place in the post-Constantine period, it should be remembered that the freedom which the Church acquired in the so-called Edict of Milan was fundamentally a freedom of cult. In order to evaluate properly what this meant for Christians, it should be noted that for over two hundred years the cult had been the main item in the 'roster of crimes' for which Christians had been punished by the Empire. In the early Church worship was necessarily secret and naturally restricted and curtailed by this secrecy.

This secrecy, of course, ought not to be exaggerated. We know that there were prolonged lulls in the persecution and, as we have just indicated, in many places even in the third century Christians had their own churches and worship was carried out more or less openly. And yet the cult remained tolerated at best, and was always at least theoretically prohibited. Persecution could always flare up, and the gatherings of the faithful could always be condemned as illegal assemblies. Naturally this could not fail to be reflected in the form and spirit of early Christian worship. One need only read (in the *Apostolic Tradition* of Hippolytus of Rome) the list of professions forbidden by the Church to her members (all connected in one way or another with the official paganism of the state) to be convinced of the truth of K. Heussi's opinion that the life of Christians in the age of persecution was 'monastic.' 'If we can imagine,' he writes, 'the position of the early Christians and Christian communities within the pagan world, their complete separation from the life of society, from the theatre, the circus, from all religious and imperial holidays, and the narrow confines within which their external life was passed, then we will understand the monastic character of the world of early Christians, living in the world but as if separated from it. . . .'[3] However, while we stress this mutual rejection of the Church and the world, it should not be forgotten that its basic cause lay in the connection of the Empire with paganism, that is from the Christian viewpoint, the connection of the Empire with a false and demonic religion and a false cult. If the Empire persecuted Christians for 'atheism,' for their renunciation of the imperial gods, the Church renounced the world only to the extent that the world considered itself as living *sub auspiciis deorum* and had joined itself to paganism. 'Our quarrel is not with flesh and blood . . . but with the spirits of evil in this world . . .' (Eph. 6:12). The tragedy of early Christianity, as its apologists knew and keenly experienced, was that as a result of this poisoning of everything by paganism the early Church was really unable to 'put into practice' her positive attitude toward the world, the whole force of her power to make the world—and in it, human life—intelligible, the whole of her cosmic inspiration. She was unable to manifest them fully and was therefore compelled to proclaim them schematically, so to speak, within her cult. Liturgical historians have taken insufficient notice of the fact that the persecutions, conflicts, sufferings and isolation of Christians are almost completely unmentioned in the prayers and liturgical texts of early Christianity. The worship of the early Church was not only more 'majestic' and triumphal than later Byzantine worship, it was in some sense even broader in its 'scope' and inspiration. It resounds with cosmic thanksgiving and embraces in its vision the whole of creation, the whole of history. 'Thou hast manifested the eternal order of the universe through the powers which work within it; thou, O Lord, hast created the world; thou, steadfast in all things, righteous in judgment, marvellous in thy power and glory, omniscient in thy creation and works. . . .' This prayer from the Epistle of Clement of Rome plays in richest chords on the biblical note of the God of Creation, Providence and Salvation. The Church saw herself at the very centre of the world, she confessed herself as the salt and salvation of the world. But the world was opposing her with all the evil of the 'spirits of this world' and so she could not fully reveal to it her purpose and blessing. Thus the freedom of cult bestowed by Constantine was, first of all, an opportunity for her to express at last what she had hitherto been unable to express fully. Externally this expression might appear to be 'revolutionary.' But if we look more carefully into this exuberant growth of cult, we will see its evident continuity with the early Christian cult as defined by the apostolic *lex orandi*. It is really impossible to speak of a 'liturgical revolution' in the fourth century, if by this we mean the appearance of a type of worship differing radically from that which had gone before.

It is also difficult, however, to deny the profound change which after all did mark the Church's liturgical life beginning with the epoch of Constantine. Only it seems to us that the numerous explanations of this change have frequently been untrue or incomplete, and developed out of inadequate historical perspectives. In them we can see signs of the limitations of that method of studying the history of worship which could be defined as 'liturgical formalism.' This method (well formulated in the work of the great Benedictine liturgiologist of the beginning of this century: Dom F. Cabrol [4]), reduces the whole study of the history of worship to the analysis of liturgical texts, to the classification of various 'liturgical families' and their subdivisions, to the study of their influence on one another, and so on. But the Church's worship did not develop in some airless place isolated from all other aspects of her life. We must recognize that one of the most important factors in this development is something which is present in every age and yet capable of changing from one age to another. We are speaking of piety, or the 'religious sense.' Such historians as Bremond, Huizings, Febvre and G. P. Fedotov have discovered the simple fact that the objective content of religion, i.e. what we find in its 'official statements,' in dogma, cult, doctrinal definitions, etc., can be variously accepted and experienced (psychologically speaking) by the religious communities of different periods, depending on the various cultural, spiritual and social peculiarities of the period. A 'coefficient of refraction' determines the 'piety' or 'religious sense' of the period, and this in turn affects the further development of the religion itself in its objective content.

This religious sense can be defined as liturgical piety. This is the psychological acceptance of the cult, its experience within the religious mind, its refraction within the consciousness of the believer. Above all it is important for the historian of worship to know that the 'liturgical piety' of an epoch can in various ways fail to correspond to the liturgy or cult of which this piety is nevertheless the psychological perception or experience. This means that piety can accept the cult in a 'key' other than that in which it was conceived and expressed as text, ceremony or 'rite.' Liturgical piety has the strange power of 'transposing' texts or ceremonies, of attaching a meaning to them which is not their plain or original meaning. This is not a question of not understanding their meaning, or of inadequate perception. It is a question here of a definite colouring of the religious consciousness which sets up between worship as it actually is and its inner acceptance a unique prism, refracting the reality and compelling the believer to experience it in a given key. There are countless examples of this. We shall limit ourselves to two illustrations, taken from areas which we shall have occasion to deal with later in more detail. The explanation of the Eucharistic liturgy as a symbolic depiction of the earthly life of Christ is an artificial explanation for any one who is even slightly familiar with the history, prayers and structure of the liturgy. And yet not only has it been since Byzantine times the most popular and widely accepted explanation, it may also be regarded as the occasion for a whole series of additions and accretions in the ritual of the liturgy which have tended to destroy its original structure. The success of this interpretation can only be explained by the pressure of a definite liturgical piety. My second example has to do with the so-called All-night Vigil. There is no service in our liturgical tradition which in its purpose, wording and structure is more 'majestic,' more triumphal, more solemn with the solemn joy of Easter and, to put it somewhat impressionistically, more gloriously white in its colouring, than the All-night Vigil. And yet in recent years Russian piety has come to accept the All-night Vigil in an almost opposite 'key,' as a hushed, dimly-lit, penitential, sorrowful service of forgiveness. And in our Russian liturgical piety it is one of the most popular services. Conservatism and love of the traditional forms of cult plus an extraordinary flexibility in their interpretation; the ability to accept and experience these forms in new ways and to 'project' into them psychological and religious experiences stemming often from completely alien sources—such are the characteristics of liturgical piety.

In the light of all this we feel that it is impossible to understand either the history of worship or its condition in any given era without first taking into account the factor of liturgical piety. As G. Dix has said : 'It is one thing to know the history of worship, that is when such and such a custom was introduced, and where; it is a much more difficult task to understand the real causes leading to these changes.' [5] And we must regard the evolution and development of liturgical piety as one of the major causes. It is in the profound reformation of liturgical piety and not in new forms of cult, no matter how striking they may seem to be at first glance, that we must see the basic change brought about in the Church's liturgical life by the peace of Constantine. The novelty of forms, as we have already indicated, was not so great that under more careful analysis one could not trace their connection with the forms of the preceding age. It was rather the change in liturgical piety which introduced a complexity and peculiar dualism into the development of worship, and which leads us now to see in that worship the continuation or revelation of elements contained within it from the very beginning and, at the same time, a certain real 'metamorphosis' which made the Christian cult in part something other than what it was in the early Church. We must now characterize this change in liturgical piety.

For all the formal continuity of the Jewish and Christian cults, the liturgical piety of the early Church was determined also by a consciousness of the absolute newness of the reality manifested and embodied in the Church and her cult. But we have seen that this newness was not a newness in the sense of a complete revolution, something unexpected, unheard of, going beyond the limits of the accustomed categories of thought and experience. From the viewpoint of the sacred history of salvation or (in the terminology of the Apostle Paul) of the mystery of salvation, this newness was a 'natural' completion and fulfilment. The One who had been expected had come; what God had spoken of from the very beginning had come to pass. Thus the 'newness' of Christianity not only could but also had to be expressed in relation to the Old Covenant, in the categories of the Old Testament messianic experience. The newness of the Christian cult was expressed naturally in the forms and language of the Jewish liturgical tradition. The newness, nevertheless, was absolute. 'The old has passed away, now all things are new.' This meant that in the light of the coming of the Messiah, as a result of His saving work, everything 'old' had acquired

78

a new meaning, had been renewed and transformed in its significance. The 'old' cult of Moses was based wholly on the principle of mediation and this principle was expressed in the three fundamental 'categories' of Old Testament worship : the Temple, the priesthood and the institution of sacrifices. This was a 'cult' and a 'religion' in the deepest sense of these words, in the sense of mediation, of a connecting of, a system of contacts and relationships with the 'holy,' with 'God.' In a remarkable book devoted to the evolution of the idea of the Temple in the Old Covenant and early Christianity, Fr. Congar demonstrates clearly the 'renewal' of these categories in the Church. This was a renewal which made all of them in equal measure an inevitable and necessary path to the New Covenant, and at the same time filled them with a completely new content. Describing the complex system of Temple restrictions (the court of the Gentiles, the Porch of Women, the Porch for the entrance of Jews in a state of ritual purity, the places for the priests and Levites, the altar accessible only to those conducting the service and, finally, the 'holy of holies,' entered only once a year by the high priest) Congar says : 'these rules were justified and sensible : they pointed to that contracting of the whole nation into the Person of its true High Priest Jesus Christ, who contains us all and "represents" us before the Father. But they were temporary, since the Holy Spirit had shown that "the way into the sanctuary was not open as long as the former tabernacle still stands" (Heb. 9 :8). In Christ, when He had finished all things in Himself (John 19 :30), this system of mediation disappeared. Now in fact we have "boldness to enter into the sanctuary by the blood of Jesus Christ, by a new and living way, which He has opened for us through the curtain, that is, through His flesh" ' (Heb. 10 :19–20). 'The newness of the Christian cult,' Congar continues, 'is even more radical. It is not just a question of a transition from a system of mediation to a system of personal contact with the deepest Reality. Or it would be better to say that if this is what it is, then it is because the highest Reality has revealed and communicated Himself in a new way, so that there can be no greater or more profound communion. The time has come for worship "in spirit and truth." ' [6] This change or newness was expressed best of all in the Christian 'reception' of the Temple, priesthood and sacrifices. Congar rightly indicates the ease and naturalness which marked the 'transposition' of the idea of the Temple, as a building, as the place and condition for mediation, into the idea of the Temple as the Church and the community of believers. 'As soon as we encounter the question of the Temple in Christianity after Pentecost,' he writes, 'we at once meet the fully articulated affirmation : This Temple is the Church herself, the community of the faithful.' The same can be said about the priesthood : in its New Testament transposition it ceases to be an expression of mediation and becomes an expression of the Church herself, as a sacred body, as the priesthood of Christ. And finally, spiritual sacrifices are offered in this spiritual Temple. This is not simply a reference to the great 'spiritualizing' of the bloody sacrifices of the Old Testament in the Christian offering (the Eucharist), but a revelation of the newness of the sacrifice itself : 'the Temple is spiritual, and the sacrifices are spiritual, since they are now nothing other than man himself.' [7] In other words, the significance of the Eucharist as sacrifice is not the idea of mediation but that the Eucharist is a manifestation and actualization of the sacrificial character of the Church herself as the people of God who participate 'in Christ,' in the complete, only and consummate sacrifice of all sacrifices.

We repeat, the regeneration of the Hebrew cult within Christianity was not the regeneration of its external forms but of its significance and function as rooted in the Church's own faith in herself, in her ecclesiological consciousness. It is a mistake to see the essence of the change as a 'spiritualization,' as liberal Protestant theology has done, i.e. as a simple purification and ennobling of the cult, which then, we are told, became less 'materialistic, ritualistic, etc.' Contemporary research has established clearly the liturgical nature of the early Church, the central place of worship in the Church, and indeed of worship externally analogous to the Jewish worship of the time. The chief significance of the change was rather in the appearance of a new understanding of the cult, of a new liturgical piety wholly determined by the faith of Christians in the ontological newness of the Church as the eschatological beginning in this world, in this aeon, of the Aeon of the Kingdom. Only by understanding the eschatological and ecclesiological basis of this 'metamorphosis' can we properly understand what constitutes historically the innate antinomy of the Christian *lex orandi* : its unquestionable continuity with Jewish tradition and its equally unquestionable newness. The Old Testament cult was viewed by Christians not only as a providential preparation for and prototype of the new, but also as its necessary foundation, since only by the 'transposition' of its basic categories—Temple, priesthood and sacrifice—was it possible to express and reveal the newness of the Church as the revelation of what had been promised, as the fulfilment of what had been hoped for, as an eschatological fulfilment. We can even say also that the cult remained a cult, i.e. an Ordo, a rite, a 'rule of prayer,' because only a cult can express or manifest in 'this world'—this aeon—the holy, the wholly-other, the divine, the supra-worldly. But this cult was subjected to an eschatological transposition, since within the Church as the Body of Christ the wholly-other was realized as something given, fulfilled, communicated to people, something already belonging to them. Not a mediation between the sacred and the profane, but the fact of the accomplished consecration of the people by the Holy Spirit, their transformation into 'sons of God'—herein lies the newness of the content and significance of this cult. It received its purest expression in the Eucharist—in a cultic act whose significance was not the renewal of mediation but the actualization of the identification of the Church with the Body of Christ and of the fact that she belonged to the Aeon of the Kingdom. But it was expressed also in the liturgy of time, in the eschatological cycle of the Lord's Day, in the Christian reception of the Passover and Pentecost. This liturgical piety of the early Church, which can be called quite accurately eschatological and ecclesiological (just as the eschatology and ecclesiology of the early Church may well be defined, in the words of Fr. N. Afanasiev, as Eucharistic and liturgical), gave a completely unique character to the Christian worship of the first three centuries, revealing the significance of its *lex orandi.*

For an understanding of the liturgical tradition and piety of early pre-Constantine Christianity we must do more than indicate their Jewish antecedents. It is no less important to indicate the relationship of the Church to that 'liturgical piety' which was characteristic of the epoch of the spread of Christianity in the Graeco-Roman world and which can be defined as 'mysteriological.' The question of the relationship of the Christian cult to the pagan mysteries and the mysteriological piety connected with them has passed through many stages, of course, and it is probably still too soon to say that it has been finally decided. Only now in fact has it really been set forth in its true significance. Let us recall briefly that this question began with the thesis advanced by the representatives of the comparative school in the history of religions—Reitzenstein, Bousset, Reinach, Loisy. According to this thesis Christianity was at a very early date, still in the apostolic era, reborn as a mysteriological religion, under the influence of the mystery cults widespread in the Hellenistic world. Whatever its Jewish-Palestinian origin may have been, it spread through the Graeco-Roman world and conquered it as a 'mystery'; it was, according to Loisy, 'nothing more than a particular instance of a general movement.' [8] As we have already pointed out, this thesis did not reign for long. A more scientific study of the Jewish roots of the Christian cult, and also a deepening exegesis of the New Testament—especially of the Pauline use of the term 'mystery'—exploded this thesis.[9] An 'antithesis' came on the heels of the 'thesis' : the denial of any genetic connection between the Christian cult and the pagan mysteries. In all this the problem of their mutual relationship was never really solved. The opponents of the mysteriological theory (Lagrange, for example) who had challenged the obviously anti-Christian 'animus' of Loisy's idea, rightly demonstrated the superficiality and hasty generalizations of this theory.[10] Not being themselves either liturgiologists or historians of cult, they directed all their attention on its weakest point, that is, the affirmation of the genetic connection between Christianity and the 'mysteries.' They successfully refuted this affirmation, but in the meantime the question of the essential nature of the Christian cult remained open and unanswered, i.e. whether the cult was not in reality—even without outside influence—a mystery. It was in fact just such an assertion which was advanced by the noted Benedictine liturgiologist Dom Odo Casel, head of the liturgical movement at Maria-Laach. Here was a synthesis reconciling and removing the conflict between the thesis and antithesis mentioned above. His *Mysterienlehre* was the beginning of an extraordinary rehabilitation of the connection between Christianity and the mysteries, of its acceptance not as a concession to the anti-Christian and tendentious simplifications of Loisy, but as a norm innate in the Christian cult.[11] In the literature of the contemporary liturgical movement there is no more popular term than *mysterion*. The explanation of Christian worship begins and ends with this word, and it is advanced as the most adequate term for the definition of its essence. According to Casel's theory *mysterion* is the necessary and organic form of cult in general, and therefore also of the Christian cult; and the latter, even though genetically independent of the pagan mysteries, was, first of all, a mystery in its form and essence and, second, the natural and complete 'fulfilment' of those beliefs and expectations and that spirituality which found expression in the Hellenistic mysteries.[12]

While not denying Dom Casel's great services in the task of reviving the liturgical question, or the depth and truth of many of his views, we must nevertheless regard his basic assertion—concerning the mysteriological nature of the Christian cult—as mistaken. We feel rather that the early Church openly and consciously set herself and her cult in opposition to the 'mysteries,' and that much of her strength was devoted to a struggle with this mysteriological piety in the first and decisive period of her confrontation with the Graeco-Roman world. The fundamental and constant distinction between the Christian liturgical tradition and the mysteriological piety of the Hellenistic world is a fact which, in our opinion, is no less important for the historian of worship than the antithetical relationship between the Christian and Jewish cult mentioned above.

Once again it is necessary to distinguish between the forms of the cult (its structure, language and ceremonies) and its acceptance or experience by the community. Certainly marks of similarity may be found between the Christian cult and the mysteries when viewed from the external, formal standpoint, although this similarity should not be exaggerated. But the real issue, of course, does not lie in these external differences and similarities. What we are concerned with here is the tremendous difference in the understanding of the significance and function of the cult; or to put it even more accurately, we are concerned with the interrelationship of faith and cult. In the broadest terms mystery or mysteriological piety can be defined as a faith in cult, in its saving and sanctifying power. If the idea of mediation was the unifying principle in Old Testament worship, then the idea of sanctification stands in the foreground of the religion of mystery. Through participation in the mystery man is sanctified, initiated into higher secrets, receives salvation, acquires 'sanctity.' In form the mystery is the religious, dramatic and ritual expression and re-enactment of a myth, of a 'drama of salvation.' But it is characteristic of mysteriological piety that the myth plays a secondary role and is wholly subordinated to the cult and disclosed in the cult. It is not faith in the myth being enacted which is required of the participants in the mystery, but simply faith in the saving and sanctifying power of the enactment, faith in the cultic act itself. The representation of the myth is therefore in some sense more real than the myth, since only within the cult and by participation in it is the idea of the myth communicated to people. The cult is primary; the myth is defined by the cult and grows out of it. Hence the symbolicalness of the mysteriological cult, its dramatic character, the elaboration in it of all the details of the myth. Its whole meaning is in the precise re-enactment of the drama of salvation, since the drama does not exist outside this cult.[13] The great success of the mysteriological cults, as Juvenal has correctly pointed out in his satire, lay therefore in their 'liturgy' and not at all in their dogma or ethics. They were preached and proclaimed precisely as a cult, as a cultic initiation, and not as a truth or doctrine.

The original success of Christianity must therefore be explained by opposite causes, and it is the failure to accept this conclusion which is, it seems to us, the main error both of the anti-Christian theory of Loisy as well as the profoundly reverent and well-intentioned theory of Casel. Christianity was preached as a saving faith and not as a saving cult. In it the cult was not an object of faith but its result. Historians have not sufficiently emphasized the fact that cult had no place in the preaching of Christianity, that it is not even mentioned in its *kerygma*.

This is so because at the centre of the Christian *kerygma* there is a proclamation of the fact of the coming of the Messiah and a call to believe in this fact as having saving significance. A New Aeon is entering into the world as a result of this fact, is being revealed in the world; faith is what brings man into this New Aeon. The cult is only the realization, the actualization of what the believer has already attained by faith, and its whole significance is in the fact that it leads into the Church, the new people of God, created and brought into being by faith. Here also we see the fundamental difference between the Christian and the mysteriological cult, a difference both in function and content. In the mystery the 'myth' is subordinated to the cult and is indeed a myth, acquiring whatever reality it has only from the cult, while in Christianity what is primary is fact, with its historicity and reality, the cult having reality only in so far as the fact is real. If in the mystery the historical authenticity of the drama reproduced and enacted in the cult is secondary and has no decisive significance, in Christianity the 'historicity' of the fact is the *alpha* and *omega* of its whole faith and preaching. 'If Christ has not risen from the dead, our faith is vain . . .' and so the cult is vain also. On the one hand the mystery cult is not only primary, it is an end in itself; mysteriological piety knows only a cultic society. The cult is the sole content of the cultic society, outside it the society has neither reality nor purpose. Its purpose in performing the cult is to 'communicate' to its members what they are looking for in the cult : sanctification, happiness, etc. On the other hand in Christianity the cult establishes the reality of the Church. Its purpose is not the individual sanctification of its members, but the creation of the people of God as the Body of Christ, the manifestation of the Church as new life in the New Aeon. It is not an end, but a means, or, if it is to be regarded as the end and content of the life of the Church, then only to the extent that it is sharply distinguished from the cult of 'mediation' and the cult of 'sanctification,' only to the extent that in it the very idea of cult is regenerated and acquires a new value—that it is to be now the revelation of the eschatological fullness of the Kingdom, in anticipation of the 'Day of the Lord.' This difference in the function of the cult and its interrelation with the faith and life of the society performing it also determines its difference in content from the mysteriological cults. The mysteriological cult is symbolic in so far as the myth depicted in it is void of historical authenticity; it is only in the cult that the myth becomes a reality at all. Hence the necessity to reproduce it in all detail, to portray the saving drama, to repeat it in the cult. The drama is conceived of as efficacious and saving only in this repetition. The Christian cult, on the contrary, is not experienced as a repetition of the saving fact in which it is rooted, since this fact was unique and unrepeatable. The Christian cult is the proclamation of the saving nature of this fact and also the realization and revelation, the actualization of its eternal efficacy, of the saving reality created by it. 'To proclaim the Lord's death, to confess His resurrection'—this is not at all the same thing as repetition or portrayal. It is quite evident historically that the early Church knew nothing about the later 'symbolical' explanation of her ceremonies of worship. Of course Baptism and the immersion in water was a 'likeness' (ὁμοίωμα) of death and resurrection (Rom. 6 : 5). But in the first place it was a likeness of the death and resurrection of the believer and not of Christ, and second, this act was possible only on the basis of faith in the saving nature of the fact of Christ's death and resurrection, which were not 'symbolized' in the cult at all. The water in Baptism is the figure of a new life, a new creation, a new reality created by Christ, and the one who has come to believe in Christ is immersed in it, is revived and regenerated by it, is led into it. This act does not fall within the definition of mystery given by Casel : 'A sacred and cultic act by means of which the redemptive act of the past is made present in the form of a specific ceremony; the cultic society performing this sacred ceremony is united with the redemptive act being recalled and in this way accomplishes its salvation.' [14] In Baptism Christ does not die and rise again, which would be its essence if it were a mystery, but the believer actualizes his faith in Christ, and in the Church, as Salvation and New Life. Nor is the believer united to the death and resurrection of Christ as if they were separate events mysteriologically reproduced in the cult, instead he is united to a new spiritual reality, a new life, a New Aeon, created by these unrepeatable events. The conditions for this communion are repentance (μετάνοια)— the death of the old 'I'—and faith—the resurrection of the new man 'in Christ.' And these are actualized in the Sacrament : 'that we too might walk in newness of life' (Rom. 6 : 4). In the early Eucharist there was no idea of a ritual symbolization of the life of Christ and His sacrifice. This is a theme which will appear later (cf. the Office of Oblation—*Proskomidia*), under the influence of one theology and as the point of departure for another (see below). The remembrance of Christ which He instituted ('This do in remembrance of Me') is the affirmation of His 'Parousia,' of His Presence, it is the actualization of His Kingdom. People gain access to this Kingdom through His death and resurrection, but once again the Eucharist does not reproduce or symbolize these events, instead it manifests their efficacy and the Church's participatian in the Body of Christ established by these events.

INTRODUCTION TO LITURGICAL THEOLOGY

The early Christian cult not only did not have the main features of a mysteriological cult, but the Church consciously and openly set herself in opposition to mysteriological piety and the cults of the mysteries. The best forces of the Church were sent into the struggle against the mysteries in the pre-Nicene epoch, since mysteriological piety was then the chief danger for Christianity, as the piety of the Law and the cult of mediation were in the period of Judeo-Christianity. It is no accident that cult, and precisely a mysteriological cult, stood at the centre of the life of the gnostic sects, the Church's main enemy in this period. The conflict with gnosticism was the conflict of the Church against the danger of dissolving her *kerygma* in myth. The radical newness of the Christian *lex orandi* and of the 'liturgical piety' determined by it—a newness in relation both to Judaism and to mysteriological paganism—provides us therefore with a vantage point from which we may understand the changes in the Church's worship which came as a result of the peace of Constantine.

2

The change which began gradually to come into being in Christian worship as a result of the changed position of the Church in the world may be seen in the assimilation by the Christian cult of a mysteriological character, in the adoption of that understanding and experience of the cult which we have called mysteriological. Let us stipulate at once that we consider this neither a 'metamorphosis' nor a 'revolution.' This was not the simple and unqualified acceptance by the Church of that religious mood, that liturgical piety and those forms of cult which she had rejected in the preceding epoch as being incompatible with the cult 'in the Spirit and the Truth' which was given to men by Christ. If this had been so then it would certainly be possible to regard the post-Constantine liturgical development of Christianity as a transformation or fall of the Church, her surrender without resistance to the reigning 'piety,' her complete dilution within this piety. But we categorically reject the understanding of the peace of Constantine as a 'pseudo-victory' of Christianity—victory bought at the price of compromise. In fact this process of development was far more complicated, and as we have already said, it is as wrong to regard it as a 'victory' as it is to see it as a 'defeat.' For an understanding of the Byzantine liturgical synthesis to which this process finally led there must be an elucidation of the host of different and often contradictory factors operating in this process.

First of all it should be recalled that the liturgical development after

Constantine was closely related to the new missionary situation in which the Church found herself after her reconciliation with the Empire. The Church experienced this reconciliation and her new freedom as a providential act destined to bring to Christ people then dwelling in the darkness and shadow of death, in the realm of idols. The first problem to come before the Church in all its complexity was that of the conversion and Christianization of the masses, as distinct from the problem of individual conversions.[15] This was a problem of the Christianization of society itself with its organized life, customs and, most important, its religious psychology. The Church 'came out from behind the door she had been compelled to bolt, and took the inquisitive world of antiquity beneath her vaulted arches. But the world brought in its own alarms and doubts and temptations—it brought both a great longing and a great presumption. The Church had to satisfy this longing and conquer this presumption.' [16] This meant that she had to incorporate society into the new life 'in Christ' not just in an external sense, but also internally.

We must accept as a characteristic feature of this new missionary situation the fact that it was the cult which became the centre of the attention and religious interests of the mass of newly converted people who streamed into the Church after her official reception by the Empire. The new and now peaceful meeting of the Church and world can be characterized as a meeting on the ground of cult. The 'conversion' of this world was to a remarkable degree a 'liturgical' conversion. It is not difficult to understand the reason for this. For paganism as a whole and especially for the pagan common people religion and cult were identical concepts. Paganism was first of all a system of cults. It is no accident therefore that in the Edict of Milan religious freedom was granted precisely as freedom of cult. Both Constantine himself and the masses which followed him naturally brought into Christianity their own cultic understanding and experience of religion, their own liturgical piety. This identification of religion with cult so typical of the times, also meant that a new meaning was attached to the liturgical life of the Church, a function different from that which it had in the early Christian period. But in order to understand the Church's reaction to this new 'liturgical piety' it should be remembered that long before Constantine the development of worship had been at least in part determined by the increasingly complicated and ever-growing institution of the catechumenate.[17] From the beginning of the fourth century the problem of catechizing and receiving pagans into the Church was complicated still more. It must be remembered that paganism, which the Church had been fighting with all her strength, was not so much a doctrine as it was a cosmic feeling connected in the deepest organic way with the whole fabric of the social, political and economic life of the times. To destroy the idols, to demolish the temples and to prohibit the offering of sacrifices certainly did not mean the end of paganism as a cosmic feeling. The history of 'double faith,' which still exists among almost all peoples of Christian culture, bears eloquent witness to the vitality of the pagan outlook. The struggle against paganism reached a special pitch when the Church collided with the 'village,' i.e. with that stratum of the population for whom the pagan cult was an organic part of man's relationship to nature. The struggle against paganism could not be limited to a negative thrust : the exposure and overthrow of idols and sacrifices. The Church had to fill up that empty space created by the elimination of the pagan cult, and this forced the Church to take upon herself the religious sanctification of those areas of life which had formerly been 'served' by paganism. To put it briefly, Christianity, in order to 'convert' the world, had to take on the function of a religion : the sanction, defence and justification of all those aspects of the world, society and life from which it had been cut off during the epoch of persecution. This new missionary situation demanded at least some partial adaptation of the Christian cult, and the cult became one of the most important and convenient instruments for the 'churching' of the masses.

We have already defined this adaptation as the acceptance by the Church, at least in part, of the mysteriological understanding of the cult, with the immediate qualification that this was not a metamorphosis or radical regeneration of the *lex orandi* which had existed from the beginning. Turning now to a demonstration of this hitherto *a priori* position, we must repeat that the process was extremely complicated. The following stages can be distinguished. At first there was an elemental break-through of 'mysteriological piety' in the life of the Church, producing a double reaction or dualism : its acceptance by some and resistance by others. After this there was a gradual 'digestion' of this new 'liturgical piety,' a period of unstable equilibrium; and finally, the third period, which we have called the Byzantine synthesis, with its expression in the *Typicon,* the crystallized *lex orandi* of the Orthodox East. Let us proceed now to as brief an analysis as is possible of these three moments in the dialectic of the Byzantine Ordo.

Certainly the evolution of the layout and significance of the church building, or in general of the location of the cult in the liturgical life of the Church after Constantine, should be placed in the forefront of the process which we have defined as the 'break-through' of mysteriological piety. We have already noticed the 'transposition' which the idea of the temple underwent at the very beginning of Christianity, a transposition which separated the Church from the Jewish theology of the Temple. We reduced the Christian idea of the Temple to the simple formula : Here is the Church, and here is the believer, as a living temple of the Holy Spirit and as the Body of Christ. It would be no exaggeration to say that in the pre-Constantine Church the temple as such, i.e. the building within which worship was carried on, played no special role at all. Its function was, so to speak, instrumental : simply the place for a gathering, for the *ecclesia*. Moreover a clearly anti-temple tendency can be noticed in Stephen's speech before the Sanhedrin, a tendency which was of course not limited to Stephen alone : 'The All Highest does not live in temples made with hands' (Acts 7 :48). Of course for a long period Christians were deprived of the opportunity to build churches, but it would be a mistake to explain the absence and want of development of a temple piety in the early Church by exclusively external reasons. In the centre of the faith and consciousness of the early Christian community there was the experience of the Church as the reality of a living temple, actualized in the Eucharistic assembly. Thus the whole significance of the building in which the assembly took place (*domus ecclesiae*—a term appearing in various places quite early) was that it made possible this realization, or fullness ($\pi\lambda\eta\rho\omega\mu\alpha$) of the Church in a given place. As with all things in the experience of early Christianity, the idea of the temple or church building was subordinated to the idea of the Church, and was expressed in the categories of Eucharistic ecclesiology.

Beginning with the conversion of Constantine, a great change occurred in this understanding of the church building and its significance. There is no need here to set forth the history of church construction during and after the reign of Constantine. Professor A. Grabar has analysed it brilliantly in his book *Martyrium*.[18] What interests us is its general significance, and this is clear enough. The church building was gradually freed from subordination to its ecclesiological meaning, acquired its own independent significance, and the centre of attention was shifted from the Church assembled and realized within it to the church building itself, as in fact a sanctified building or sanctuary. The intense interest in church construction of Constantine himself, from his first steps in the Christian life, was of course not something accidental. Here was an expression of that liturgical piety which was to make itself felt ever more strongly in the mind of the Church in the years to come. This was a church-sanctuary, a place for the habitation and residence of the sacred, capable therefore of sanctifying and communicating the sacred to whoever entered it.[19] Professor Grabar demonstrates very clearly the twofold origin of Christian church construction as it developed after the beginning of the fourth century. On the one hand there was the Christian reception of the ancient *heroon* (ἡρόων) or temple-memorial raised over the tomb of a martyr or saint, or at the place of his theophany. On the other hand there was the *basilica,* the place for public assembly and the state cult. Both forms gradually merged, but characteristically their merger took the form of the 'hero's temple' or sanctuary. Uppermost was the understanding of the church as the place of residence of the sacred. Even more striking was the gradual uniting of the altar—the Lord's Table, the place of Eucharistic offering and administration of the Holy Gifts—with the tomb of a saint, and then the placing of relics in the altar.[20] This also testifies to the new experience, of the church building as a sacred place. Already we have deposited here the whole future Byzantine theology of the church building, which found expression later in the rite for the consecration of a church—so extraordinarily complicated in its symbolism and its sacred 'materialism.' This was the beginning of that church piety which little by little became one of the most characteristic features of Christian society. It is not difficult to trace the growth of this evolution in the memorials of the early Byzantine epoch. In John Chrysostom, however, one can still hear an echo of the old understanding of the church building, even the wish to check the wild growth or—as we have called it—the breakthrough of the new piety. In his treatise 'On the Cross and the Robber' Chrysostom says : 'But when Christ came . . . He purified the whole earth, and made every place suitable for prayer. If you wish to know how the whole earth finally became a temple. . . .' This is completely in the spirit of Stephen's speech : '. . . heaven is my throne, and the earth is a footstool for my feet . . .' (Acts 7 :49). But already in the Areopogitic writings, one of the basic memorials of the new mysteriological liturgical piety, the Church is defined as a sacred building, separated from the profane and opposed to it by reason of its sacredness. This idea will be repeated and developed in countless commentaries which Byzantine piety will later devote to the symbolism of the church building.

As another example of the new experiences of the cult, related to the first and complementing it, we must point to the rapid development in this same period of the veneration of holy places, the growth of an intense interest in sacred 'topography.' Once again the contrast of this interest with the concerns of the early Church is striking. It is sufficient to recall that before the special attention shown by Constantine toward Jerusalem as the main centre of the earthly life of the Saviour, this city was the object of no special veneration, and the

Bishop of Aelia Capitolinus was even at the beginning of the fourth century still only a 'suffragan' of the Metropolitan of Palestinian Caesarea. Like the idea of the church-temple, the idea of Jerusalem or Holy Zion, so central in the Jewish understanding of the messianic fulfilment, was subjected to a 'transposition' in the Christian faith and was grafted into its Eucharistic and eschatological ecclesiology. We see no attempts on the part of the Jerusalem Church to make appeal to her exclusive place of residence or to conclude from this that she had any kind of seniority. In that period the authority of the local Church already included the concept of the authority of the Apostle who was her founder, but not yet the idea of the sacredness of the place as such. Here again the source of this 'indifference' lies not in the want of development of a particular category in the mind of the early Church, but on the contrary in the powerful and exclusive experience of the Church herself as *Parousia,* as the Presence of the Risen Lord, as the Beginning of His Kingdom. This was not a weakness of historical interest, but the faith that the meaning of the historical events described in the Gospel was fulfilled in the Church, in the new life given by the Church. But from the fourth century on, parallel to the change in the idea of the church building and in connection with it, there gradually arose another form of experience of the 'sacred place,' rooted in the mysteriological piety of the age. Once more the attitude of Constantine himself is extremely typical and his influence was decisive. At first in Rome, then in the East and in Palestine he introduced the cult of holy places by the erection of churches and by the special religious veneration which he displayed toward these places. This marked the beginning of local cults connected with specific events or persons, and it was these cults which for the most part explained the success of the *heroon*-churches.[21] But it is important to emphasize that the significance of this local cult was not in its ability to arouse historical interest so much as it was in the fact that it expressed the sense and need of the sacred as something materialized, localized, and introduced into the very fabric of natural life as its religious sanction or 'consecration.' It was characteristic that where there was no 'sacred place'—the tomb of an Apostle or martyr, or perhaps a memorial of a theophany—there was resort to an artificial creation of these things by means of the discovery or translation of relics, and by the relating of secondary events in biblical history to specific places. The discovery of the relics of Stephen the first martyr in A.D. 415 became a kind of prototype for such phenomena, so extremely popular in Byzantine piety.[22] Characteristic also was the connection of these holy places with civic life, the evident tendency to 'sanctify' the life and activity of the city, the society, the Empire. The building of memorial-churches in the sacred centres of Christian history (The Holy Sepulchre in Jerusalem, the tomb of the Apostle Peter in the Vatican) testifies to the adoption by Christianity of norms of liturgical piety which were common to all antiquity, and the building of a church in the centre of a city indicated its setting within the old idea of the temple as the mystical core of the city, sanctifying its life and rendering it *sub auspiciis deorum.* This was especially noticeable in the case of Constantinople, the new capital built by Constantine, where he was for the first time able to embody his idea of a Christian πολίτευμα.[23] In line with this idea Constantinople came to be accepted as the sacred centre of the Christian Empire. This idea was later expressed in a whole liturgical cycle of Imperial and specifically Constantinopolitan feast days. In studying this aspect of Constantine's activity, however, we must not forget that here more than anywhere else he was the voice of his age, the one who expressed its moods and world view, its religious psychology. This is borne out by the extremely rapid success of his plans. His own liturgical piety, shared as it was by a whole epoch, could not fail to be reflected in the development of the form and content of Christian worship nor fail to define at least in part its ultimate destiny.

We have dwelt first on church building and the cult of holy places because together they form one of the chief causes and at the same time manifestations of that upheaval in liturgical piety which marked the early Byzantine era, and which we regard as decisive in the history of Byzantine worship. They radically altered the external setting of Christian worship; they made at least its external adaptation to the new conditions inevitable. It is enough to glance at the dimensions of the churches and basilicas of the early Byzantine period which have been preserved (even partially) in order to understand at once that the worship carried out in them could not retain its former style and had to be arrayed in a new vesture. The character of this change can be best understood perhaps 'in reverse,' from an example taken from our own time. In the first years of the Russian emigration, when worship had to be celebrated in cellars and garages converted into churches, we became aware of the complete impossibility of celebrating it 'as it should be,' according to all the canons of elegance and solemnity proper to the synodical style of Russian Orthodoxy. This became especially apparent on the days of services conducted by the archbishop or on special solemn festivals. In a very short time a piety was created which was not only by necessity but also in essence opposed to any show of pomp or external solemnity in worship, which would endure such pomp with suffering, as something undesirable and inappropriate to the nature of the Christian cult. For many people these wretched garage churches will remain forever connected with the fullness of liturgical experience, something which becomes impossible in churches of magnificent and grandiose design. The same process began in the Church—only in the opposite direction—when large and more or less costly churches began to appear. Christian worship of the first and second centuries was perforce limited to simplicity and reduced to its most basic and necessary 'lines.' It was devoid of external pomp. A few indispensable actions and ceremonies had to 'express' all its inner movement, its liturgical dynamic. Externally it was almost static: the bishop seated, surrounded by presbyters facing the assembly, the Supper Table, on which the deacons placed the gifts which were being offered, preaching, prayer, the *anaphora* and the distribution of the Holy Gifts—here in sum was the entire rite of the Eucharist, which can still be readily distinguished in our contemporary liturgy beneath the accretions of a later period. But in the great, magnificent and indeed solemn basilicas the complication and 'decoration' of worship was inevitable, if only because if it had been celebrated in the old way it simply would not have reached the eyes and ears of those assembled. In studying the earliest types of the Liturgy and its basic structure, which is preserved to-day, one realizes the extent to which it 'presupposed' a small assembly and room, and what an 'amplification' was needed when the external conditions of its celebration were changed. Later we shall touch again on the particular details of this process of complication. Here it is enough to say that the development of that solemnity which henceforth became a fundamental and necessary characteristic of the Christian cult was based precisely on these altered external conditions. In liturgics, or rather in the phenomenology of cult, it is high time that a distinction was made between inner and outer solemnity. Inner solemnity lies in the fullness of religious meaning invested in an action, no matter how simple it may be: the breaking of bread, the lifting up the hands, etc., or more accurately, it is the complete awareness and acceptance of this meaning by those who are performing the ceremony or who are present at it. This is inner solemnity because any one who does not believe in it or who does not know the meaning of this ceremony simply does not perceive or experience it as a solemn action. In order to see the assembly of the little group of disciples—'who met together on the first day of the week for the breaking of bread' on the third floor of one of the tenement houses of Troas—in order to see this as a glorious and solemn occasion, as the 'Day of the Lord' and a participation in the feast of the Kingdom, one had to be of one mind and faith with those who had gathered, and it was this faith which created the inner solemnity of the action. External solemnity, on the other hand, consists in the sacralization of sacred ceremonies and actions, in emphasizing that they are not 'simple,' in building around them an atmosphere of sacred and religious fear which cannot fail to influence the way they are received and experienced by the participants in the cult. In the light of this distinction one can say that early Christian worship was profoundly solemn with an inner solemnity, and devoid of external solemnity. First, because the pagan cults were shot through with this external solemnity and Christians regarded this style of worship as *pompa diabola;* and second, of course, because external conditions themselves made such solemnity impossible. But the external setting of the cult was changed radically in the fourth century, and the official abolition of paganism rendered external solemnity less dangerous for the Church. From the missionary viewpoint—with the attraction of the 'masses' as an objective—it even seemed useful now to borrow from paganism everything that could be borrowed without distorting the basic meaning of the Christian faith. Moreover, we probably should not regard the pagan cults as the main source for this new outer solemnity of Christian worship, but rather the Imperial court ceremonial, which was religious in character and was a typical feature of the Hellenistic monarchies.[24] This Imperial liturgy was more 'admissible' for the Church than the pagan ceremonies, in view of the miraculous recognition of the Roman monarchy in the person of Constantine on the day of the fateful battle near the Ponte Molle.

The complication of ceremonial which is evidenced in the numerous memorials from this new era must be placed in the category of this external solemnity. For example, we may point to the ceremony of processions which became one of the typical forms of the cult. A complex system of entrances, exits and litanies, of the movement of the whole praying congregation from one place to another, was introduced into worship, and this of course gave to worship not only an inner but also an outer dynamic, a dramatic and symbolic significance. Another example is the rapid and extravagant growth of hymnody, the ever more complicated system of church singing, which in the course of time began to occupy such a disproportionately large place that quite often the original biblical and eschatological material was displaced. Finally the complication and development of the 'material' side of the cult (vestments, incense, candles, etc., the growth of that complex cultic organization or economy so typical of Byzantine ecclesiastical piety) must also be explained at least partially by this court influence.

The new attitude toward the church building, the cult of holy places, the development of ceremony in its aspect of outer solemnity and 'symbolicalness'—all this is to be related for the most part to the form of worship, to its external setting. No less important, however, in this process of adoption of a 'mysteriological' colouring by the Christian cult, were the substantial changes made in the very content of worship, the inclusion within it of new elements and new 'emphases.' In one of the chapters of his book Dix has defined the essence of this change as a 'reconciliation with time.' [25] Formerly eschatological, the Christian cult now became historical. This meant that the separate events of the history of salvation stood out in it as objects of special cultic commemoration, in which their redemptive significance was in some way connected with the various aspects of human life and history. Sacred history, which in the early cult, in Dix's view, was contrasted with profane history, was now as it were introduced into natural life, became its correlative, as the principle of its sanctification and meaning. This is how Dix explains the rapid development of cycles of festivals dedicated to the separate events in the earthly life of the Saviour, the merging of the eschatological Day of the Lord with the natural day of rest, etc. In the opinion of other historians this whole aspect of post-Constantine liturgical development must be explained by the influence on the cult of the great theological controversies—triadological and Christological—which so deeply marked the early Byzantine era.[26] Drawing a conclusion from his painstaking investigation of the development of the feasts of Christmas and Epiphany, Dom B. Botte writes: 'These festivals . . . were developed in centuries which were filled with theological and Christological controversy. . . . They were not created with a polemical purpose, but they unquestionably furthered the assimilation of the Orthodox faith, the dogmas of Nice, Ephesus and Chalcedon. Thus when I refer to them as the festivals of the Incarnation, I am speaking not only about the commemoration of the fact of the Incarnation, but also about the mystery (*mysterion*) and dogma of the Incarnation.' [27] According to this theory, therefore, the significance of the liturgical commemoration is not so much in the history as it is in the dogmatic significance of the feast: 'the purpose of the festival and cycle of Christmas was not to recall in all detail the facts of Christ's life, but to manifest, comprehend and as far as possible to experience the mystery of the Word made flesh.' [28]

Although they are right fundamentally, both these last theories provide only a partial explanation of the development of feast days in the Church and in general of that 'symbolicalness' which became an element of worship after Constantine. Here we can trace with maximum clarity the adoption by the mind of the Church of that mysteriological experience of cult and its inclusion in her liturgical piety. We already know that the early Christian cult was devoid of 'historicism' in the sense of symbolism and repetition, even in the sense of marking the particular events of the Gospel story. 'Remembrance' was directed then not to details but to the saving character of the whole work of Christ, and it was just in this sense that the apostle Paul used the term μυστήριον—the mystery of Salvation not revealed to angels but manifested and communicated to men in Christ. With certain qualifications it is possible to call this cult and this remembrance synthetic. 'In them attention and feeling are concentrated not on the significance of individual elements, but, on the contrary, these elements are recognized and taken into account only to the extent of their significance for the faith of Christianity—its on-going experience and life response. The Eucharist and its day—the Day of the Lord—are not the symbolization of the whole drama of the Cross and the Resurrection, even though they are clearly dedicated to the remembrance of the Lord's Death and Resurrection. Only faith, i.e. the knowledge and acceptance of the Gospel, turns this solemn supper into a remembrance, and neither the Eucharist nor its special day have any symbolic relationship to the event remembered. The festivals of the early Church, especially Easter, were also by nature synthetic, and the Passover of the Cross became the Passover of the Resurrection not within a scheme which would liturgically represent these two events in sequence, but within the realism of the Baptismal Sacrament. From the fourth century onwards the cultic 'emphasis' began to change and in it the idea of liturgical remembrance—the idea of the feast day—was also gradually changed. We have seen the changes in the understanding of the church and of holy places; these in turn played an important role in the development of festivals or, more accurately, in the development of the very concept of festival. The interest in a holy place was rooted in the religious imagination, in an extraordinary spiritual curiosity about the details of the 'drama of salvation.' Where these details were lacking, religious imagination invented them, a process which can provisionally be called 'mythification.' The drama which was later 'portrayed' liturgically arose or rather was first 'formulated' in this mythification. And of course a 'holy place' makes an ideal setting for a 'cult of portrayal.' Gradually there arose a form of worship designed to help the participant relive—psychologically and religiously—the events or series of events with which the place was connected. It is no accident therefore that Jerusalem and Palestine in general became one of the first centres of this representational cult.[29] We have a rather complete description of it in the writings of Sylvia of Aquitain.[30] Having grown at first out of a remembrance of the particular events in the Saviour's life, it later included within its development the veneration of the Mother of God and John the Baptist. It is characteristic that almost all the festivals having to do with the Theotokos originated in the construction and dedication of churches in the places of particular events in her life : the Nativity, Assumption, etc. Let us qualify this at once by saying that unlike the pagan mysteries these festivals have always kept their factual basis, a connection with a real event and not with a 'myth.' The Christian cult will always remain historical in the sense of the historicity and reality of the events which are remembered in it. But this 'historicity' gradually acquired a mysteriological formulation.

One of the clearest examples of the influence of the new mysteriological liturgical piety is the complicated history of the nativity cycle and its liturgical 'institution.' Whatever its 'prehistory' may have been, it is clear that this cycle of historical remembrance gradually grew up out of some sort of 'synthetic' festival of Epiphany including the Nativity, the Baptism, the Purification (in the East) and (in the West) the Adoration of the Magi. We see here an unwavering tendency to 'detailization,' and this tendency is clearly connected with the new forms and requirements of the cult. This does not mean, of course, that we should minimize the significance—in the development of the nativity cycle—of either the theological controversies (the struggle with Arianism in particular, which Culmann stresses so heavily) or the Church's struggle with the pagan cult of the sun. But this is precisely the point, that these doctrinal influences now found a point of application in the cult, that worship itself became the instrument and at the same time the expression of the new position of the Church in the world, of her new tasks, and of her new relationship with the world.

In view of the examples just cited we are now able to try to define the nature of the acceptance and partial adoption in the mind of the Church of the mysteriological understanding and experience of cult. Let us remember that we are speaking here only about the first of the three stages in the evolution of worship after Constantine as mentioned above. Later we shall turn to an analysis of the Church's reaction to this thesis, that is to the antithesis, and only after this will we be able to set forth our concept of the Byzantine synthesis which, it seems to us, expressed the Byzantine understanding and reception of the Ordo.

As we have already said, the acceptance in the Church of that liturgical piety which was natural for the masses of people pouring into the Church following her reconciliation with the Empire must be acknowledged as the starting point of the process with which we are concerned. The basic idea in this liturgical piety was the distinction between the profane and the sacred and, consequently, the understanding of the cult as primarily a system of ceremonies and ritual which transmits sacredness to the profane and establishes between the two the possibility of communion and communication. The pagan mystery was basically just such a consecrating and sanctifying act. But as a system of sanctification or means of communion between the sacred and profane, the mystery thereby inevitably presupposed not only a precise distinction between these two spheres, but also their ontological incompatibility and immutability. For all the dramatic nature of the cult, for all its 'historicity' in the sense of a portrayal of the drama of salvation, the mystery did not presuppose any history of salvation whatever, no historical process leading to a final and decisive event having not just an individually sanctifying significance, but also a cosmic scope and meaning. 'Salvation' is not the restoration of an order broken by sin but simply deliverance, whether from suffering or sin or death; the latter being acknowledged as 'normal' for a profane world and a part of it. What is missing in this mysteriological piety is eschatology. We know that Christianity set itself in opposition to the mystery religions on this point. It professed salvation not as the possibility of an individual or even collective deliverance from evil and sin, it professed sanctification not as the possibility for the 'profane' to touch the 'sacred,' but proclaimed both as the eschatological fulfilment of the history of salvation, as the event leading man into the Aeon of the Kingdom of God. History and event, and the uniqueness of the saving fact with which the Kingdom was approaching and being revealed, these were the basic categories for Christians, and in this plan it was precisely the eschatology of the Christian cult, its foundation in the 'event of Christ,' which drew a line between it and the mysteriological or sanctifying cults. The acceptance by the Christian consciousness of these categories of sanctification with their accompanying distinction between 'profane' and 'sacred' was therefore fundamental to the 'mysteriological breakthrough' of the fourth century. We have already investigated the evolution of the concept of the church building as a 'sacred place' or sanctuary, and also the new religious experience of holy places. But these were only partial manifestations of that whole general process of change which was felt more and more plainly after the beginning of the fourth century and which will develop especially in the Byzantine religious mind. The cult will become more and more a sacred action in itself, a mystery performed for the sanctification of those participating. This is most noticeable in the evolution of the external organization of the cult: in the gradually increasing separation of the clergy (who 'perform the mystery') from the people; in the emphasis by means of ceremony on the mysterious, dreadful and sacred character of the celebrant; in the stress which is laid henceforth on ritual purity, the state of untouchableness, the 'sacred' versus the 'profane.' A detailed analysis of this process of the 'sacralization' of Christian worship under the influence of its mysteriological experience and reception would require a large and specialized research. Here we can only sketch its general character. Again it is important to stress that what was changed was not worship itself in its objective content and order, but rather the reception, the experience, the understanding of worship. Thus the historian can easily establish not only a continuity in the development of Eucharistic prayers, but also the essential identity of their basic structures. The assembly of the Church, Scripture, Preaching, the Offertory, the Elevation and finally the Communion—this structure of the Eucharist remains unchanged. But if we were to take each of these unchanged elements and trace its particular evolution, it would become clear how it has gradually been set in a new 'framework' and become overgrown with ritual actions designed to stress its 'mysteriological' essence. What is characteristic of the process is the gradual reformation of the very notion of the assembly of the Church. It is evident from early memorials that the act of assembling was experienced as the first constitutive moment of the Eucharist, as its beginning and necessary condition. The first name of the Eucharist— the 'breaking of bread'—already emphasized this indispensable correlationship between the Liturgy and an assembly, between the Eucharist as the actualization of the Church, as *ecclesia,* as a gathering. In the writings of Justin, Irenaeus, Ignatius and others the assembly of the Church is thought of as the self-evident and necessary condition for the Sacrament, its beginning and at the same time its final purpose. The remembrance of Christ is celebrated so that we might always 'live at one with each other.' [31] In the Byzantine epoch the emphasis was gradually transferred from the assembly of the Church to the exclusive and actually self-sufficient significance of the clergy as celebrants of the mystery. The Sacrament was celebrated on behalf of the people, for their sanctification—but the Sacrament ceased to be experienced as the very actualization of the people as the Church. One of the final stages of this development will be the transferring of the name 'holy doors' from the doors of the church building to the doors of the iconostasis, with the prohibiting of all but ordained persons to enter these doors. But long before this a whole series of ritual changes (the evolution of the Little Entrance, the moving of the *Proskomedia* to the beginning of the Liturgy, the separate entrance of the celebrants, etc.) had already begun to express this gradually developing reformation in the understanding of the Sacrament.[32] No less typical was the gradual development in the explanation of the Eucharist as a sacramental ('mysterio-logical') representation of Christ's life, an explanation which acquired tremendous popularity in Byzantium.[33] This was the replacement of the ecclesiological understanding of the Eucharist by one that was repre-sentational and symbolical—the surest sign of a mysteriological reformation of liturgical piety. The appearance of a whole new part of the Eucharist was connected with this reformation, i.e. the *Pros-komedia*—wholly and exclusively symbolic in nature and in this sense 'duplicating' the Eucharist. Finally, this shift to a 'sanctifying' under-standing of the Eucharist was nowhere more strongly revealed than in the change in the practice of administering communion. The idea of communion as a corporate liturgical action 'sealing' the Eucharistic breaking of bread was modified into the idea that it was an individual-sanctifying action, related to personal piety and not at all to the ecclesiological status of the communicant. In the practice of administer-ing communion one can indeed speak of a 'revolution' since the under-standing of communion as an individual action obscured its original ecclesiological and truly liturgical meaning.

On the theological level this mysteriological liturgical piety expressed itself mainly in the idea of consecration or initiation, which in Byzan-tine thought became the major if not the only ecclesiological category. The idea of consecration or initiation is connected in the most profound way with the concept of mystery. One is initiated into the mystery— and the mystic, as one who is initiated ($\tau\epsilon\lambda o\acute{u}\mu\epsilon\nu o\varsigma$), is set over against the uninitiated. The early Church lived with the consciousness of her-self as the people of God, a royal priesthood, with the idea of election, and she did not apply the principle of consecration either to entry into the Church or much less to ordination to the various hierarchical orders.[34] Baptism was understood as a man's rebirth into the new life bestowed by Christ, not as initiation into a 'mystery,' and Chrismation preserved all the symbolism of a royal anointing, that is of the ordina-tion of the newly baptized to a ministry in the 'royal priesthood' of Christ. In other words the idea of consecration in the early Church was the continuation and transposition of the Old Testament idea of con-secration as a Divine election and institution in the service of God, and not the mysteriological understanding of initiation as a step by step elevation through the degrees of a sacred mystery. But it was just this second understanding which began gradually to enter the Byzantine consciousness and which was finally established in it. It was, of course, closely connected with the new experience of the cult as a sanctifying mystery, as a means of rising by way of initiation from the profane to the sacred, from the material to the spiritual, from the sensual to the *noumenal.* We find the first pure expression of this theory of the cult and initiation in the writings of Dionysius the Areopogite: 'Beware that you do not blasphemously violate the most holy among all holy mysteries—take care and honour the Divine mystery by means of spiritual, intellectual and invisible concepts—keep yourself from contact with every kind of profane impurity, do not speak publicly about the sacred truths, since only to holy people are these seen as sacred things, holy insights. . . .' [35] At first this category of consecration was still applied to the whole Church, to all the faithful. For Dionysius the Areopogite all are consecrated (ἱερωμένοι) as distinct from those who do not belong to the Church (ἀνίεροι). Baptism and Chrismation are defined therefore as consecrations. But, writes Fr. N. Afanasiev, 'the doctrine of consecration did not remain on this narrow edge, since the idea of consecration has its own logic. Byzantine thought came to the conclusion that the true mystery of consecration was not Baptism, but the sacrament of Ordination. In the light of this theory the majority of those who had earlier been regarded as 'consecrated' were now 'deconsecrated.' [36] It is important to emphasize that the basis for this evolution was in the new and mysteriological experience of the cult. Having become a mystery, the cult also began to be performed by initiates, began to require a special initiation. It was removed from the unconsecrated not only 'psychologically' but also in its external organization. The altar or sanctuary became its place, and access to the sanctuary was closed to the uninitiated.

But these changes were not the only ones which marked the complicated early Byzantine epoch. Before evaluating this period as a whole, before indicating its general significance in the formation of the Byzantine synthesis, we must consider the other stream which led into this synthesis, the other liturgical 'pole' of the post-Constantine era; i.e. the influence of monasticism.

3

In order to understand the unique role which monasticism has played in the history of worship it is necessary first to recall the general ecclesiastical significance of monasticism, its place and meaning in the age when it appeared. It is a known fact that the origins of the monastic movement have been sought and found in the most varied influences,[37] but the time when scholars were carried away by these fantastic hypotheses has happily ended. The close relationship of the basic monastic ideal to the ideal and cosmic sense of the early Church and the origins of early monasticism in the ethical and spiritual maximalism of the pre-Nicene epoch may be regarded as established and proved. This fundamental connection does not exclude, of course, either the newness of certain forms of life and asceticism which were adopted by monasticism; or the possibility of external influences experienced during its development; or, finally, the well-defined pluralism of monastic 'ideologies,' a pluralism in the understanding of its purposes and paths of development. In the main, however, there is an undoubted connection with the early Christian summons to 'the one thing needful.' And it was precisely this profound connection between monasticism and the original Christian *kerygma* which explained its extraordinary and rapid success from almost the very first years of its existence in the Church. Very quickly monasticism became a kind of centre of attraction in the Church's life, one of the great poles of the ecclesiastical community. It seems to us that Bouyer is right when he traces both the nature and success of monasticism to its eschatological character, i.e. to its embodiment of the other-worldly substance of the Gospel at the very moment when the Church was in danger of being dissolved in the 'natural' order, and of forgetting that she belonged to the Aeon of the Kingdom of God.[38] Monasticism arose as an almost unconscious and instinctive reaction against the secularization of the Church—not only in the sense of a reduction of her moral ideal or pathos of sanctity, but also in the sense of her entrance, so to speak, into the 'service of the world'—of the Empire, civic society, natural values; into the service of everything that (after the downfall of paganism) was waiting to receive from Christianity a religious 'sanction' and 'sanctification.' 'Properly speaking,' writes L. Bouyer, 'monasticism brought nothing essentially new into the Church. It was only the expression, in a new form evoked by new circumstances, of that eschatological character of Christianity of which the first Christians were so powerfully aware and which for them had been embodied in martyrdom.' [39] If in monasticism the renunciation of the world took on certain radical forms, so that it almost dissolved the original cosmic element in the Christian faith and sometimes became a denial of the worth of the world and man, this could be explained partially by fear of the secularization of the Church's membership, and it is possible to judge the extent of this secularization by reading the homiletical texts which have come down to us from the Byzantine period. From this standpoint we can begin to understand the *de facto* agreement made by the Church's hierarchy with monasticism, which in Byzantium led to the actual control of the Church by the monks. The influence of monasticism on the liturgical development of this period must also be explained in the light of this basic correlation between the monastic movement and the new position of the Church in the world.

Several periods must be distinguished in the history of monasticism. These periods refer first of all to the mutual relations between monasticism and the Church as a whole and, second, to the development and crystallization of the monastic 'consciousness,' i.e. to monasticism's theological reflection upon its own nature and task. Both of these processes determine to a large extent the liturgical role played by monasticism.

It is necessary first to remember that monasticism began as a lay and indeed private movement. Neither of the founders of organized monasticism—St. Anthony and St. Pachomius—had any sacerdotal order; both in fact regarded it as incompatible with the monastic vocation. Early monasticism must be defined as 'private' in the sense that it did not begin as an establishment or institution of the Church. It was something elemental and sporadic. It was not only a departure out of the 'world' but also in some sense a departure from the organized life of the Church. We must qualify this at once by saying that this departure was neither a setting of oneself in opposition to the Church nor a protest against her. There was not even a hint of catharist or montanist feeling in early monasticism. Dogmatically monasticism not only thought of itself as part of the Church, it also regarded its way as a realization of the ideal bestowed to and in the Church. Nevertheless this anchoritism or separation was the real novelty of monasticism as it developed from the beginning of the fourth century. It was unprecedented in the life and consciousness of the Church. And if we recall the 'ecclesiocentricity' of the early Christian cult, its significance as a manifestation and 'realization' of the Church, its inseparability from the idea of the assembly of the people of God, then it becomes evident that the 'liturgical situation' of monasticism in the first, basic and determining stage of its development was something radically new.

Historians speak of a 'liturgical revolution' brought about by monasticism. Skaballanovich ascribes to monasticism the attempt to create a new form of cult, a new form of worship which 'refused to be reconciled with what had been developed up to that time.' [40] Out of the new liturgical situation created by the separation of monasticism from the ecclesiastical community there came a conscious reform of the cult, with monasticism setting itself in liturgical opposition to the Church and her worship, her liturgical tradition. It seems to us, however, that this approach and the conclusions drawn from it are incorrect. The error lies in a false historical perspective. A certain liturgical theology or understanding of the cult is ascribed to early monasticism which in fact it never possessed. If the devotional rules and 'typicons' of monasticism were later 'formalized' this was not the result of a definite plan or effort to produce a liturgical programme, or to create a new cult in the place of the old one, but rather the evolution of monasticism itself, its transformation into an institution of the Church, about which we shall have more to say below. We regard as false any attempt to ascribe a special liturgical ideology to early monasticism. This could not have been, because monasticism was a 'lay' movement and in any case was never anti-ecclesiastical. If it had been a sect it would certainly have created its own worship as the expression of its sectarian faith and doctrine. But the cult of the Church remained the one lawful cult of monasticism, and the monastic cult was never suspect in the eyes of the Church. In the beginning monasticism did not even think of itself as a special part of the Church, since in its first expression—the hermit life—it was for the most part alien to any kind of collective consciousness; while in its second expression—the cenobitic life—it was more inclined to regard itself as the realization of the 'ideal Church,' as a return to the early Christian community, than as a special 'institution.' All this means that monasticism cannot be understood as a liturgical movement. The newness of its liturgical situation lay in the fact that it was to a large extent cut off from the common ecclesiastical cult, which remained always the one constant and self-evident norm for monasticism. Monasticism did not contemplate any replacement of the old cult, it had no special liurgical programme. The real significance of early monasticism for the liturgical life of the Church must therefore be sought not in some imaginary 'liturgical thelogy,' but in those motives which compelled the monks to prefer the anchorite life to participation in the Church's cult, to the general 'ecclesiocentricity' of early Christianity. These motives have been defined clearly enough in contemporary studies of monasticism. They included, first of all, a hunger for moral perfection, a longing for the maximalism of early Christianity which had begun to weaken in the comparatively 'secular' communities beginning in the second half of the third century. Again this was the early Christian understanding of the life of the believer in terms of a struggle with the 'prince of this world,' with 'the spirits of evil in this world,' which moved the maximalistically inclined believer to 'overtake' the devil in his last refuge—the desert. The singularity, the whole paradox of early monasticism lies here—in this consciousness that to attain the goal set for the Church, to realize the eschatological maximalism related to this goal, it was necessary to separate oneself from the ecclesiastical community and yet not break away from it or condemn it. Here in this central nerve or motive of monastic 'anchoritism' we can discover how the relationship of monasticism to cult really came into being.

Two elements must be distinguished. On the one hand, as we have just said, there can be no doubt about the complete acceptance of the Church's cult by early monasticism—as a norm and as an ideal, even when it could not be fulfilled. All the early monastic memorials, for example, emphasize the participation of the monks in the Eucharist on the Church's regular liturgical days : Saturday and Sunday.[41] Very characteristic is the stress on both of these days, not just one, indicating a subordination to the Eucharistic rhythm of the church, in spite of the fact that monks must often have had to come from considerable distances for this purpose. In addition, although fasting was one of the main and constant disciplines of the monks, they felt obliged to observe with increased strictness the periods of fasting in the general Church, especially the Forty Days. Irenaeus, describing the Egyptian cenobites, notes that although the fast was the same for them throughout the year, the time of the meal was changed 'after the eve of Pentecost, to preserve in this way the Church's tradition. . . .' [42] The devotional rule was made stricter on other feast days also. Finally, the very earliest descriptions of specifically monastic worship laws leave no doubt that it was based on that common Ordo or structure evidenced in earlier, pre-monastic memorials, which in the last analysis may be traced back, as we now know, to the early Judeo-Christian *lex orandi*.

The second element to be distinguished is the special stress laid by monasticism on prayer and the chanting of psalms. 'A love of psalmody gave birth to monasticism,' St. Augustine once remarked. The command to pray constantly was of course not new in Christianity—'Pray without ceasing' (1 Thess. 5 :17). Again monasticism was the continuation of the early Christian tradition. What was new here was the idea of prayer as the sole content of life, as a task which required a separation from and renunciation of the world and all its works. In the early Christian understanding prayer was not opposed to life or the occupations of life, prayer penetrated life and consisted above all in a new understanding of life and its occupations, in relating them to the central object of faith—to the Kingdom of God and the Church. 'Everything you do, do heartily, as for the Lord and not for man' (Col. 3 :23). 'And so whether you eat or drink or do any other thing, do all to the glory of God, since the earth is the Lord's and all that is therein' (1 Cor. 10 :26, 31). Therefore, 'pray at all times by the spirit' (Eph. 6 :18). Work was controlled, enlightened and judged by prayer, it was not opposed to prayer. And yet monasticism was a departure out of life and its works for the sake of prayer. It was rooted in the experience of the times, when the original eschatological aspiration of Christians, which had made possible the simple relating of all work to the 'Lord's Day,' was becoming complicated, hesitant, modified. No matter how strange it may seem from the standpoint of contemporary categories of Christian thought, it was just this clear eschatological differentiation of the two Aeons—of the Kingdom and the Church on one hand and of 'this world' on the other—which made the attitude of the first Christians toward life in 'this world' so simple. Their belonging to the Church and their participation in the Lord's Day neatly defined the value and meaning of each of the tasks and concerns of 'this world,' and 'prayer in the spirit' meant above all a constant recollection of this relatedness and subordination of everything in life to the reality of the Kingdom manifested in this world. The change in the Christian consciousness, symptoms of which can be noted at the end of the second century although it becomes obvious only at the end of the third, consisted in an almost unnoticed, subconscious transposition in this hierarchy of values, in the gradual 'subordination' of religion, i.e. faith, cult and prayer, to life and its demands. The emphasis shifted from the Church as an anticipation of the Kingdom of God to the Church as a sacramentally hierarchical institution, 'serving' the world and life in it in all its manifestations, providing it with a religious and moral law, and sanctioning the world with this law. There is no better evidence of this change than the gradual extinction in the Christian community of the eschatological doctrine of the Church, the replacement of the early Christian eschatology by a new, individualistic and futuristic eschatology. 'The Kingdom of God,' Salvation and Perdition came to be experienced as primarily individual reward or punishment depending on one's fulfilment of the law in this world. The 'Kingdom of God' or eternal life, having become 'ours' in Christ, paled in the experience of believers (not dogmatically, of course, but psychologically), and no longer appeared as the fulfilment of all hopes, as the joyous end of all desires and interests, but simply as a reward. It was deprived of the independent, self-sufficient, all-embracing and all-transcending content toward which all things were striving : 'thy Kingdom come!' Previously 'this world' acquired its meaning and value from its relatedness to the experience of the Church and the Kingdom. Now the Church and the Kingdom began to be experienced in relation to the world and its life. This did not mean a reduction of their significance or a weakening of faith in these realities. The Church remained more than ever in the centre of the world, but now as its protection and sanction, as its judge and law, as the source of its sanctification and salvation, and not as the revelation of the Kingdom 'coming in power' and bestowing in this world (whose form is passing away) communion in the 'age to come' and the 'Day of the Lord.'

Monasticism appeared as a reaction against this change, this sub-conscious 'utilization' of Christianity, and it is just in this sense that we must keep in mind the definition of monasticism as an 'eschatological' movement. It was an affirmation of the primacy of the Kingdom as the 'one thing needful,' the affirmation of its dissimilarity to everything pertaining to 'this world.' It is true that this eschatology was also torn away from the experience of the Church herself as an eschatological reality, was reformed as an individual eschatology; basically, however, in its understanding of the relation of the Kingdom to the world, in its view of the whole of life in terms of two 'aeons,' monasticism was undoubtedly a reaction against both the ethical and the psychological 'secularization' of the Church.

Hence the exclusive and central significance of prayer in the monastic ideal. If in the first early Christian view every undertaking could become a prayer, a ministry, a creating of and bearing witness to the Kingdom, in monasticism prayer itself now became the sole under-taking, replacing all other tasks.[43] The labour prescribed by the monastic rules (the weaving of baskets, making of rope, etc.) was in this sense not a 'task.' It had no significance in itself, was not a ministry or vocation. It was necessary only as a support for the work of prayer, as one of its means. This is not the illumination of life and work by prayer, not a joining of these things in prayer, not even a turning of life into prayer, but prayer as life or, more properly, the replacement of life by prayer. For monasticism was born out of the experience of failure, of the weakening of the original order of things, out of the experience of the impossibility of uniting the two halves of the funda-mental Christian antinomy : that which is 'not of this world' and that which is. The second half, that which is 'of this world' must simply be discarded so that the first might become realized, and so 'anchoritism'—the physical and spiritual departure out of this world, the withdrawal into the desert or the monastery, the drawing of a line between oneself and the world. Prayer has become the sole task and content of life, the spiritual expression of 'other-worldliness,' and communion with the reality of the Kingdom. The ideal of the monk is to pray always with-out ceasing, and here we approach the significance of this view of prayer for liturgical history. Devotional rules and an ordo of prayer did indeed appear in monasticism (of both types : cenobitic and anchorite) at a very early time.[44] But for the liturgiologist it is essential to understand that these rules developed not as an ordo of worship, but within what might be called a 'pedagogical' system. They were needed to guide the monk on his way toward 'spiritual freedom.' Their origins are completely different from the origins of the liturgical ordo or what we have been calling the *lex orandi*, which is essentially the embodiment or actualization of the *lex credendi* of the Church's faith and life. The purpose of the liturgical ordo is to make worship the expression of the faith of the Church, to actualize the Church herself; the purpose of the monastic devotional rules is to train the monk in constant prayer, to inculcate in him the personal work of prayer. In the liturgical ordo there are no categories of 'long' or 'short' prayers, while its relation to seasons, times and hours is rooted in a definite understanding of these times and hours. In monasticism, however, times and hours as such have no great significance. What is important is the division of prayer in such a way that it will fill up the whole of life, and for this reason it is set in a framework of time. But time itself has no meaning at all other than as the 'time of prayer.' The monastic rule knows only the rhythm of prayer, which due to the 'weakness of the flesh' is interrupted occasionally by sleep and the reception of food. Hence the great variations in devotional rules which developed in the different centres of monasticism. It could involve the whole Psalter, or a rule of sixty prayers by day and sixty prayers by night, or the Psalter read in conjunction with Scripture—a great many different rules have come down to us, but it is typical that in the early monastic literature the stress is always on the practical value of a given rule, its usefulness from the point of view of the monk's ascetical growth. Thus in the legend of the ordo given by an angel to St. Pachomius the Great, the angel replies to St. Pachomius' question whether the rule did not contain too few prayers by saying: 'I have ordained enough that the weak might conveniently fulfil the rule. The perfect have no need for a rule, since alone in their cells they pass their whole life in the contemplation of God.'

We can see then that the monastic rule of prayer is radically different in origin, purpose and content from the liturgical ordo of worship which the Church had known from the beginning. It was conceived neither as a reform nor as a replacement of the Church's worship, as Skaballanovich and other historians have thought, for by nature it stood outside the sphere of liturgics. Even when part of this devotional rule was inserted into the liturgical ordo (we shall speak more about this) its unrelatedness to other elements of the liturgical tradition is evident. Thus 'Compline,' which is formally recognized as one of the services of the daily cycle, is still an essentially 'non-liturgical' service. It can be sung 'in the cell,' i.e. it can be part of the individual's devotional rule; it does not presuppose an 'assembly of the Church' and an officiating minister; its structure consists of a simple sequence of psalms and prayers without any definite 'theme,' while a theme is characteristic of Vespers and Matins.

But if it is impossible to regard the monastic devotional rule as an attempt to create a new kind of worship which would replace the old, it is equally wrong to deny the profound influence exerted on worship by this rule or understanding of prayer, an influence which became decisive in the development of the liturgical Ordo. The causes and the inevitability of this influence were embedded in that 'liturgical situation' in which monasticism found itself. We have emphasized that monasticism not only did not deny the liturgical norm of the Church but strove with all its power to retain it. And yet as a result of the actual withdrawal of monasticism from the Church's communities it inevitably acquired new and special features and these features, in turn, gradually created a new 'experience' of worship, or in our own terminology, a new liturgical piety.

The relationship of monasticism to the central action of the Christian cult—the Eucharist—will illustrate this evolution. We have seen that originally the norm was the participation of the monks in the Church's Eucharist. At the same time there are very early indications of the reservation of the Holy Gifts by hermits and of their self-communication. 'All the hermits who live in the desert, where there is no priest,' writes St. Basil the Great, 'reserve the Communion where they live and communicate themselves.' [45] The practice of reserving the consecrated elements at home and of self-administration is also supported by evidence from the early Church, and there was perhaps nothing new in this practice. But the motives in each case were completely different. 'Private' Communion in the early Church was a kind of extension on weekdays of the Sunday Communion in the Eucharistic assembly of the Church. This assembly (ἐπὶ τὸ αὐτό) on the Lord's Day, the triumphal and joyous feast of the people of God, remained the primary and major obligation. Piety, prayer and asceticism could in no way become a reason for separation from the assembly, since the whole 'spirituality' and liturgical piety of the early Church could be summed up in the words of St. Ignatius of Antioch : 'Try to be together as much as possible.' The novelty of monastic private Communion lay in the fact that it was precisely piety or a particular experience of the Christian life which caused it. The Eucharistic Gifts and Communion were still the necessary conditions of this life, since the 'poison of evil demons consumes the monks who dwell in the desert, and with impatience they wait for Saturday and Sunday to go to the springs of water, that is to receive the Body and Blood of the Lord, that they might be cleansed from the filth of the Evil One.' [46] But without being noticed the receiving of Communion was subordinated to individual piety, so that piety was no longer determined by the Eucharist (as in the early

Church). Instead the Eucharist became an 'instrument' of piety, an element of asceticism, an aid in the struggle against demons, etc. 'They say of the Abbot Mark of Egypt that he spent thirty years without once leaving his cell, a presbyter usually came to him to celebrate for him (ποιετν αὐτῷ τὴν ἀγ προσφοράν) the Holy Sacrifice.' [47] This would have been impossible in the 'liturgical piety' of the early Church. And yet it became if not the rule then at least a normal observance in monasticism.[48] Let us emphasize once more that the change here was not a reduction of the place and significance of Communion, but a change in the way it was experienced and understood. It was included within the general scheme of monasticism as an ascetical act and a form of individual 'self-edification.' In this sense the view of the Eucharist as the actualization of the Church (as the people of God) and as the eschatological feast of the Kingdom was not denied or disputed. The emphasis simply shifted to the view of Communion as a beneficial asceteic act. The Eucharistic service was now seen as an opportunity to receive spiritual succour. This was in fact a change in liturgical piety.

As for the liturgy of time, the influence of the monastic 'liturgical situation' and monastic piety was expressed first of all in the gradual joining of the devotional rule with the Ordo of the Church's worship, that is, in the joining together of elements which were originally unrelated both in content and purpose. In the conditions of monastic life this process was inevitable. We know that at first monasticism was deprived of the regular worship of the Church and yet continued to regard it as a self-evident norm. Thus in all monastic ordos the same hours were set aside as those 'sanctified by common worship' in the world. The general structure of all three cycles of the liturgy of time was retained. Everything which could be preserved in this structure was preserved : psalms, prayers, chants, in exactly the same order in which they came in the Church's ordo. In this way the Ordo of the Church's worship was kept intact—although in different ways in different places. But since it was often celebrated without ecclesiastical 'formulation,' i.e. without the clergy and sometimes not in the church but in cells, this service naturally merged gradually with the monastic devotional rule, and was in fact transformed into a part of this rule. A good example of this merging is the Sinai Vespers of Abbot Nilus, described by Cardinal Pitra from the manuscript discovered by the Abbot.[49] Here both Vespers and Matins have an obviously common ecclesiastical structure, but between the elements of this structure there is inserted a devotional rule in the form of chanted psalms (the whole Psalter divided into three parts in the course of one Vespers service).

There were many sometimes very different ways of joining the two forms of worship. What is important is the fact of this merging of the Church's liturgical tradition with a private ascetical rule. It is important because both elements were partially reformed in this merger : once included in the Ordo the monastic rule acquired a liturgical character and came to be thought of as an inviolable and integral part of worship (cf. our reading of *kathisma* and the inclusion of the non-liturgical services of Compline and Nocturne in the daily cycle), while liturgical worship began to be experienced less in its specific content and intention and more as prayer, as an ascetical act in a devotional rule. The indifference nowadays with which Vespers is transferred to the morning and Matins to the evening shows how firmly established in the mind of the Church is this attitude toward the service as an ascetical act, significant in its own right rather than as an expression of a definite plan or *lex orandi*.

Both these examples—the evolution of the attitude toward the Eucharist and the merging of the ascetical rule with the liturgy of time—clearly show that there was a metamorphosis of liturgical piety within monasticism, in this case just the reverse of the one which was connected with the 'churching' of the masses. In monasticism it may be termed an individually ascetical or 'pietistic' metamorphosis, rather than 'mysteriological.' Again it should be stressed that in both cases it was not the Ordo which changed, not worship in its basic structure and content, but its acceptance and understanding. A kind of polarization occurs in the liturgical piety of the Church on the basis of the one cult, the one liturgical tradition. It is this polarization which is the real starting point for the Byzantine synthesis and the Byzantine *Typicon*.

This synthesis became possible as a result of the evolution first of the place of monasticism in the Church, and second, of its own self-understanding and theology. Up to now we have spoken only of the first phase in the history of monasticism, of that period which will be regarded as a golden age within the monastic tradition. It is important to emphasize that in that stage monasticism was a lay movement and one which was separated not only from 'the world' but also in some sense also from the community of the Church. This stage was very short-lived. Or rather, alongside this experience of monasticism there appeared another new understanding and form of monasticism, which must be regarded as its second stage. Its general significance was the return of monasticism into the community of the Church and its gradual regeneration as an ecclesiastical institution; indeed as a very influential institution connected with all aspects of the Church's life. There is no reason for us to enter here into all the details of this rather complicated and many-sided process. Expressed in the actual physical 'return' of monasticism, in the erection of monasteries in the cities (the very centres of 'this world') and, somewhat later, in the transformation of monasticism into a unique 'elite' in the community life of the Church, this process must not be explained as the secularization of monasticism or as a reduction of its original maximalism, or as a change in its basic opposition to the world. On the contrary, one of the main causes of this process was the very success of monasticism and the Church's acceptance of its 'ideology,' the acknowledgment that this ideology was true and possessed saving power. This paradoxical blending of the whole structure of the Christian οἰκουμένη with the basic monastic affirmation of salvation as a renunciation of the world, as an ascetical departure out of the world, must be accepted as the basic feature of the Byzantine period of the Church's history. Not all can become monks in the full sense—one might summarize this Byzantine theory—but all are saved by their approximation of the monastic life. We have already written about the significance of this internal victory of monasticism and its ideal in another place. Here it is enough simply to recall what happened. In saving Christian maximalism from reduction monasticism returned it to the Church in the form it had developed and elaborated. This was a transfer of the 'desert' into the world, a victory of the 'anchorite' idea of withdrawal and renunciation in the very centre of the world. The monastery in the city became a kind of ideal society, a witness and summons to Christian Maximalism. It was natural that this ideal society should become a centre of influence upon the world, and on the Church as a whole as well as on her individual members. The role played by the monks in the resolution of the great theological controversies and at the ecumenical councils is well known. No less significant was their role as 'confessors' and religious leaders of society. All this helps to explain the tremendous influence which the monasteries exercised in the development and formulation of worship. In the last analysis the monastic ordo of worship became the Church's Ordo or, rather, its general and determining form. But does this mean that it simply displaced and over-whelmed the 'liturgical piety' which we have called 'mysteriological'? Our reply to this last question brings us face to face with the problem of the Byzantine liturgical synthesis.

We shall try to show that simultaneously with the return of the monasteries into the world and their establishment in the Church there occurred an evolution in the monastic self-understanding, or more accurately, that monasticism adopted a specific theological interpretation of its own nature. We have spoken of the 'lay' character of early monasticism. We must now mention also its non-Greek character. The monastic movement began in the non-Greek border lands of the Empire and its founders were the Copts. The absence of Hellenistic culture in this first stage explains the absence of a coherent theological 'doctrine.' This was a pre-theological stage, when the monastic 'idea' was expressed more in categories of ascetic endeavour. L. Bouyer has analysed these categories very well in his book on St. Anthony the Great. Early monastic literature is devoted more to the patterns of monastic life, to the great examples of asceticism, than to an analysis of the monastic task. Analysis of this sort combined with theological explanation came from the Greeks. 'It was some time later that Greeks appeared in the ranks of the anchorites and cenobites,' writes Fr. George Florovsky, 'and it was precisely the Greeks who first synthesized the ascetical experience and formulated its ideal. And they formulated it in the old familiar categories of Hellenistic psychology and mysticism. The ascetical world view was organically connected with the traditions of Alexandrine theology, with the doctrinal position of Clement and Origen.' [50] It was the mystical explanation of monasticism, its interpretation in terms of the speculative tradition with its 'conscious borrowing of neo-Platonic and mysteriological terminology' which is so interesting from the standpoint of the history of worship, since it was just this interpretation which made possible the Byzantine liturgical synthesis and erected a bridge from one 'liturgical piety' to the other. There is no need for us to enter here into an examination of the question of the genesis of this mystical monastic tradition. What is important is that this 'Greek reception' of monasticism, marked by the names of Evagrius of Ponticus, the Cappadocians, Pseudo-Dionysius, etc., came very close to that new mysteriological interpretation of worship or liturgical theology which was developing in the same epoch under similar influences. The 'mysteriological' terminology became a kind of common language for describing the rise of monasticism and for speaking of the sanctifying quality of worship. It was no accident that from the fifth to sixth centuries onwards monasticism was the major interpreter of and commentator on the Church's liturgical life. In this new spiritual and mystical understanding worship became the central concern of monasticism, and monasticism itself was experienced as a 'sacrament of initiation,' as a sort of mystical equivalent of Baptism. What we have called the Byzantine synthesis was determined by the crossing of these two paths, by the suppression of the old liturgical 'polarization' between monasticism and the community of the Church. We must now briefly outline the history of this synthesis, since it is in essence the history of the Orthodox *Typicon*.

INTRODUCTION TO LITURGICAL THEOLOGY

FOOTNOTES TO CHAPTER THREE

[1] Dom B. Botte, *Les Origines de la Noel et de l'Epiphanie*, Louvain, Abbaye du Mont César, 1932.

[2] H. Delehaye, *Les Origines du Culte des Martyrs*, Bruxelles, Société des Bollandistes, 1912, pp. 29ff.

[3] K. Heussi, *Der Ursprung der Moenchtums*, Tübingen, J. C. B. Mohr, 1936, p. 39.

[4] Dom F. Cabrol, *Les Origines Liturgiques*, Paris, Letouzey et Ané, 1906, pp. 193ff.

[5] Dix, *The Shape of the Liturgy*, p. 303.

[6] Yves M. J. Congar, *Le Mystère du Temple*, Paris, Cerf, 1958.

[7] ibid., p. 181.

[8] A. Loisy, *Les Mystères Paiens et le Mystère Chrétien*, Paris, 1930, second edition, p. 13.

[9] cf. G. Bornkam, 'Mysterion' in *Theol. Woerterb. zum N. Test.*, III, p. 821.

[10] cf. Articles by Lagrange in *Revue Biblique* ('Les mystères d'Eleusis et le christianisme,' 1919; 'Attis et le christianisme,' 1919; 'Attis ressuscité,' 1927) and also his *Introduction à l'Etude du Nouveau Testament*, IV, 'Critique historique, 1, Les Mystères: l'Orphisme,' Paris, Lecotte-Gabalda, 1937.

[11] Dom O. Casel, *The Mystery of Christian Worship and Other Writings*, Westminster, 1962; cf. Dom E. Dekkers, 'La Liturgie, Mystère chrétien,' in *Maison-Dieu*, 14, 1948, pp. 30–64.

[12] I. Dalmais, *Initiation à la Liturgie*, Paris, Desclée de Brourver, 1958, and also his 'Le Mystère, Introduction à la Théologie de la Liturgie' in *Maison-Dieu*, 14, 1948, pp. 67–98.

[13] F. Cumont, *Les Religions orientales dans le Paganisme romain*, Paris, P. Geuthner, 1929, pp. 86ff.

[14] Casel, op. cit., p. 162.

[15] cf. A. Dufourcq, *La Christianisation des Foules; Etude sur la fin du paganisme et sur les origines du culte des saints*, Paris, Plon, 1903.

[16] G. Florovsky, *Vostochnye Otsy 4-go veka* (The Eastern Fathers of the Fourth Century), Paris, Y.M.C.A., 1931, p. 7.

[17] cf. Dom P. de Puniet, art. 'Catechumenat' in *Dict. d'Archeol. et Liturgie chrét.*, 2, 2, 2579–2621.

[18] A. Grabar, *Martyrium; recherches sur le culte des reliques et l'art chrétien antique*, Vols. I–II, Paris, College de France, 1946.

[19] cf. M. Eliade, *Traité d'Histoire des Religious*, Paris, Pagot, 1953, pp. 315ff.

[20] Grabar, op. cit., Vol. I, pp. 487ff.

[21] Grabar, op. cit., I, 314ff., 385ff.

[22] Delehaye, *Les Origines du culte des martyrs*, pp. 96–8.

[23] Grabar, op. cit., I, 227ff.

[24] On the imperial cult cf. E. Beurlier, *Le Culte Imperial: son histoire et son organisation depuis Auguste jusqu'à Justinian*, Paris, 1891; L. Bréhier and P. Batiffol, *Les survivances du culte imperial romain*, Paris, 1920; N. H. Baynes, 'Eusebius and the Christian Empire' in *Annuaire de l'Institut de Philol. et d'Hist. Orient.*, Mélanges Bidez, I, pp. 13–18.

[25] Dix, *The Shape of the Liturgy*, pp. 303ff.

[26] O. Culmann, *The Early Church*, London, S.C.M., 1956, pp. 21–38.

[27] Botte, *Les Origines*, p. 85.

[28] ibid., p. 85.

[29] On the liturgical significance of Jerusalem cf. Baumstark, op. cit., pp. 149ff.; H. Vincent and F. M. Abel, *Jerusalem, recherches de topographie, d'archéologie et d'histoire*, Paris, Lecoffre, 1924–6, Vol. II, pp. 154–217; Abel, 'Jerusalem' in *Dict. Arch. Lit. Chrét.*, VII, 2304–2374; H. Leclercq, 'La Liturgie à Jerusalem,' *Dict. Arch. Lit. chrét.*, XIV, 65–176; F. Cabrol, *Etude sur la Peregrinatio Sylviae: les églises de Jerusalem, la discipline et la liturgie au IVme siècle*, Paris, 1895.

[30] Etherie, 'Journal de Voyage,' ed. and trans by H. Petré, *Sources chrétiennes*, 21, Paris, Cerf, 1948.

[31] Justin Martyr, *Apol.*, 45–7; cf. B. I. Sove, 'Evkharistia v drevnei tserkvi i sovremennay praktika' (The Eucharist in the Ancient Church and Present Practice) in *Zhivoye Predanie* (Living Tradition), Paris, Y.M.C.A., 1952; H. de Lubac, *Corpus Mysticum: l'Eucharistie et l'Eglise au Moyen Age*, Paris, Aubier, 1944.

[32] These changes can be followed in the work of Dom Placide de Meester, 'Les origines et les developpements du texte grec de la liturgie de St. Jean Chrysostome' in *Krisostomika, studi et ricerche*, Rome, 1908, pp. 245–357; and also his 'Liturgies grecques' in *Dict. Arch. Lit. chrét.*, VI, 2, 1591–1662.

[33] cf. the most famous of such explanations: Nicolas Cabasilas, *Explication de la Divine Liturgie*, Introd. and trans. by A. Salaville, Paris, Cerf (*Sources chrétiennes*, 4), 1943, especially pp. 115ff.

[34] cf. Afanassiev, *Sluzhenie miryan v tserkvi* (The Ministry of the Laity in the Church).

[35] M. de Grandillac, *Oeuvres completes du Pseudo-Denys l'Areopagite*, Paris, Aubin, 1943, p. 245.

[36] Afanassiev, *Sluzhenie*, p. 15.

[37] For a review of these theories cf. K. Heussi, op. cit., pp. 280–304.

[38] L. Bouyer, *L'Incarnation de l'Eglise Corps du Christ dans la Théologie de St. Athanase*, Paris, Cerf, 1943, pp. 16ff.

[39] ibid., p. 24.

[40] Skaballanovich, *Tolkovy Typikon*, p. 197.

[41] ibid., p. 210.

[42] Quoted in Skaballanovich, op. cit., p. 237.

[43] cf. P. Pourrat, *La Spiritualité chrétienne*, Vol. I, Paris, Gabalda, 1931, pp. 198ff.; Com Anselme Stolz, *L'Ascèse chrétienne*, Prieuré d'Amay, Chevetogne, 1948, pp. 172ff.

[44] Skaballanovich, op. cit., pp. 208ff.

[45] ibid., p. 45.

[46] cf. texts collected in D. Moraitis, Η λειτουργία τῶν προηγιασμέιον (The Liturgy of the Presanctified), Thessalonika, 1955; cf. my review of this work in *St. Vladimir's Sem. Quarterly*, 1957, No. 2, pp. 31–4; and also the article by I. Ziadé in *Dict. Arch. Lit. chrét.*, XIII, 77–111.

[47] Skaballanovich, op. cit., p. 210.

[48] ibid., p. 211.

[49] J. B. Pitra, *Hymnographie de l'Eglise grecque*, Rome, 1867, p. 44.

[50] G. Florovsky, *Vizantiiskye Otsy V–VIII vekov* (Byzantine Fathers of the fifth-eighth Centuries), Paris, 1933, p. 144.

CHAPTER FOUR

THE BYZANTINE SYNTHESIS

I

As a history of the synthesis between these two lines of development in the Ordo, the history of the *Typicon* falls naturally into two periods. If the rule of prayer at the end of the third century is taken as the point of departure for this process, then the first period extends from the fourth to the ninth centuries, and the second from the ninth century down to the present. The first period was a time when both types of worship—parish and monastic—developed simultaneously, the period of their gradual merging and influence upon one another. This process may be regarded as complete by the ninth century. The second period is a time of the development of the Ordo within an already completed synthesis, and of the conflict and interaction between its different variants. This division into periods can be found in every history of the Ordo. However, historians of the *Typicon* usually concentrate all their attention on the second period, and this is because written evidence in the form of complete texts of the Ordo have been preserved only from this period. We know very little about the first era which, in the words of Skaballanovich, 'was the most decisive period in the formation of our liturgical Ordo.' 'Information concerning the extensive activity of that period,' he writes, 'is very meagre, falling far short of what we know from the periods preceding and following.' [1] As far as our own work is concerned, it is just this period which is of special interest, in so far as the synthesis of the original Christian *lex orandi* with the new 'emphases' of liturgical piety, and their 'digestion' by the mind of the church, occurred during this time. While granting the necessarily hypothetical character of our general presentation, we shall therefore concentrate our attention on this period of the formation of the Byzantine synthesis.

If we were to take everything out of the *Typicon* that was introduced into it after the ninth or tenth centuries, during the era of its finalized form and structure (and it would not be difficult to do this, since this process of accumulation is rather well documented in the numerous manuscripts which have been preserved), three basic 'strata' would remain, corresponding to the three concepts or views of the 'rule of prayer' which we have been analysing. There would be, first, the ordo which arose out of the synagogical and Judeo-Christian foundations of the Christian cult. Second, there would be those elements which are connected with the new liturgical piety of the 'parish church' and are rooted in the new relationship of Church and world created by the conversion of Constantine. There would be, finally, the monastic 'stratum.' The problem of the historian is to define each of these layers separately, and also to discover their inter-relationship within the final synthesis, within the one design or Ordo. The problem is a difficult one, since the whole significance of this Byzantine synthesis is that these three layers were not simply 'linked' to one another in some kind of mechanical unity, but transformed within a genuine synthesis, changed in accordance with a general design, a general theology of the Ordo. The problem has not yet been resolved, and this has deprived both the historical and theological study of the Ordo of all perspective.

First, then, there is the question of the early Christian or pre-Constantine 'layer' of the Ordo. In the most general terms this question can be formulated as follows : 'What elements in the Church's contemporary "rule of prayer" must be traced back to this fundamental layer?' In the chapter devoted to the origin of the Ordo, we have tried to demonstrate the source of the very idea of ordo—i.e. of structure, order—in the fundamental *lex orandi,* and also to show the general connection between this order and the liturgical traditions of the synagogue. Now we can make this description more detailed, on the basis of texts from the third century, when the liturgical life of the early Church can be regarded as rather well defined and the factors related to the crisis of the fourth century had not yet begun to have their effect. Our brief analysis will fit naturally into the scheme already familiar to us : the three cycles of the liturgy of time, and then their relationship with the Eucharist as the Sacrament of the Church.

Two basic services in the worship of the daily cycle have special significance : Vespers and Matins. Both undoubtedly originated in the pre-Constantine layer of the Ordo not only because of their place in the general order of worship, but also because of their liturgical structure. We now know much more about the original substance of these services than was known in the time of Duchesne and Battifol. The methods of comparative liturgics have helped us, together with the ever deepening study of the synagogue worship. In the words of Hanssens, author of one of the more recent studies of the history of Matins, 'the theory concerning the monastic and local origin of these services in the fourth century must be regarded as inadmissible.' [2] In our present order for Vespers and Matins three basic elements, which in combination form their ordo, must be traced back to this original layer. These are : (a) the chanting of psalms, (b) eschatological material, and (c) hymns. These three elements stem in one way or another from the worship of the synagogue. What was borrowed from the synagogue was first the very principle of the liturgical use of the Psalter, with its divisions into separate psalms and their habitual use at set times in worship. We may assume also that certain groups of psalms were borrowed—for example, the use of psalms of praise at Matins, which was 'one of the most widespread customs,' in the words of A. Baumstark, the father of comparative liturgics.[3] From the evidence of early texts the morning and evening worship of the Church developed around certain psalms or groups of psalms. At Matins there was the morning psalm (ἐωθινός)—psalm 63; and at Vespers the evening psalm (ἑσπερινός)—psalm 141. To these could be added the psalms of praise (148, 149, 150) at Matins, and the 'candlelight' psalms (15, 142, 132, 130) at Vespers. These psalms still form an unchanging part of the daily cycle. As for the way in which these psalms were used, there is still no agreement between the defenders of the theory of the musical dependence of the early Church on the synagogue, and those who think that the psalms (and the prophets) were originally read, and only later, at the beginning of the third century, in the struggle against gnostic hymnography, became 'the Church's song.'[4] There can be no doubt, however, about the existence of some form of psalmody as a basis of the daily office in the pre-Constantine Ordo.

The prayers also may be traced to the early Judeo-Christian worship. In the contemporary Ordo both the morning and the twilight prayers have become secret and are read by the officiant one after another during the reading of the Psalter. But it is plain from their text that they were related originally to particular moments of worship, and actually alternated with the psalms and hymns.[5] Their rubrics in early manuscripts give evidence of this usage: 'prayer of the 50th psalm,' 'prayer at the praises,' etc. In content these prayers were close to the *tephilla*—the intercessory prayers of the synagogue worship, which points to their early inclusion in the Ordo of the daily offices.[6] The *Syrian Didascalia* and other texts connected with it refer to these prayers as an important part of these offices.

In St. Paul we find mention of psalms, hymns and spiritual songs (Eph. 5:19; Col. 3:16), and this list, in the words of E. Wellecz, 'is understood uniformly now by every student of comparative liturgics. These three groups correspond to the three kinds of singing usually found in Byzantine ritual. They originate in the Hebrew worship of the synagogue, which the disciples of Christ attended daily.'[7] A list of the first hymns used in the Church has been preserved in an Alexandrian codex of the fifth century,[8] but there are good grounds for believing that they were used in Christian worship even before Constantine.[9] This list includes our present ten Old Testament songs, which later formed the canon, and also the Great Doxology, the Song of Simeon the God-receiver, the Prayer of King Manasseh, etc. Using the comparative method, Baumstark shows the gradual 'formulation' of this early hymnological tradition, in which the Song of the Three Children represents, in his opinion, the original element. What is important for us here is simply the fact that there were hymns in the Ordo of the earliest daily offices. As far as the term 'spiritual songs' is concerned, in Wellecz's opinion these are chants of the 'melismatic' type, of which the *alleluia* is a major form.[10] It is clear to any one familiar with the order of our worship to-day that our present use of *alleluias* clearly suggests that they had a greater significance in ancient times. Here too we can establish the connection with the synagogue tradition. It is demonstrated, for example, in the musical structure of the *alleluias* of the Ambrosian liturgy, the earliest form of *alleluia* which has come down to us.[11]

To this list of the primitive elements of Matins and Vespers we must also add (1) the undoubtedly liturgical character of these services; both the *Didascalia* and the *Apostolic Constitutions* (in their descriptions of these services) invariably mention a leading person, an officiant, and both clergy and people, i.e. the 'pleroma' of the Church [12]—these were not private prayers, therefore, but liturgical actions, performed by the Church and in the name of the Church; and (2) their structural similarity to the first part of the Eucharistic assembly (the pre-anaphora), which supports Dugmore's conjecture [13] that these services—constructed on the pattern of synagogue worship—formed the first part of the Eucharist on the days of its celebration, and on other days were independent offices.[14]

In our present study it is not too important to us whether these services were conducted in all places and at all times in the first centuries of Christianity (for example the words 'every day in the morning and the evening' were inserted into the *Didascalia* by the compiler of the *Apostolic Constitutions* at the end of the fourth century). What is important is their general similarity to the cult of the synagogue, pointing to their very early acceptance by the Church, and also the universality of their basic pattern, which has been clearly demonstrated by specialists in the field of comparative liturgics.

There can be no doubt whatever about the existence of the weekly cycle—the Eucharistic cycle of the Day of the Lord—in the earliest layer of the liturgical tradition. We should make some brief mention here of two questions which have so far not received adequate answers. These are the questions of the liturgical character of the Sabbath and of the daily reception of Communion. In the East, at the end of the third century, the Eucharist was celebrated not only on the day of the Resurrection but also on Saturday, and Saturday preserves this liturgical character even now in the Orthodox liturgical Ordo.[15] Opinions of scholars differ on the explanation of this fact. Skaballanovich believes that the tendency to celebrate Saturday on a par with Sunday arose only at the beginning of the third century, as a result of the gradual weakening of the anti-Jewish feeling among Christians.[16] But in the opinion of other scholars the development of Saturday simply continued the Judeo-Christian tradition in the Eastern Churches, a tradition discarded at an early date in the West.[17] We repeat, this question deserves special study. In the meantime the second hypothesis seems more probable and to correspond more nearly to the early Christian theology of time. It should be remembered that Judeo-Christianity in the broad sense of this term (as it is used, for example, by Fr. Daniélou in his *Theology of Judeo-Christianity*) was not at all a sort of spiritual Judeophilism. Thus the 'Epistle of Barnabas' is not only a memorial of the anti-Jewish polemic but also a memorial of Judeo-Christianity, i.e. of Christianity expressed in the language and concepts of *Spaetjudentum*. We have spoken of the correlation of the 'eighth Day' or first day of the week with the seven days ending with Saturday within the Judeo-Christian tradition. It can hardly be doubted that the Judeo-Christian communities continued to celebrate Saturday as a holy day, above all as a commemoration of the Creation.[18] The joining of this holy day with the celebration of the Eucharist was probably not something which happened at the very beginning, but it occurred naturally under the influence of the view of the Eucharist itself as a festival, and was possibly a reaction against the overly 'Judaized' Christians. An echo of this view of the Saturday Eucharist can be found in one of the memorials of the Ethiopian Church, a memorial from a later date, of course, and yet in view of the century-old isolation of Abyssinian Christianity, one which probably reflects a rather early tradition. In 'The Confession of Claudius, King of Ethiopia,' it is said : 'We observe it (Saturday) not as the Jews, who drink no water and kindle no fire on this day, but we observe it by celebrating the Lord's Supper and the feast of love, as our fathers the Apostles commanded us and as it is prescribed in the *Didascalia*. But we also observe it not as the festival celebration of the first day (Sunday), which is a new day, of which David spoke : "This is the day the Lord has made, let us rejoice and be glad in it." ' [19] The liturgical observation of Saturday could hardly have grown out of local and later customs. It is more reasonable to suppose that it reflects the early Christian theology of the week, which began to pale after the

'Lord's Day' was 'naturalized' and returned into the time of this world as a day of rest.

In early Christian texts we see the development of Wednesday and Friday as fast days.[20] This raises two questions : one concerning the reason for the setting apart of precisely these days; the other concerning the place and significance of fasting in the early tradition. Until very recently there has been a widespread opinion that these days were established in opposition to the Hebrew fast days—Monday and Thursday, i.e., were motivated by anti-Judaism.[21] After discovery of the Qumran documents, however, it may be considered as proved that the origins of this tradition lie in the ancient sacred calendar which the Essenes observed and which in all probability was accepted by the Judeo-Christian communities in Palestine.[22] Wednesday and Friday have special significance in this calendar. Christians appropriated these days and later added a new meaning to them—as commemorations of the days of Christ's betrayal and His death.[23] These days were described as days of fasting or *station days,* and this raises the question of the meaning of fasting and its relationship to the Eucharist. The evidence which has come down to us is, outwardly, conflicting. Thus, according to St. Basil the Great,[24] the Eucharist was celebrated on Wednesday and Friday, while in the words of Socrates : 'Alexandrians read the Scriptures and their teachers expound them on Wednesday and on the day of preparation, as it is called; on these days everything is done as it usually is, except for the Mysteries.' [25] Much earlier, in the work of Tertullian, one can find an echo of the African controversies over whether Communion should be received on the station days.[26] In studying this question it should be remembered that the early pre-Constantine and pre-monastic tradition understood fasting primarily as a one-day fast involving the complete abstinence from food, and not as abstinence from certain foods, as it came to be understood later on. This complete abstinence continued to the ninth hour (3 p.m.). Such a concept of fasting (again, borrowed from Judaism) could be defined as liturgical. It was connected with the concept of the Church as being 'not of this world' and yet existing 'in this world.' Fasting was the 'station' of the Church herself, the people of God standing in readiness, awaiting the *Parousia* of the Lord. The emphasis here was not on the ascetical value of fasting but on the expression—in the refusal of food, the denial of one's subjection to natural necessity—of that same eschatological character of the Church herself and her faith which we have discussed above. 'Fasting was regarded,' Skaballanovich remarks, 'as a form of festival or solemn celebration.' [27] Hence the correlation between fasting and Communion as between waiting for and being fulfilled by and receiving the food and drink of the King-dom. According to the *Testament of the Lord* : 'The sacrifice must be offered on Saturday and Sunday only and on the days of fasting.' [28] Differences concerned only the question whether there should be a Communion in the Eucharist itself or by means of the Pre-sanctified Gifts. It may be supposed that where there was a practice of receiving Communion by the Pre-sanctified Gifts, it was received on Wednesday and Friday at the ninth hour, and later, after this practice was abolished or restricted, the complete Eucharist began to be celebrated on these days, but in the evening, so that the Communion would terminate the fast or vigil; while the Liturgy of the Pre-sanctified Gifts was cele-brated during Lent. All the early rubrics concerning the pre-Easter fast bear witness to the connection between fasting and the Sacrament.[29] The Lenten fast developed out of the practice of catechumens fasting in preparation for Baptism and entry into the Church. 'Let them fast before Baptism,' the *Didache* teaches, 'and let the baptized and others too if they can fast also with the catechumens.' [30] According to St. Justin, the newly converted 'are instructed to beg God with prayer and fasting for forgiveness of sins, and we too pray and fast with them.' [31] Baptism is a Sacrament of the Kingdom—the whole Church participates in it and is enriched by it, so that the preparation for it is a 'station'—i.e. a state of waiting and purification. Baptism was celebrated at Easter, and the fast was ended after the Baptismal and Paschal festival. Tertullian speaks of the prohibition of fasting during the Fifty Days, when the 'need for joy and thanksgiving' keeps us from fasting.[32] Monasticism will introduce a great change in this concept— with its view of fasting as primarily an individual ascetical exploit. In the late Byzantine *Typicon* these two concepts of fasting are inter-woven—which explains the curious contradictoriness of the prescrip-tions on fasting in the period of Pentecost. We shall have more to say about this change later. Here we must say once again that in the pre-Constantine Ordo fasting was related to worship, to the liturgical rhythm of the Church's life, since it corresponded to the Church as a vigil and waiting, to the Church as being in this world and yet directed toward the fulfilment of the Kingdom in the *Parousia* of the Lord. It was therefore related to the Eucharist as the Sacrament of the *Parousia,* the Sacrament in which the coming of the Lord and participa-tion in this Kingdom was anticipated. This original tradition concern-ing fasting is essential for an understanding of the further develop-ment of the Ordo.

Finally we know that the Church Year, in its general structure, undoubtedly originated in the pre-Constantine Ordo, in the annual

cycle of Easter and Pentecost. We have spoken of the relationship of
these festivals to the Hebrew year on the one hand, and to the eschatological theology of time on the other. Recent studies seem to indicate
a remote Judeo-Christian foundation for the Feast of Epiphany also,
and therefore for the liturgical cycle of the Nativity which is connected
with it and which later developed out of it. This thesis cannot yet be
considered as proved, and so we shall limit ourselves here to a general
outline of its main features.[33] It begins with the question why, having
kept the Passover and Pentecost in her liturgical tradition, the early
Judeo-Christian Church did not keep the third great messianic and
eschatological feast of late Judaism—the Feast of Tabernacles. What
led scholars to this question was the undoubted presence of the symbolism and ceremonies of the Feast of Tabernacles in the New Testament,
especially in the Johannine literature, where the Feast of Tabernacles
is connected with the messianic vocation of the Saviour and also with
the theme of the water of life, i.e. with Baptism (cf. John 7 : 10, 37–8).
In his analysis of these texts and the symbolism of the Apocalypse,
P. Carrington writes : 'It is clear from the Gospel of John and from
the Revelation that the Feast of Tabernacles was a living tradition in
Johannine circles.' [34] In the Synoptics the symbolism of the Feast of
Tabernacles is evident in the description of our Lord's entrance into
Jerusalem. 'Everything here,' writes Fr. Daniélou, 'reminds us of the
Feast of Tabernacles—the branches from palm trees, the singing of
Hosanna (Psalm 118, which was prescribed for use at this festival
and mentioned also in the Apocalypse), the procession itself. . . .' [35]
Thus the theme and symbolism of the Feast of Tabernacles in the New
Testament literature is connected with the theme of Baptism on the
one hand and with the messianic entrance of the Saviour into
Jerusalem on the other. Carrington has proposed that the Gospel of
Mark is constructed as a series of liturgical readings for the year—
beginning with the Baptism in Jordan and ending with the entrance
into Jerusalem (the chapters on the Passion forming a separate cycle,
in his opinion).[36] But Mark's calendar—as A. Jaubert has recently
shown [37]—is an ancient sacerdotal calendar according to which (in
contrast to the official Jewish calendar) the year was counted from the
month Tishri, i.e. September. In this calendar the Feast of Tabernacles
coincided, therefore, with the end and the beginning of the year. Thus
it may be supposed, and Daniélou defends this thesis, that the earliest
Judeo-Christian tradition did include a Christian 'transposition' of the
third great messianic festival. On the one hand the final feast day of
the Saviour's earthly ministry—His entrance into Jerusalem (the end of
the year)—and on the other hand the theme of Epiphany or Baptism

(the beginning of the year) were, in this theory, the main themes of this transposition. What happened then? In Daniélou's opinion there was a branching out or separation of the traditions, related to the difference in the calendar. The first stage was the adoption by the Judeo-Christian communities outside Palestine, especially in Asia Minor, of the official Jewish calendar as opposed to the ancient one still retained by the Essenes. This change is reflected in the Johannine literature, as A. Jaubert has demonstrated brilliantly in her work on the Lord's Supper.[38] In the official calendar the year began with the month Nisan (April), in the period of the Passover. Thus also the Christian year was reconstructed, extending from the theme of Baptism-Manifestation ($\epsilon\pi\iota\phi\acute{a}\nu\epsilon\iota a$) to that of the messianic Entrance into Jerusalem. Our contemporary Ordo preserves traces of the calculation of the Church year from Passover to Passover: Quasimodo Sunday is called the 'New Week' and marks the beginning of the counting of weeks. Moreover—and this tends to support Daniélou's hypothesis—immediately after Easter we begin the reading of the Gospel of John, and in fact with the chapter on the Baptism. Thus also here—as in the conjectured original structure of Mark—the Gospel corresponds to the Church Year, which opens with the theme of the Baptism and ends with the theme of the Entrance into Jerusalem. In this shift from one reckoning of time (that of the Judeo-Christians in Palestine) to another, the Feast of Tabernacles was as it were dissolved in the Feast of Easter —which became also the festival of the transition from the old into the new year. 'We can then begin to understand,' writes Daniélou, 'the significance attached in Asia to the date of Easter, as evidenced in the controversies on this subject. It was the key to the liturgical year, the beginning and the end, the transition from the old into the new year as a figure of the transition from the old into the new life. It combined all the Hebrew festivals into one Christian festival.' [39] But if one part of the symbolism of the Feast of Tabernacles—embodied in the narrative of the Entrance into Jerusalem—retained its relationship to Easter, then the other—connected with the Lord's Baptism and His $\epsilon\pi\iota\phi\acute{a}\nu\epsilon\iota a$—was developed as a special feast. For the Gentile Church neither of these Jewish calendars could have any real significance, since this Church was already living by the official calendar of the Empire, beginning in January.[40] But even here the tradition of the general order of the Christian Year remained in force, as the cycle of our Lord's messianic ministry with its beginning in the Epiphany and its ending in the messianic entry into Jerusalem. The January Feast of the Epiphany, as a festival of beginning and renewal, grew out of this tradition, as well as being influenced by other and external factors.

Perhaps it is not accidental that in the course of the Gospel readings at the end of the year, in December (both in the East and in the West), Christ's eschatological sermon is read, a sermon that followed His entry into Jerusalem and was connected with it by a common messianic theme. No matter what the ultimate fate of these hypotheses may be, what has been said points to the major place of the idea of the Church (or Liturgical) Year in the early, pre-Constantine Ordo, and to the undoubted origin of this idea in that eschatological and ecclesiological theology of time which was the basis of the early Christian *lex orandi* and the first stratum in the Church's liturgical tradition.

2

Let us turn now to the second layer, to those elements or features of the Ordo which owe their place in it to the liturgical changes of the post-Constantine period and are connected with what we have called the new liturgical piety. We will define this layer provisionally as 'secular,' in contrast to the liturgical elements introduced by monasticism. No full description or ordo of this 'secular' worship has come down to us, which would show us how it was formed and developed in the epoch of exuberant liturgical growth in the fourth and fifth centuries. Nevertheless it is possible to distinguish the main features or 'emphases' of this type of worship. Apart from isolated pieces of evidence scattered in various memorials, the basic sources here are two documents whose extraordinary significance for liturgical research has long been acknowledged by such scholars as Dimitrievsky and Mansvetov. We have in mind the remarkable *Typicon of the Great Church* published from a Patmos manuscript of the tenth century by A. A. Dimitrievsky,[41] and the text of an *Asmatiki Akolutheia* (Sung Service) of the fifteenth century as described by Simeon of Thessalonica.[42] Neither of these texts, of course, can be accepted as first hand testimony from the era which interests us. They contain many later accretions which still require a great deal of painstaking work before they can be clearly defined. And yet they do give a general picture of the worship which Baumstark has called 'cathedral rite,' and undoubtedly they reflect an earlier era than the one in which they were written. Baumstark has shown that the Patmos text for the most part may be traced back to the Constantinople *Typicon* of 802–806.[43] As for the Sung Service, Simeon himself remarks that it is 'no longer observed either in Constantinople or in other places, having been replaced by another Ordo.'[44] These facts would seem to indicate that the Ordo of St. Sofia in Constantinople (described in both memorials) was not an exception to the general rule, was not radically different from the worship in other churches. Nor can the Patmos *Typicon* or the text of the Sung Service be traced to one Constantinopolitan tradition. 'The fundamentals of the Sung Service,' Mansvetov wrote, 'and its general type of service precede the epoch when particular ordos appeared. In it are found all the original and fundamental norms which were in one way or another worked out in subsequent practice. In the usage of the Great Church this archaic order of service was retained and elaborated with few departures from the original pattern; the honour of creating this order, however, did not belong to her. . . .' [45] It is true that this respected liturgiologist falls into self-contradiction when he ascribes this honour to monasticism, since a little farther on he himself asserts that the 'make-up of the prayers of the chanted service have their origin in the liturgical order of the early Christian Church.' [46] What is important for us here is not this contradiction, which may be explained by Mansvetov's general approach to the history of the *Typicon,* but rather his conclusion—concerning the significance which the ritual described by Simeon had for the whole Church. We have in it an important witness to the development and elaboration which the original Ordo underwent as a result of the new 'liturgical situation' created after Constantine.

Let us give here a general characterization of this type of 'secular' worship which will embrace all the cycles and individual services of the Church's liturgy. Its basic features were, first, the new and great importance acquired by chanting in worship; and, second, the dramatic nature of its ritual. We have said that the chanting of 'songs and hymns and spiritual songs' was an essential part of Christian worship and was inherited by it from the Hebrew tradition. In spite of this demonstrated inheritance by the Church of Hebrew chant forms and traditions, however, there can be no doubt that here again after the fourth century a profound change gradually occurred. This was not a change or development in musical theory or technique, but a change in the function of the Church's chanting, its new place in the general structure of worship, its acquisition of new liturgical significance. This change is best demonstrated by the peculiar duality in the place and function of chanting in our modern worship. On the one hand, a 'singing quality' has been assigned to almost every word pronounced in Church; western rubrics still speak of the 'chanting' of the Gospel by the deacon, and the manner of reading the psalms or *parimia* is close to being a form of chant. In using the term 'chant' ancient ordos had reference to the entire service, which was thought of in all its parts as a singing of praise to God. We find the same definition of worship as chanting in the New Testament. In the Revelation the elders sing a new song before the Lamb, and the Apostle Paul summons the faithful to 'teach and admonish one another . . . by grace singing in your hearts to the Lord' (Apoc. 4:9; 14:3; 15:3 and Col. 3:16). While not dealing here with the heart of the question, whether there was here a 'Semitic' concept of liturgical chanting,[47] we may note simply that the first meaning of chanting in our Ordo and worship corresponded precisely to this Semitic concept. This does not mean that early Christian worship recognized no difference between the various types of chanting and made no special provision for 'hymns'—i.e. for material written expressly to be sung (for example, the biblical 'song'). But their function was the same as that of prayers and psalms and litanies—all were to the same degree the prayer of the Church, all were subordinated equally to the general scheme of worship.

On the other hand there is within our Ordo a second, narrower, more specialized concept of chanting. This is the chanting which is set in contrast to reading. A whole great area of worship (the *Oktoichos,* for example) consists almost exclusively of hymnody : *tropars, canons,* versicles, etc. Moreover the musical execution of this material, its division according to tones, stylistic similarities, etc., represents its main purpose. It can be said that here chanting acquires its own independent significance, is set apart as a special element of worship distinct from all others. If in the first view all worship is expressed melodically, and *is* chanting in some sense, then in this second view chanting is isolated and acquires its own special function in worship. So much significance is attached to this function that the Ordo directs the chanting or non-chanting of a given text depending on the festal nature of the service. One of the earliest Church hymns or canticles—the Great Doxology—is in our modern Ordo directed sometimes to be sung and sometimes to be said. Chanting has become the expression and sign of festival character, of a festal day (by means of the number of versicles, etc.). Secondly, chanting has acquired its own special material, which has gradually taken a central place in worship.

In this evolution of the place and significance of chanting in the Ordo we must distinguish the historical factors which brought it about, and also the interpretation which was given to it and permanently fixed its significance in Byzantine liturgical theology. We have already pointed out its general cause : the change in the external conditions of worship which marked the period after Constantine, reflected first of all in huge church buildings, with their need for a corresponding 'amplification' of liturgical material. The influence of the Imperial court ritual undoubtedly played a great role in this 'amplification' and development in worship of external festal solemnity. We may assume that the terminology of the Hellenistic cult of the emperor was partially appropriated by the Church even at an earlier date—and applied to Christ. It cannot be doubted that after Constantine both the language and the form of this cult were received into Christian worship and became one of its characteristic 'expressions.' [48] Hymnographical material (greetings, anthems such as 'long live the Emperor,' etc.) played a very prominent part in this cult.[49] The experience and view of chanting as a special liturgical function, as a manifestation of festal solemnity, was a natural result of the new liturgical piety—i.e. the understanding of the cult as primarily a sacred, solemn ceremonial. But if Christian worship acquired its general concept and experience of the function of liturgical chanting from this 'secular' source, this source did not determine the content of Christian hymnography. Modern studies of the history of Byzantine chanting point clearly to the Church's resistance to 'Hellenic' poetry, even when vested in Christian clothes.[50] This is not the place for a detailed description of this antagonism. In his *Hymnography of the Greek Church,* Cardinal Pitra has stressed the fact that the Church rejected the forms of classic poetry even when the early Fathers were its authors, preferring a more 'lowly poesy.' [51] Since then the purely technical study of Byzantine Hymnography has taken a great step forward, and it may be accepted that the decisive influence both in form and content was not Greek but Semitic poetry.[52] The earliest forms of this hymnography—the *tropar* and *kondak* —show a dependence on Syrian poetry (the so-called *memra* or preaching homily [53]) and, as Wellecz notes, 'the music of the Byzantine Church developed directly out of the music of the early church.' [54] Thus the position of chanting in Byzantine worship was determined by two 'co-ordinates.' Its place in the structure of worship, what we have been calling its liturgical function, may be traced to the ceremonial, 'festal' concept of cult, characteristic of Hellenic liturgical piety, while its content and poetic form may be traced back to the early Christian, biblical and 'Semitic' tradition. These two co-ordinates reach a synthesis in that theologically liturgical interpretation of the Church's chanting which we find first clearly expressed in Pseudo-Dionysius, which in turn defined the whole subsequent development of the Church's hymnography within the framework of the Byzantine Ordo. According to Dionysius the hymns, songs and poems used in Church are a 'resounding' or echo of the heavenly chanting, which the hymnographer hears with a spiritual ear and transmits in his work. The Church's hymn is a copy of the heavenly 'archtype.' [55] We recognize here that familiar principle of consecration to a higher order, a hierarchical ascent to an invisible reality. The Church's canticles are proclaimed by angels, and therefore the hymnographer must follow the established types of heavenly origin (hence the significance of the 'model' in Byzantine hymnography, understood as a 'metaphysical' concept rather than as an object of simple imitation). We shall have more to say about this theology below, as a decisive factor in the Byzantine liturgical synthesis. Here it is important only to take note of this new understanding of the Church's chanting as a special element in worship, an understanding clearly connected with the experience of worship as a festal and mysteriological ceremony.

Simeon's description of the *Sung Service* in all probability reflects a rather early stage in the development of this type of worship—since in it the chanted material is still closely bound to biblical texts and has not yet developed, as it did later, into an independent hymnody. His description is interesting, first, because already there is an unusual stress laid on chanting. 'All catholic Churches in the whole world,' he writes, 'have observed it (the *Sung Service*) from the beginning and have uttered nothing in worship except in song' [56]; and second, because of Simeon's contrasting of this—from his point of view—ancient and universal type of worship with the monastic type, celebrated without chanting. 'Of course,' he remarks, 'this latter institution was brought on by necessity and was determined by pastoral authority.' [57] By necessity 'all the sacred monasteries and Churches followed this Ordo and only a few retained for a while the Ordo borrowed from the great Church of Constantinople.' [58] Simeon's service is undoubtedly an early one; this is indicated by its antiphonal structure and, more important, by the absence of an elaborate hymnody in the form of independent *canons* and groups of *tropars*. For this reason we can see in it all the more clearly the point of departure for the general path of development of this hymnody—from refrains to verses of psalms, from biblical songs to hymns actually displacing the biblical texts. (Thus, for example, to the verses of the ancient Vespers psalm 'Lord I have cried . . .': the refrain was added, 'Thy life-giving Cross we glorify, O Lord . . .' this being the embryo of future hymns based on 'Lord I have cried.') There is no need here to set forth the further development of hymnody, since although the forms of hymns were later modified (*tropars* developed into *kondaks, kondaks* into *canons*), the liturgical function of chanting and its general place in worship remained unchanged. This process of development, as modern research is showing, was very complicated, influenced by a multitude of different factors. One thing is sure : there was a gradual complication and expansion of hymnody; increasingly hymns took a central place in the

I

liturgical life of the Church. Pitra has indeed called the introduction of the *tropar* a 'revolution' in the common prayer of the Church. This did not mean simply the addition to the service of new material more suitable to its festal and ceremonial nature. It was the result of a profound change in the very understanding of worship. 'It would be easy,' writes Pitra, 'to find many analogies between a solemn service of the Greek rite and the ancient Greek drama. It has already been noted that the choirs and semi-choirs correspond to the antiphonal chanting of psalms, the *idiomelia* and *katabasia* to the monostrophes and parables, the anthems to the responsive verses, etc. Undoubtedly we must attribute the terms *kathisma, katabasia,* etc., whose mystical etymology is extremely obscure, to the significance of groups either moving or standing still during the singing of sacred songs. It may be that the term *oichos* refers simply to the groups arranged in a circle around the leading chorister or precentor as he recited a poem, which was then continued in a musical form since given the name *kontakion* . . .' [59] Again let us note that the details of this complicated process—leading to the substitution of the *kondak* by the *canon,* etc.—have been set forth in special studies, and there is no need for us to repeat them here. In these works one can also trace the gradual growth of *troparions* and *heirmologia*—their slow organization in the form of the *Oktoichos.* All this belongs to a special field in the history of the Church's chanting.[60] From the viewpoint of the history of the Ordo it is important simply to point out the general fact—this rapid growth of hymnody and the transformation of chanting into a very special and complex stratum in the Church's liturgical tradition.

The growth of hymnody is organically bound up with the second main feature of 'secular' worship as it developed after the fourth century, what we have called the dramatic nature of the ritual. Worship gradually acquired the form of a symbolic drama with a complicated system of entrances and exits, processions, etc., and as a corollary to this, the church building itself, where the drama was performed, was overgrown with complicated symbolism. There is a description of the Sunday Matins given by Simeon of Thessalonica.[61] The service begins in the entrance of the church, before the closed royal doors, 'in which there is a representation of eternal paradise and heaven or, rather, which actually lead into paradise and heaven.' The royal doors are closed, 'inasmuch as by our sins we have closed off and are still closing off for ourselves both paradise and heaven. . . .' The beginning of Matins is announced by the priest, 'as a mediator and one who has the form of an angel.' Then the Six Psalms are sung, and 'both sides of the church take up the refrain alternately.' During the chanting 'the priest opens one door of the church at the holy words "Look upon me, O

Lord, and be merciful unto me," showing us that the door of heaven has been opened to us by the incarnation of the Lord, who looks upon us from heaven, and who was made man through the heavenly and living door of the Theotokos.' During the chanting of the words 'Let my inheritance abide before thee, O Lord,' the priest opens the doors wide and sings loudly the introit with the alleluias and all enter (the church) as if it were heaven itself, following the priest who carries the cross and represents the Lord who saves us by the Cross. Three candles are set in the cross, signifying the light of the three suns. In the meantime both groups, standing in the middle, sing the remainder of the psalm antiphonally, and also the Song of the Three Children. During this chanting the priest goes up, in the company of all, to the altar, as to the throne of God, representing the Lord's ascension and sitting down (with the Father) in heaven.' We find also in Simeon the most detailed explanations of the symbolism of censing, and of literally every moment of the officiant and the congregation. Of course Simeon is a late author and he comes at the end of the long tradition of symbolic explanation of worship so popular in Byzantium. Nevertheless, the 'Catechetical Instructions' of Cyril of Jerusalem, the 'Diary' of Sylvia of Aquitain, and many other memorials which do not give such a complete picture but which reflect the same liturgical theology, all bear witness to the fact that this tradition began at an early date and was certainly connected with the new 'liturgical piety' of the post-Constantine era.

On the basis of this general characterization of what we have called the 'second layer' of our Ordo, we may now try to note briefly what its effect was upon the structure of worship, what it added to the pre-Constantine Ordo. Clearly it introduced into the services of the old cycle first a new view of chanting in worship and, second, a complication of ceremonies, a system of entrances and processions. Basically the 'secular' Matins and Vespers as described in the Patmos *Typicon* and by Simeon preserved their original structure. They are made up of a series of antiphons, the chanting of psalms and biblical songs, the deacons' litanies and the priest's prayers. Simeon notes that many people were surprised at the similarity of chanted Vespers to the first part of the Liturgy. This similarity in ordo only witnesses to the preservation in the 'secular' rite of the original antiphonal structure of the ancient services. That this structure was more ancient than that of our present Vespers is indicated by several of the 'Candlelight' prayers read now by the priest during the appointed psalms, which are nothing more than paraphrases of the antiphons sung at a chanted Vespers. In the latter the officiant's prayer repeats the antiphon—'that through the priest all might be offered up to God.' For example, our first Candle-light Prayer ('O Lord Bountiful and compassionate . . .') is an exact paraphrase of Psalm 86, which was, according to Simeon, a part of the first antiphon of the *Sung Vespers*. But of course the main thing to note is the result of this line of development : hymnographical elaboration. In our contemporary worship the chant 'Lord I have cried . . .' is regarded as a kind of preface to the chanting of the canticles 'I have cried unto the Lord,' and usually only a few verses of the evening psalms are sung—at the beginning and end, where they denote the number of the canticles (10, 8, 6, etc.) So too at Matins the Six Psalms on the one hand and the 'psalms of praise' on the other are regarded as the beginning and end of Matins, while originally they formed its main content, and the whole of the mid section is now taken up by the *canon* with its special (seated) psalms and *kondaks*. In the so-called *irmos* the connection with the original biblical songs is preserved only by their use of the traditional biblical themes and figures. The chanting of Psalm 119—the 'psalm of the innocents'—disappeared, but the chanting of the 'Tropar of the Innocents' is preserved, and so on. All this was the result of the shifting of the centre of gravity brought about by the new 'liturgical piety.' In modern liturgical books no less than 80 per cent of the material printed is hymnody, comparatively late hymnody at that, since whole sections have been dropped out and subsequently replaced. This does not mean that all this hymnody was developed exclusively within the realm of the 'secular' liturgy. On the contrary, monasticism played a tremendous role in its growth, and the most recent layer of hymnody (actually in use to-day) is primarily monastic. But this monastic hymnody began its development within and not prior to the Byzantine synthesis of the Ordo, while what we have called the new liturgical function of chanting was connected essentially with the 'secular' form of the liturgical tradition. The same can be said about the ceremonial complication of worship. It will be adopted and 'integrated' within the final Ordo from this 'secular' liturgical usage, above all from the festival cathedral ceremony of the church of St. Sofia. Once adopted and received, however, it will be reinterpreted in categories of monastic mystical theology.

But of course nowhere has the influence of the new liturgical piety been felt so powerfully as in the evolution—in the era after Constantine—of the liturgical year. It was here especially that our second 'stratum' in the Ordo was of decisive importance. Without going into the details of this process (we hope to dwell more fully on this in a special section of this study dealing with holy days), we want to indicate here its general meaning and path of development. Its general meaning lay in the transition from the original eschatological concept of the liturgical year to its acceptance in historical and mysteriological terms. We have already indicated that even in the last phase of its pre-Constantine 'formulation,' at the end of the third century, the structure of the Church year continued to be an expression of the original theology of time or, to put it another way, of the theology of the Church as the Sacrament of the Kingdom in time. This theology also determined the Christian 'transposition' of the Jewish year, the Church's reception of Passover as the central festival of the passage from the 'aeon' of this world into the 'Aeon' of the Kingdom, as the beginning of the time of the Church, of her messianic and eschatological 'fulfilment.' The Church and her time were a triumph of the 'new day' over the old conquered time of this world. The Church herself, especially in her Eucharistic expression, in her fulfilment as the feast of the Kingdom, was a participation in the new life, the new time. In the fourth century the idea of feast changed, and this change was connected with the reformation of the eschatological self-consciousness of the Church. As Dom Odo Casel has written : 'The original and fundamental idea of the feast is to be contrasted with another which historically re-presents every event and saving act. Of these two concepts one concentrates on the work of Christ in its historical, the other in its metaphysical dimensions.' [62] Also bound up with this shift of emphasis was the multiplication of festivals, which is a characteristic feature of the fourth century. We already know that one of the major causes of this multiplication was the Church's need to replace the pagan festivals, to carry out the new missionary task which was suddenly set before her. 'There was a need in the now Christian Empire,' writes Daniélou, 'to replace the old pagan festivals with Christian festivals which would answer the demand basic in every society for holidays celebrating the most important moments in natural life. Clearly this kind of festival was unknown to early Christianity. For it the end of time was felt to be at hand. Baptism introduced each person into the only Feast— the eternal Passover, the Eighth Day. There were no holidays—since everything had in fact become a holy day.' [63] The introduction of these holidays and their multiplication, while fully justified from the missionary standpoint, could not fail to alter the idea of holy days already existing in the Church. Holy days naturally acquired the meaning which they had in the minds of those for whom they were introduced : i.e. a mysteriological meaning. They acquired the significance of commemoration as a cultic re-enactment of the central actions in a given event, as a communion in this event, as a reception of its meaning, power and special efficacy. This is the mysteriological concept of a holy day. The word 'sacrament' (μυστήριον), which in St. Paul's writing and in early Christianity as a whole meant always the whole Body of Christ, the whole of salvation, was now as it were narrowed down and used to define separate holy days, sacred actions and ceremonies, in which the essence of the individual actions of our Saviour were remembered by and communicated to the faithful. 'Here is another work of Christ, another sacrament!' exclaims St. Gregory the Theologian on the Feast of the Epiphany, 'Christ is transfigured, and we also will shine gloriously with Him. Christ is Baptized, let us also descend with Him, that we may also rise with Him. . . .' [64] 'Let us note this use of the word *mysterion* in connection with the "sacraments" of Jesus as a key to the new understanding of liturgical festivals,' writes Daniélou. 'This usage, so closely related to the mysteriological cults, appeared only in this period.' A similar evolution was taking place at the same time in the West. 'It is necessary to look in the works of St. Ambrose and later St. Augustine,' writes P. de Chellink, 'for the source of that terminology which Pope Leo was to popularize half a century later and which involved the application of the word *sacramentum* to every dogma and feast of the liturgical cycle. *Sacramentum incarnationis, passionis, resurrectionis redemptionis, ascensionis. . . .*' [65] As it acquired its own identity in contrast to other holidays, each holiday naturally became the expression of a definite theological idea, became a dogmatic feast. Holidays were set apart not only as commemorations of individual events in Christ's life but also as the expression and affirmation of separate elements in the Church's doctrine. It has been noted more than once that the multiplication of feasts went hand in hand with the great theological controversies and was in a way a reflection of the results attained in these controversies. Thus the development of the nativity cycle was connected on the one hand with the necessity to Christianize and 'church' the dates of the great pagan feasts of December 25 (*natale invicti solix*) and January 6 (the birth of Ion or Dionysius), and on the other hand with the fight for Nicene orthodoxy, for the term ὁμοούσιον.[66] Typical was the substitution by the Cappadocians of the earlier name of the feast—ἐπιφάνεια—by a newer and more theological term : Θεοφάνεια, God-manifestation. Christmas is simultaneously the feast of the triumph over the darkness of paganism (the manifestation of the 'sun of truth'), and of the triumph of Nicaea over Arianism (the affirmation of the divine nature of Christ).[67] The content and purpose of the liturgical mystery came to be the revelation and communication to its participants of a definite saving truth about God and Christ, which in turn led to the rise of the 'Feast Day' in its pure form, for example, the Feast of the Circumcision of the Lord in the nativity cycle, or the special day of the Holy Spirit after Pentecost.[68]

In the development of the Nativity cycle we have the best example of the process which led to the new concept and function of a Feast Day in the liturgical life of the Church. First a 'missionary' factor determined the substitution of the pagan *natale solix* by the feast *Natale Christi,* the manifestation of the Saviour to the world. Then, under the influence of the historico-mysteriological concept of a Feast Day on the one hand, and of the dogmatic controversies on the other, this ancient Feast of the Epiphany was splintered : the date of December 25th became a special commemoration of the God-made-Man, January 6th of the Lord's Baptism as a Divine Epiphany, i.e. the first manifestation of the Trinity in the world. And finally, a third 'historical' stage is seen in the further development of the cycle : the appearance of the special weeks before Christmas of the Forefathers and the Fathers, the intermediate Feast of the Circumcision, and the final Feast of the Purification. This was wholly analogous to the development of the Paschal cycle—with its gradual completion in the special historical commemorations of Holy Week, the Ascension, and the Descent of the Holy Spirit.[69]

But the real and in a way paradoxical result of this development and multiplication of Feast Days was the gradual weakening of the idea of the Church year as a liturgical whole. The dogmatic and mysteriological concept of the feast as a kind of special and isolated liturgical event gradually changed its 'relationship' to the whole, to any single theology of time embracing the whole liturgical life of the Church. No matter how strange it may sound, there was a greater connection with time, a greater 'cosmic' content in the original and eschatological concept of worship and its rhythm than in the elaborately detailed and perfected Church Year of a later era. This is explained first of all by the fact that every Feast Day in this 'mysteriological' piety became an end in itself. As such it acquired a depth, beauty and richness of content which indeed transmitted the inexhaustible 'joy of the Church,' in the words of Fr. S. Bulgakov. But at the same time it ceased to be really connected with time, to be its real fulfilment as 'the new time,' as the manifestation in the time of 'this world' of the fullness of the Kingdom. Feast Days came to be experienced as a series of 'break-throughs' into a sort of other world, as communion in a reality in no way connected with 'this world.' It would not be hard to show that our present Church Year has no real, organic wholeness. It is divided into a series of festal cycles frequently interwoven with one another, yet inwardly dis-unified and out of harmony. Theoretically the Paschal cycle embraces the whole year. But a multitude of other cycles and feast days have been inserted into it, each subject to another 'key' and unconnected with it on the calendar. The idea of the year as a unit and as real time within which the Church dwells for the purpose of its fulfilment is so weak that the Byzantine list of months begins with September, a month which in our present calendar has no special liturgical 'significance' whatever. In the Nativity cycle the original theme of the yearly renewal, the end of the 'old time' and the beginning of the 'new,' which connected this feast with the annual 'birth' of the sun and the return of light to the world, although it is reflected in our liturgical texts, is so little understood by the mind of the Church that the 'Church's New Year' is separated from the world's New Year quite painlessly. The date of the Feast became in fact indifferent—since the liturgical formula 'On this day . . .' ('On this day the Virgin bore the Eternal One') is in no way connected with time. The whole meaning of the Feast Day is to give us a vision of the eternal 'this day,' i.e. of the supra-temporal, ideal substance of the enacted 'mystery.' The traditional interest of the Church in the calendar (cf. the controversies over the old and new style of dating) is completely academic. Least of all is there an interest here in real time. On the contrary, there is a conscious or unconscious faith in a 'sacred calendar' having no direct relationship with real time.

Very striking in this respect is the later development of secondary Feast Days and cycles. If in the Paschal and Christmas cycles there is still at least a theoretical connection with the year (time) and its rhythm; this disappears completely later on. The dating of the Feast of the Transfiguration of the Lord on August 6th has no explanation other than that this was the date of consecration of three churches on Mount Tabor.[70] Before its 'formulation' as a separate Feast Day, however, the commemoration of the Transfiguration was certainly connected with the Paschal cycle and this is still indicated in the *tropar* and *kondak* for this day: 'Let them look upon Thee crucified. . . .' And in the west the Gospel account of the Transfiguration is still the lection for the first Sunday of Lent. On the other hand, among the Armenians this Feast Day enters into the calendar of liturgical weeks. This is a vestige of the time when the Transfiguration was a part of every cycle of time. Once torn away from the whole it became overgrown with its own cycle of 'pre-festal' and 'festal' material, and has become isolated from the general structure of the liturgical year. Even more interesting is the history of the Mariological festivals. Veneration of the Mother of God was first expressed in the form of 'supplementary' feast days (*fêtes concomitantes* in the words of A. Baumstark). The Feast of the Cathedral of the Most Holy Virgin must be regarded as the first of these days, directly connected as it was with the Nativity of Christ (and by analogy also with the commemoration of John the Baptist after the Feast of our Lord's Baptism). Here it was still related to the general structure of the cycle, it still occupied a definite and 'logical' place in it. In the West there was an accompanying development of the *Natale Sanctae Mariae* on January 1st, noted in several ancient liturgical texts. In the East—in the Syrian tradition— there were also the two last Sundays before Christmas, called 'Annunciation Sundays,' dedicated one to the memory of the Mother of God and the other to that of John the Baptist.[71] All this points to the primitive connection of the veneration of the Mother of God with the Nativity cycle, which in turn was defined originally by the idea of the year. This connection was weakened as the idea of the Feast Day was isolated from the general structure of the liturgical year. Our present cycle of great Mariological feasts cannot really be called a cycle at all. The dates of these feasts are accidental, with the exception of the date of the Annunciation—which has a purely artificial connection with the Nativity cycle (nine months before Christmas).[72] The Feast of the Assumption, on August 15th, originates in the consecration of a church to the Mother of God located between Bethlehem and Jerusalem,[73] and the dates of September 8th [74] and November 21st [75] have a similar origin. Outside the Mariological cycle there appeared, for similar reasons, the Feast of the Exaltation of the Cross (connected with the consecration of the Holy Sepulchre),[76] and the Feast of the Beheading of John the Baptist on August 29th (the consecration of the Church of St. John the Baptist in Samaria at Sebaste).[77]

The development of the 'liturgical year' in the Byzantine era may be defined far more accurately as a development of Feast Days. The new historico-mysteriological idea of the Feast Day was after all not connected with time or the theology of time, or with any clear understanding of how the Church (the new people of God belonging to the Aeon of the Kingdom) was related to 'this world,' to the old aeon. Instead it was rooted in a special concept of commemoration in which an event of the past is 'made present' in all its saving and sanctifying power. The original understanding of the Feast Day, which we find in the early Christian experience of the Lord's Day or of the Passover, was rooted primarily in the awareness of the Church herself as a Feast Day, as the actualization of the 'eschaton' in this world. Hence its profound connection with real time, with the time of 'this world.' The early Christian theology of the 'eschaton' did not destroy, did not empty time, or abolish its significance, but transformed it into the 'time of the Church,' into the time of salvation. Within the Church time becomes a progressive movement toward the fullness of the

Kingdom of Christ, toward His cosmic and historical triumph. This world is condemned by the coming of Christ 'in the fullness of time'; by His death and resurrection heaven and earth are done away. But by this same coming the world is saved in 'the children of light,' in the new people of God, in the Church, where it acquires the life of a new creation. So then a 'Feast Day' is in fact the fulfilment in the Church of the new life, a communion through the Church in the 'New Aeon.' In 'this world' where Christ was condemned to death a true Feast Day is impossible . . .'in this world you will be sorrowful.' In this world the Church is 'possible' only as a 'station,' an expectation, a preparation, as an ascetical action. But Christ overcame the world and triumphed over it; in Him there was accomplished a renewal of nature and a new creature was born, there was the beginning of a new life. The Kingdom of God was at hand. Those who are in Him now overcome the world, which means that they receive their life in Him as new life and have the power which comes with a new and pure communion with Him. In other words their very life in this world is already a new life—a life in grace—in and through which the world itself is renewed. 'For the pure all things are pure.' This same condemned world becomes in the Church the 'matter' of the Eucharist, is transformed into the Body of Christ. The Church does not simply dwell in this world, waiting for the end of the world. The very fact that she is dwelling in the world is its salvation. The Church condemns it to exhaustion and death, but she also is its resurrection and the beginning of new life. The Feast Day in the early Church was escatological because it was the manifestation and actualization of the Church herself, as the new life, as an anticipation of the unending day of the Kingdom. This was the sole content of 'Feast Day' for Christians dwelling in 'this world.' But to the extent that such a day was eschatological it was connected also with the real time of 'this world,' since it was only for the sake of this world 'which God so loved' that the Church was created, with her vocation to be the world renewed by the power of Christ's victory in it and over it. Hence the significance for the early Church of a 'reckoning of time,' a calendar, a correspondence between the liturgical year and the 'cosmic' year, a significance which is becoming ever more apparent to historians who have delivered themselves from a one-sided and false understanding of the 'eschatology' of early Christianity as complete indifference to the world. One could even go so far as to say that only in early Christianity were the categories of time—the week and the year—real, and real from the liturgical standpoint, since the Church's liturgy itself was rooted in a theology of time, in a contrasting conjunction of the time of this world and the time of the Kingdom. The new idea of the Feast Day which developed out of its acceptance as something 'mysteriological' was a departure from this theology. Its object was not the time of the Church but the history of salvation understood mysteriologically, as something liturgically commemorated and repeatedly experienced in the cult in all its saving significance. The connection of such a Feast Day with real time, i.e. with the world and its life as measured by time, was more or less accidental. If in the comparatively early Nativity cycle both the theme and the content of the Feast were to a certain extent defined by its place in 'real time,' by its date in the cosmic year, then in the later liturgical development any date (even one chosen at random) acquired all its significance from the Feast celebrated on that day. The Church calendar which was formed as a result of this process is simply a listing of the dates of separate feasts and cycles more or less artificially set in the framework of 'real time.' In mysteriological theology the commemorated or celebrated event is in itself an extra-temporal eternal reality and the meaning of the celebration consists in the spiritual contemplation of this reality and communion with it, by way of its liturgical performance and elucidation. Such celebrations are set in the framework of the calendar and form in it a series of sacred as opposed to non-sacred, profane or 'working days.' This distinction changes nothing in time itself, since it is not the bringing into old time of the principle of its renewal and conquest by the 'new life'; there is here no inner subordination of the old time to the Aeon of the Kingdom, nor is old time illuminated by the New Aeon. Rather it is the setting apart and 'sacralization' of separate bits of old time and their conversion into 'sacred time' to mark the contrast with time that is profane. In the early eschatological theology of time, time as such, i.e. the time of 'this world,' could not become 'sacred,' since the 'form of this world was passing away.' It could not become the Kingdom; it was ultimately condemned, and 'lay in evil.' The Lord's Day is not 'one out of several' days of the week and does not belong to time, just as the Church is 'not of this world,' and cannot be a part of it. But at the same time the Lord's Day, the first and eighth day, does exist in time and is revealed in time, and this revelation is also the renewal of time, just as the existence of the Church in the world is its renewal and salvation. In the eschatological consciousness of the early Church the central categories were not 'sacred' and 'profane' but 'old' and 'new'; the fallen and the saved; the regenerated. For believers, for those who had been baptized and regenerated and who had tasted the Kingdom, participation in the new time meant that the whole of time became new, just as in their new life the whole world was being renewed. Their life was not divided up into 'profane working days' and 'sacred feast days.' The old had passed, now all things were new. So then their calendar could not be merely a rhythmic alternation of 'profane' and 'sacred' days. It expressed the antithetical conjunction of the Church and the world, in which 'this world' and its time—not by being sanctified as such but rather by dying away—is transformed into a 'new creation,' becoming a new time, rising into a new life. This calendar was not symbolic but real, just as real as the 'new life' in Christ and the victory 'overcoming the world—even our faith.' But the antinomy disappears in the categories of 'sacred' and 'profane.' Sacred feast days belong wholly to the time of this world, they are distinguished only as being 'holy' days. They can delimit time—by being usually associated with certain dates, and can 'break into' time—by the mysteriological commemoration of a certain event. They can, in other words, introduce into time a kind of 'other world,' an alien reality; but they do not transform it into new time, they do not renew it from within.

The evolution of the 'Lord's Day' must be regarded as the first instance of this departure from the eschatological understanding of the Feast Day. Constantine's decree made Sunday the official holy day and the day of weekly rest. In doing this he returned it to the week, setting it within the rhythm of the 'old' time, with its alternation of holy and working days. But in this sanctioning of the day of Resurrection there was a weakening of its understanding and experience as the New Day, as the manifestation of the new time in the old. Sunday simply replaced Saturday, acquiring all its sacred functions. But in the Old Testament, in the Judaic tradition (as we have pointed out) even the sabbath had a connection with the eschatological reckoning of time. It was not only the commemoration of the cosmic 'It is very good' of Creation but also of the Last Day, thus pointing to its own fulfilment in the 'New Sabbath' of the messianic Kingdom. In the context of the Hellenistic understanding of a sacred day, the day of the Resurrection was 'naturalized,' was finally merged with the idea of the natural cycle of work and rest. Later this same idea was transferred to other Feast Days. Once the Feast Day became in content the mysteriological commemoration of a certain extra-temporal reality having no essential connection with time whatever, it acquired the character in the Church's Calendar of a 'holy' day, an interruption of work, a holiday.

It is true that what developed as a result of this evolution of Feast Days was in fact a Christian year, that is, a general scheme or Calendar which was gradually filled out by custom, traditions, special local circumstances, etc., etc. Natural social and family life was in some sense in harmony with this Calendar. From this viewpoint the 'missionary victory' of the Church should not be minimized. Nor should it be exaggerated, however, as it often is by those who see this linking of the life of the common people with the dates of the Calendar as the major expression of the 'churching' of life and the cosmic victory of Christianity. This victory was at best equivocal. We are unable to dwell here on the countless examples of 'double faith' in the Church, the preservation of pagan customs and beliefs under the mask of Christian Feast Days. It is no accident that this 'double faith' was revealed most strongly precisely in the annual liturgical cycle. Most important, the ambiguity of the victory was a theological and liturgical ambiguity. For although, as we shall see below, the Feast Day preserved its ecclesiological and eschatological content and meaning in the depths of the Church's consciousness—in the deep and ultimate 'logic' of the Church's *lex orandi*—neverthelss this content was expressed least of all in the 'Christian Year' or Calendar as it existed in the empirical life of the Church. That theology of time and the Church which the Feast Day 'actualizes' liturgically finds only a partial, incomplete and oblique expression in the Calendar, and is almost completely rejected in our present 'liturgical piety.' Feast Days and festal cycles remain disconnected and isolated. Many aspects and moments of man's life in the world are marked and adorned by these days, but in the understanding of 'liturgical piety' they do not appear as the new time, the time of the Church, which alone can truly renew the life of 'this world' and transform it into the life of the New Creation.

Last but not least in our description of the second 'stratum' of the Ordo, we must take note of the extraordinary and rapid growth of the veneration of saints which marks the history of worship from the fourth century on. Since the early work of the Bollandists the study of the cult of saints has developed into a specialized and complex science, and there is no need for us to describe here in any detail the process of the inclusion of an ever-increasing number of memorials to the saints in the Ordo.[78] It would be hardly an exaggeration to say that at present no less than half of all the liturgical texts of the Orthodox Church have some connection with hagiography and the glorification of the saints. In the overwhelming majority of cases the 'rubrics' give preference to this material over the texts of the *Oktoichos* (the weekly cycle), so that the *Menaion* can really be called the most frequently used of all the liturgical books. The attention of liturgical historians has been for some time directed at this virtual inundation of worship by the monthly calendar of saints' days. Certainly this inundation is a significant and striking fact in the whole development of liturgical piety. It is now known that the veneration of saints began in the local

cult. It was at first the veneration by the local Church of her own martyrs and leaders. 'The primitive sanctorale,' writes Baumstark, 'was
rooted in a strictly local and two-faceted tradition: the *memoriae* of
local martyrs and bishops, whose commemoration was inseparably connected with their place of burial. It is this connection which gave birth
to the system of stations, touching all liturgical functions. This principle of stations was by nature in keeping with the primitive form of
the sanctorale, with its connection of a specific liturgical commemoration with a specific location.' [79] The local character of the cult of
saints was preserved up to the end of the third century, and the
close connection between this veneration and the grave or body of the
saint must be regarded as its essential and distinctive feature. It is an
accepted fact that the early Church knew nothing of our distinction
between glorified or canonized saints and 'ordinary' members of the
Church. Holiness pertained to the Church and all those who constituted
the Church were holy because they were members of a holy people.[80]
The setting apart of the bodies of the martyrs for special liturgical
veneration was rooted therefore not in any specific opposition of holy
to non-holy, but in the early Church's faith that Christ appeared (was
revealed) in the martyr in a special way, bearing witness ($\mu\alpha\rho\tau\upsilon\rho\iota\alpha$)
through the martyr to His own power and victory over death.[81] The
body of a martyr was therefore a witness left to the Church, a pledge
of the final victory of Christ. Hence the connection from earliest times
between the Eucharist and the *natalia,* the memorial days of the
martyrs.[82] This connection points not to a liturgical emphasis on the
saint's name in the original cult of saints (commemoration in the
modern sense of the word) but rather to its eschatological character, to
the early Christian faith that the Kingdom of God which was coming in
power (the new life now stronger than death) was actually 'attested' in
martyrdom. Furthermore the cult of saints in the early Church was not
mediatory. The supplication *ora pro nobis* ('Pray for us') in the *grafitti*
of the catacombs was addressed to all the faithful departed in the communion of the Church. Nor was it sanctifying, in the sense of a sanctification of the faithful by way of touching the remains of the saint.
It was sacramentally eschatological. It was 'sacramental' in the sense
that the presence of Christ attested to by the martyr's exploit was manifested in his body. It was eschatological because the martyr by his death
demonstrated the power given to him by the Church ('The water of
life whispers within me: "Come unto the Father," ' said St. Ignatius),
and because in his decision to die that he might live he manifested its
reality. In celebrating the Eucharist on the martyr's tomb the Church
confessed and revealed that she belonged to this new life and had the
same desire which St. Ignatius confessed on the way to his death: 'I

desire the bread of God, which is the flesh of Jesus Christ; I wish to drink His blood, which is incorruptible love . . .' i.e., the desire for the fullness of the Kingdom, its fulfilment in the final triumph of the Lord.

Basically the cult of the saints remained faithful to this original concept—even when the age of persecution ended, even in the period of its greatest growth. While they built martyr-churches and surrounded them with ecstatic veneration, Christians did not forget the original meaning of 'holiness' as the Church's self-attestation. From this viewpoint the results of Grabar's painstaking analysis of the influence of the cult of saints on architecture are remarkable: 'Architecture of the fourth and fifth centuries,' he writes, 'did not allow itself to be carried away by popular distortions of Christianity. From our analysis of eastern Syrian and Greek churches we must recognize the following essential fact: No matter what location was assigned in these churches for the preservation of the saint's relics or the celebration of his cult, and no matter what their architectural form, all these churches were constructed for the normal Eucharistic assembly.' [83] In other words, that whole development of the cult of saints which found expression in the connection of their sepulchres with churches and later with altars, in relating the body of the martyr to the Eucharist—all this bears witness to the development of the original and basic understanding of the place of the saints in the Church and her worship. But at the same time this area of the Church's life was subjected perhaps more than others to the pressure of the new 'liturgical piety.' At one time the theory was fashionable that the Christian cult of saints was essentially a 'transformation' of the ancient pagan cult of gods and heroes.[84] This theory, like the one which deduced the whole Christian cult from the pagan mysteries, is probably not defended seriously to-day. The critical works of such scholars as Fr. H. Delehaye, the publication of texts, the great 'theological' penetration into Church history, have brought the whole question of the veneration of saints back into a more healthy perspective. 'Almost all these supposed metamorphoses,' writes Delehaye, 'were based on superficial comparisons, and if one carefully weighs each argument advanced by critics of this tradition, one will be struck by the logical consequences of their fundamental error.' [85] This error was the simple assumption that the cult of saints originated in the cult of gods and heroes. What actually happened was that the Church's quite independent and unique veneration of saints (it was rooted, after all, in the faith and experience of the Church) began, from the fourth century on, to be coloured more and more by elements belonging to the mysteriological 'liturgical piety,' and appropriated many of its features. In the broadest terms this change may be defined as follows. The 'emphasis' in the cult of saints shifted from the sacramentally eschatological to the sanctifying and intercessory meaning of veneration. The remains of the saint, and later even articles belonging to him or having once touched his body, came to be regarded as sacred objects having the effect of communicating their power to those who touched them. Here is the basis of the cult of the saints which appeared in the Church in the fourth century. The early Church treated the relics of the martyrs with great honour—'But there is no indication,' writes Fr. Delehaye, 'that any special power was ascribed to relics in this era, or that any special, supernatural result would be obtained by touching them. Toward the end of the fourth century, however, there is ample evidence to show that in the eyes of believers some special power flowed from the relics themselves.' [86] This new faith helps to explain such facts as the invention of relics, their division into pieces, and their movement or translation, as well as the whole development of the veneration of 'secondary holy objects'—objects which have touched relics and become in turn themselves sources of sanctifying power. At the same time the intercessory character of the cult of saints was also developing. Again this was rooted in the tradition of the early Church, in which prayers addressed to deceased members of the Church were very widespread, as evidenced by the inscriptions in the catacombs. But between this early practice and that which developed gradually from the fourth century on there is an essential difference. Originally the invocation of the departed was rooted in the faith in the 'communion of saints'—prayers were addressed to any departed person and not especially to martyrs. In the new life of the Church the communion of saints in Christ (their prayers for one another and their bond of love) was not destroyed by death, since in Christ no one was dead, all were alive. But a very substantial change took place when this invocation of the departed was narrowed down and began to be addressed only to a particular category of the departed. From the fourth century onward there appeared in the Church first a practical and unnoticed but later a carefully worked out theological concept of the saints as special intercessors before God, as intermediaries between men and God. Saint Augustine was the first, perhaps, to offer a definition of the difference between prayers for the dead and prayers addressed to the saints, a distinction which lies at the heart of the whole subsequent cult of saints in the Church. 'The righteousness (*justitia*) of the martyrs is perfect,' writes St. Augustine, 'they have attained perfection through their action. Therefore, the Church does not pray for them. She prays for others of the faithful departed; but she does not pray for the martyrs. They have departed from this world in such perfection that instead of being our "clients" they are our advocates' (*ut non sint suscepti nostri sed advocati*).[87] The original Christocentric significance of the veneration of saints was altered in this intercessory concept. In the early tradition the martyr or saint was first and foremost a witness to the new life and therefore an image of Christ. Not only did the veneration of such a martyr have reference to Christ, to Christ's glorification, it was also by its very nature a manifestation of this new life, a communion with the martyr in this life. Therefore the liturgical cult included the Eucharist and the reading of the martyr's acts or a description of his trial and death (*passio*). The purpose of this reading was to show the presence and action of Christ in the martyr, i.e., the presence in him of the 'new life.' It was not meant to 'glorify' the saint himself. For the glory revealed and manifested in the martyr was the glory of Christ and the glory of the Church. The martyr was primarily an example, a witness, a manifestation of this glory, and the description of his acts therefore had a didactic significance. But in the new intercessory view of the saint the centre of gravity shifted. The saint is now an intercessor and a helper. 'The healthy person,' writes Theodoret of Syria, 'asks (the saint) for the preservation of his health; the sick, for healing. Childless couples ask the martyrs for children, and women appeal to them that they may become mothers. Those who are about to set off on a journey hope that the saints will be their travel companions, and those who return offer them thanks. They are addressed not as gods, but as divine people, who are asked to intercede. . . .' [88] Hence in the liturgical cult the shift in emphasis to the glorification of the saint's power, to the description and praise of his miracles, to his mercy and kindness towards those who turn to him for help. We know also how important in the development of Christian hagiography was the adoption of the form of the panegyric. 'A careful examination of these panegyrics,' writes R. Aigrain on this point, 'reveals often an eloquent use of rhetoric, and such a studied effort to conform to the laws of eulogy and to the rules layed down for this type of composition by the Sophists that nothing else is noticed, especially when the orator states his resolve to avoid such embellishments. The formulas used by an author to declare that he is occupied with the loftiest verities and therefore will not restrict himself to the established usages of this school remain nevertheless so clearly dependent on them that we are provided with a complete review of themes previously dealt with by the Sophist masters : Menander of Laodicea or Theo of Alexandria. . . .' [89] It was precisely this conventional, rhetorical form of solemn praise which almost wholly determined the liturgical texts dealing with the veneration of saints. One cannot fail to be struck by the rhetorical

element in our *Mineion,* and especially the 'impersonality' of the countless prayers to and readings about the saints. Indeed this impersonality
is retained even when the saint's life is well known and a wealth of
material could be offered as an inspired 'instruction.' While the lives
of the saints are designed mainly to strike the reader's imagination with
miracles, horrors, etc., the liturgical material consists almost exclusively
of praises and petitions.

We may close our brief analysis of the second layer of the Ordo
with some remarks about the development of the monthly calendar.
The honouring of saints, which little by little was separated from the
place of burial and from any direct connection with the saint's body,
fell almost at once into the category of the Feast Day which we have
described above. It became a mysteriological commemoration having as
its purpose the communication to the faithful of the sacred power of a
particular saint. The saint is present and as it were manifested in his
relics or icon,[90] and the meaning of his holy day lies in the acquiring
of sanctity by means of praising him and coming into contact with him,
which is, as we know, the main element in mysteriological piety. In
this way the idea and experience of the Feast Day is separated all the
more from time and the theology of time. In the mind of the faithful
the difference between a Feast Day marking an event in the sacred
history of salvation and a Feast Day of a saint is only one of degree,
not a difference in the 'nature' or 'function' of the Feast Days themselves. Both are holy days—both are independent and self-sufficient
occasions for liturgical pomp and ceremony, sacred days requiring a
corresponding liturgical 'formulation.' Two Feast Days which are completely different in their origin, nature and function in the Church (for
example, the Circumcision and the commemoration of St. Basil the
Great) can be celebrated at the same time, and gradually the Church's
Ordo works out a complicated system of principles to handle such
concurrences. The idea of the Feast Day as a sacred day of rest, and of
the festival as a sanctifying, mysteriological cultic act, has almost completely displaced the original meaning of the Feast as the passage constantly being realized in the Church from the old to the new, the
passage out of 'this aeon,' out of time, out of the life of this world,
and into the new time of the new creation.

3

We have already spoken about the influence of monasticism on the
development of worship, on the third 'stratum' of the Ordo. We may
recall that under the influence both of monasticism's original ideology

and of the liturgical situation in which it found itself following its 'anchorite' withdrawal from the Church's community, the determining fact in monastic worship was the inclusion in it of a devotional rule or, more accurately, the merging of this rule with the original Ordo of the Church. The beginnings and the development of this merger are very evident in the early ordos of the Pachomite monasteries, and later in the descriptions of them by Cassian. In the *Angelic Rule* the devotional rule is related basically to the hours of prayer in the Church, but consists of completely uniform rites in each of which there is a reading of twelve psalms and prayers. Its 'hours' originate in the Church's 'rule of prayer,' but its content comes from the devotional rules of the hermits. '*The Rule of Holy Pachomius,*' writes Skaballanovich, 'introduces special and more uniform services in place of the Church's services, which were inaccessible to the monks, obliged as they were to remain in the monastery without priests.' [91] In the writing of Cassian, who lived in Egypt in the last decade of the fourth century, we see a further stage in the development of this monastic Rule. The devotional rule became worship, and acquired a 'rite' (*modum*) which Cassian decribes in detail. An ascetical devotional rule has been turned into worship : 'It is to be observed,' writes Skaballanovich, 'how everything which had been developed in worship up to that time by the secular churches was eliminated : not only the litanies and special prayers (which was natural, since a person in orders was considered necessary for their recitation), but even the psalms appropriate to the hour of worship—the 141st at Vespers and the 63rd at Matins. The psalter was sung in worship simply in sequence, and the whole service was determined by this procedure.' [92] This 'chanting of the psalter in sequence' was the basic change introduced by monasticism into the liturgical Ordo. What had been characteristic of the early Ordo was the *psalmus fixus*, a specific psalm related in its theme to the structure of worship—expressing some particular element of this structure. The reading of psalms in sequence preserved in our present-day *kathismas,* and also the reading of Scripture according to the principle of *lectio continua,* separated these readings from 'structure,' or rather, introduced into the rite ascetical elements quite independent and unconnected with its general order. What is typical of monastic worship is the emphasis on the quantity of assigned readings or chants, because the quantity of texts or the length of worship has become a measure of the ascetical exploit, a measure of the strictness of the devotional rule. In the writings of Pachomius, Hieronimus and Cassian there are many indications of 'holy discord' among the monks over the length of the rule, the number of psalms, and so on.[93] 'Each according to his zeal, without remembering the weakness of others, wished to introduce into the rule what he considered to be easy of fulfilment. Some were thinking of requiring a huge number of psalms, one fifty, another sixty, while others were not satisfied with this number and felt it was necessary to assign even more.' [94] In this way the principle of inserted and structurally unconnected readings entered into the Ordo and has remained, along with the 'principle of prolongation' (the repetition of the same prayer—like the 'Lord have mercy upon us'—forty times; the supplementary readings in the liturgies for fast and feast days, etc.), an idea which regards worship not so much as a 'rite' (as a dialectical elaboration of a theme) as it is a rhythm of prayer, requiring above all—if it is to be useful—a prolonged ascetical effort.

Deprived in its very structure of 'dramatic ceremonial,' monastic worship has nevertheless made its mark on this aspect of the cult too. First of all there are the prostrations or bows, which still play such a large part in the prescriptions of the *Typicon*. Indeed, a whole type of worship is defined by this word. Cassian comments on the significance attached to bowing in the monastic devotional rule, and finds it necessary to give a detailed comparison of western and eastern practices. 'They (the Egyptian fathers) begin and end the appointed prayers,' he writes, 'in such a way that in finishing a psalm they do not immediately bend the knee, as certain of us do. . . . But, before bending the knee they pray for a while, and spend more time in this standing prayer (than in bending the knee). After this, having fallen down for a very brief moment, as if only to pay respect to the Divine goodness, they quickly rise again . . .' [95] This attention to bowing, which might appear to be a minor detail, is in fact quite significant. There is the expression here of another ethos, another experience or sense of worship, distinct from both the original and the 'secular' concepts. The bow, as a ceremony of ritual veneration, like the *adoratio* (προσκύνησις) in the imperial ritual, is subconsciously transformed into the expression of a spiritual state—the state of contrition, repentance and receptivity, and it is precisely this state which the monk seeks to embody in worship. Even in its most *kenotic* form, when it was devoid of all external solemnity, early Christian worship was still solemn in its nature and purpose, since its object was always the Kingdom, manifested, revealed, and given by Jesus the Lord. We have seen how secular and liturgical piety embodied this inner solemnity in the mode of external solemnity, in chanting, in praise, in the ritual, dramatic development of the whole cult. Monasticism, on the contrary, strove to exclude outward solemnity from its worship, since worship when seen primarily as a devotional rule is an exploit, an ascetical act, repentance, a protracted spiritual activity. 'Monks have not left the world,' says the Abbot Pamus, 'in order to make fools of themselves before God, to sing songs, to raise their voices, to wave their hands and stamp their feet. We ought rather to lift our prayers to God with much fear and trembling, with tears and sighs, with reverence and deep feeling, with a soft and humble voice.' [96] It was not just bowing as such which became an organic part of the liturgical Ordo and one of its determining principles, but also that ascetically penitential concept of worship which the bow expressed.

Special mention must be made of the way in which the theory and practice of fasting as adopted by monasticism were reflected in the liturgical Ordo. As we have seen, fasting in the Church was originally related to worship and involved the complete abstinence from food over a relatively short time. The idea of fasting was rooted in biblical typology. 'John the Baptist came neither eating bread nor drinking wine . . . the Son of Man came eating and drinking . . .' (Luke 7 :33–4). John the Baptist is the figure of the Old Covenant, of waiting and preparation for the Kingdom, and his figure is one of fasting. But in Christ the messianic Kingdom has come and is revealed—how then can the 'guests of the wedding feast fast, when the bridegroom is with them?' (Luke 5 :34). In biblical typology the Kingdom is described as a banquet, i.e., as the breaking of a fast. The Eucharist is the Banquet of the Kingdom, its eschatological anticipation, and therefore fasting is related to it—is thought of and undertaken in relation to it—as to the 'fulfilment' of the Church. In this view of fasting there is of course no differentiation between kinds of food, since it involves the complete abstinence from food. Inasmuch as 'for the pure all things are pure,' every kind of food is acceptable for Christians outside the fast. The monastic fast springs from a completely different premise. It is an ascetical fast; fasting as mortification of the flesh and as a protracted effort to restore the spiritual freedom and essence of man. Adam's tasting of the forbidden fruit enslaved man to food, and the purpose of ascetical fasting is to return man to freedom, to a life which does not depend on bread alone. What is meant here by the term fast is not a complete abstinence from food but primarily the regulation of its quantity and quality. In early monasticism much space is given in the rubrics to rules concerning hours for eating, the methods of food preparation, its quality and quantity.[97] The rule of fasting is related therefore to the devotional rule and completes it. The purpose of each is the same : to assist the monk in his ascent to perfection. But as the devotional rule became worship and began to determine worship from within, so also ascetical fasting as an individual exploit entered into the Ordo and exercised an influence upon its structure. Typical in our printed *Typicon* is the mixture of purely liturgical sections with prescriptions concerning fasting, and above all references to fasting as a liturgical principle. Under the influence of the monastic idea the principle of liturgical fasting, which occupied such a central place in the original Ordo, was relegated to a secondary position. It was transformed gradually into a disciplinary regulation for the receiving of Holy Communion 'on an empty stomach.' All this reflects the contradiction preserved in the Ordo up to the present day between the concepts of liturgical and ascetical fasting. According to the liturgical principle Eucharistic days cannot be fast days, because the Eucharist is itself both the breaking and the fulfilment of the fast. Hence the prohibition of fasting on the Lord's Day and on Saturday, as Eucharistic days (cf. Apost. Canon 66 : 'If a presbyter fasts on the Lord's Day or Saturday, let him be deposed; if a layman, let him be excommunicated'). But according to the logic of ascetical fasting the whole of Lent is one long rule of abstinence— hence the prohibition against 'terminating the fast'—even on Eucharistic days. Fasting as a condition of the Church, as the rhythm of expectation and fulfilment which is a part of her eschatological nature, was replaced by fasting as an ascetical act, and as such became the determining factor in the 'formulation' of our Ordo.

Probably the most important and profound of all the changes brought about in 'liturgical piety' by monasticism was bound up with this view of worship as a devotional rule and the idea of ascetical fasting. We have in mind the monastic theory and practice of receiving Communion. Within monasticism the receiving of Communion, while it remained at the very heart of the Christian life, was broken away from the rhythm of the Church and entered into the rhythm of the individual's ascetical life. We have already mentioned early examples of 'private' Communion by hermits from the Holy Gifts reserved for this purpose, and also the celebration of 'private' liturgies of a sort in the cells of anchorites who did not wish to break their solitude. With the 'establishment' of monasticism in the cities and the development of monastic Ordos both these practices disappeared. But the principle which first appeared in them remained : the view of Communion as an ascetical activity—as an individual act related to the individual needs or private spiritual state of the believer. It is not the variations in the Ordos or the differences in practice which are important for us here . . . whether Communion was received daily or comparatively rarely, or even only once a year. What is important is the appearance of the concept of 'frequent' and 'infrequent' Communion, a concept no longer connected with the Church's *lex orandi,* but with the spiritual state of the one receiving Communion, the decision of his spiritual director, or the discipline of the monastery, etc. What is most important (for the history of the Ordo) is the accompanying change in the place of the Eucharist in the whole structure of liturgical life. It is precisely this new view of Communion which must be related to the institution—in the monasteries—of the practice of a daily celebration of the Liturgy, of the Liturgy as something actually inserted into the cycle of the Liturgy of time and regarded as simply one of the services in this cycle. As A. Salaville has shown clearly in his article 'Messe et Communion d'après les Typica monastiques byzantine,' [98] the daily celebration of the Eucharist became the norm in monasteries in the eighth–ninth centuries. But this norm did not imply a daily receiving of Communion. Reception of Communion was governed by another, private rhythm. The daily Eucharist was the opportunity given to each one to establish his own individual rhythm.[99] Once included within the liturgy of time, the theology of the Eucharist was changed, and also the theology of time related to it, which together had formed one of the foundations of the original Ordo. In this Ordo the rhythm of the Eucharist was determined by the rhythm of the Lord's Day, of the New Time, set within the framework of real time as the principle of its renewal, but also distinct from real time, since the Eucharist does not belong to time. Thus the distinction between liturgical and non-liturgical days in the early Ordo had another meaning than that which it acquired under the influence of the monastic Ordos. In reality no day in the time of 'this world' can be 'liturgical' or Eucharistic, because as such it is separated from the 'New Time' in which the Eucharist is celebrated and of which the Eucharist is the expression and actualization. On the other hand all this old time is renewed in the Church, and she lives a new life within it in all things. It was Ignatius of Antioch who wrote that Christians always live 'according to the Day of the Lord,' [100] and Origen who stated that 'the perfect Christian always belongs by nature to the Lord, in word and deed and thought . . . and dwells always in the Lord's day . . .' [101] The customary celebration of the Eucharist on a particular day signified therefore not the opposing of one day to all others, the setting aside of a 'liturgical' day in contrast to simple (ferial) or non-liturgical days. On the contrary, it signified the antithetical relationship of the Church to time; as the first day of the week it remained within the limits of the cycle of 'old time,' but in the Eucharist this day was 'renewed' as the first day, the beginning of the New Time, as the 'eighth day,' outside the limits of the week and therefore outside the limits of old time. In this way the old time was related to the new but not confused with it. This relationship expressed not the connection of the Eucharist with a particular day, but its conjunction with that time which the Church was 'renewing' in her own life. On the other hand the customary celebration of the Eucharist on a particular day was based on the organic unity (in the mind of the early Church) of the Eucharist with the Assembly of the Church, and on the need therefore to observe at least some kind of set rhythm. In the monastic Ordo the concept of a liturgical day was altered. In practice every day became liturgical. It was the non-liturgical day which became special, a day on which for one reason or another there was no provision for a celebration of the Eucharist. In other words, the celebration of the Liturgy came to be understood as something self-evident and natural in time, while its non-celebration was regarded as a sign of the special nature of a given day or period in the Church's life. But if in its monastic origin this practice was still connected with an assembly of the community, since the daily Liturgy was still a part of the liturgical Ordo, in its adoption later by parish churches it led to a gradual separation of the Liturgy from the assembly, to an understanding of it as a service performed by the clergy and not necessarily requiring the participation of all—ἐπὶ τὸ αὐτό. Both views of the place of the Eucharist in the Church's liturgical life can be distinguished in our contemporary *Typicon,* the earlier one as well as the one which owed its appearance to monasticism. On the one hand the Eucharist is still 'prescribed' on Sunday and Feast Days, retaining its original connection with definite times and hours and its nature as a festival of the Church. In contrast to the West the practice of daily celebration has never acquired the character with us of a self-evident norm, except in the monasteries and great cathedrals and churches. It is still generally understood as a festal or at least special service. On the other hand, this same Ordo obviously assumes a daily celebration of the Liturgy. As an indication of this there is the series of apostolic and Gospel readings arranged as if the Liturgy was to be celebrated each day (this late 'lectionary' undoubtedly originated in the monastic Ordo and was simply inserted in the final synthesis of the Ordo of the Church). Then there is the already mentioned distinguishing of non-liturgical days, which would be meaningless if in the Ordo which so definitely stresses this distinction the Liturgy was not thought of as a daily office.

Without developing this thought further it is possible to say that this monastic 'stratum' is connected with one of the most important and profound upheavals ever to occur in liturgical piety, precisely the separation of the Eucharist (in the minds of believers) from its eschatological and ecclesiological significance.

4

There is sufficient reason to believe that these two lines of liturgical development—the 'secular' and the 'monastic'—began not only to move apart in the course of time, but also to come into conflict. There was a definite liturgical 'polarization' in the approach to the Byzantine synthesis. Although the principle of the Church's *lex orandi* and its application to all believers was by no means denied in monastic circles, still the general spirit of its 'transposition' within the secular post-Constantine liturgy of time certainly fell under a great shadow of doubt.[102] We have already referred to one of the Egyptian ascetics, quoted by Nikon of Chernigov. In him we heard a protest against the development of hymnody. Evidence of a similar protest is found at the beginning of the fifth century. In answer to the complaint of one accustomed to the hymns of Cappadocia a certain monk of Nitre said : 'As for the singing of *troparia* and *canons* and the use of musical melodies, this is suitable for secular priests and worldly men in order that people may be drawn into the Church. For monks, however, who live far from the world's noise, such things are not useful.' [103] From the side of 'secular' worship we can also distinguish certain signs of opposition to the monastic type. We have already seen that for Simeon of Thessalonica, an advocate of the ancient *Sung Service,* the 'simple' worship of monasticism was a kind of decline. The canonical tradition has preserved traces of opposition to the monastic view of fasting. Also the services of so-called mixed type described in certain quite late versions of the *Typicon* bear witness to the peculiar conflict between these two general tendencies.[104]

We do not know how far this polarization went or what connection it has with the controversies and doubts about monasticism clearly indicated in memorials from the fourth century (in the canons of the Council of Gangre, for example). For the history of the Ordo it is important to recognize that this polarization was temporary and that it led to the combining of both tendencies in what we have called the Byzantine liturgical synthesis. Also important is the fact that this synthesis was 'formulated' by monasticism, that our modern *Typicon* can rightly be called monastic both in its form and content. But this monastic character of the Byzantine Ordo does not mean that the process of liturgical unification was a simple victory of monastic liturgical piety over what we have called 'secular' piety. For an understanding of the real nature of this unification and the meaning of the Byzantine synthesis, it is necessary to remember that the fundamental fact in its formulation was the return of monasticism into the world, and its subsequent theological evolution. This enthronement of monasticism, this crowning of the 'anchorite' ideal of a separation from the world for the sake of the 'one thing needful' and of monasticism as the guide and conscience of the world, must be regarded as one of the great paradoxes of Byzantium. The chief exponent of this view of monasticism as the 'nerve and mainstay of the Church' (and therefore of the whole Christian society) was St. Theodore of Studion.[105] The view was crystallized in its final form after the iconoclastic crisis, which was 'monastoclastic' as much as it was iconoclastic, and was a conflict in which the main glory of victory over heretical emperors must be credited to monasticism. But the process of return actually began much earlier, and by the end of the fourth century monasteries had begun to penetrate the capitals and other cities. In 586, according to the signatures on one official document, the Eparchy of Constantinople included sixty-eight monasteries for men while the neighbouring Eparchy of Chalcedon had forty.[106] The monks became instructors, spiritual advisers and teachers of the people, and also guardians of orthodoxy. One need only recall the role they played at the time of the Christological controversies and in the ecumenical councils. These facts may help us to understand the liturgical influence which the monasteries began to exercise even at a very early date. 'Constantinople,' writes Skaballanovich, 'created a special type of monastery, and long before the first blows struck by the Crusaders it had become a legislator in the realms of cathedral and parish worship as well as that of the monasteries." [107] Chrysostom also speaks of the monasteries in the region around Antioch.[108] The relationship between Egyptian monks and the Church of Alexandria are well documented.[109] Before becoming centres of liturgical life and legislators in matters of Ordo, however, the monasteries themselves had to modify their own worship. Among the 'anachorites' in the desert, cut off from the hierarchy, the liturgical situation was much different from that which was created now in the communal monasteries of the capital, built under the special patronage of the court and aristocracy. 'It is reasonable to believe,' says Skaballanovich, 'that once separated from the life of the desert and called to satisfy the spiritual needs of the urban population, these monasteries were forced to accommodate themselves to the rites of the secular churches as developed in that time.' [110] A 'synthesis' of the two liturgical traditions was necessary and natural simply by virtue of external circumstances and the new 'status' of monasticism itself with the Church.

But operating to further this synthesis and bring it to completion was another, internal cause, no less important than these external factors. This was the evolution taking place in monasticism's understanding of itself or, as we said earlier, that new theology of monasticism which was adopted after it took root on the soil of Hellenistic culture. There is no need for us to set forth in detail the development of this mystical monastic theology, which runs from Origen through the Cappadocians, Evagrius, and Pseudo-Dionysius, down to Maxim the Confessor and the late Byzantine mystics. It is enough to say that this was an interpretation of monasticism in the language and categories of the neo-Platonic speculative tradition. In other words, it was an interpretation of monasticism in those same 'mysteriological' categories which were applied to worship from the fourth century on. The monastic life became a special initiation or mystery, and it is no accident that in Pseudo-Dionysius monasticism is counted in fact as one of the Church's Sacraments. Monasticism was an initiation into the path toward an exalted 'ecstasy,' to a flight into the 'cloud of unknowing,' which was indeed the true contemplation of God. It was the receiving of the form of an angel; and in Dionysius' teaching angels were heavenly intellects, a loftier hierarchy—united in a system of mediation with the hierarchy of men. For Dionysius monasticism was next to the highest class in the Church—standing above the catechumens and 'sanctified ones' but beneath the hierarchy. According to Dionysius, the title of monk itself was an indication of that comprehensive, undivided, 'uni-form' or monadic life which monks must lead. They must direct their spirit toward the 'God-formed monad.' Dionysius speaks in the same language and with the same concepts about worship. 'Worship is the path of deification and sanctification.' The Church, for Pseudo-Dionysius, is above all a 'world of sacraments,' a world of sacred rites by means of which one ascends from the sensual to the supra-sensual, to enlightenment and deification. In this way the two hitherto unrelated traditions acquire a common soil, a common tongue. On the one hand the success of monasticism, the acceptance by the ecclesiastical community of its ideals of asceticism and maximalism as ideals toward which even people in the world must strive according to their strength, compelled the 'secular' churches to imitate the monastic peculiarities and 'rubrics' of worship, and also made monasticism the centre of liturgical influence. On the other hand, mystical theology opened up to monasticism the world of ceremonial, the world of mysteriological liturgical piety, and moreover turned this world into a natural expression of the 'sacrament' of monastic life. Within the Byzantine synthesis the original 'emphases' and categories of both contrasting liturgical traditions were interwoven and their contradictions removed. 'Mysteriological' piety acquired an ingrafting of 'ascetical' piety, since asceticism remained an indispensable step in the mystical interpretation of monasticism. But then the ascetical, almost a-liturgical view of worship which we have found in early monastic texts also 'absorbed' the mysteriological moment. From the Areopagite down to Cabasilas we see the elaboration of one and the same theology—a theology simultaneously monastic (ascetical) and mysteriological in its whole spirit and movement. This theology was the determining force in the development and completion of the Byzantine *Typicon*.

We have an inadequate knowledge of the path of this development and synthesis, but surely it is not by chance that the Orthodox liturgical tradition has kept a memory of the two main sources of the *Typicon*, in the Ordos of the Palestine monastery of St. Sabas and the Studite monastery in Constantinople. We must conclude that these monastic centres were the places where the 'synthesis' which had been developing in various places and in various ways found its final expression and was, so to speak, 'codified.' The investigations of Mansvetov, Dimitrievsky, Skaballanovich and others show clearly, however, that neither the St. Sabas nor the Studite monastery can be regarded as the place where the *Typicon* was actually created. Furthermore, under no circumstances does either the Jerusalem or the Studite tradition represent a wholly independent line of development in the growth of the *Typicon*. 'In the first period (before the appearance of complete transcripts of the Ordo) there were certainly copies of Ordos which have not come down to us,' writes Mansvetov.[111] Yet the similarity of the Jerusalem and Studite Ordos is plain to any one who has studied their manuscript tradition. Thus we are speaking here first of centres of codification and elaboration of the Ordo; and second, of centres which due to their position and the intensity of the liturgical work which they undertook exercised a very great liturgical influence upon the Church at large.

Both chronologically and in the light of the role it played in the work of completing the synthesis of the Ordo, first place should be given to the centre in Palestine. According to a late but firm tradition it was precisely in Palestine that the Ordo was drawn up—'The ritual, rite and order, as they were given to us and authorized for us by the holy Fathers in the monasteries, that is, by Euphemius the Great, St. Sabas, Theodosius the Cenobite and Gerasimos of Jordan, who was ministered to by a wild beast, by Chariton the Confessor and Cyprian the Hermit, such an Ordo as this did the great patriarch Sophronius write down for the generations to come. But when the barbarians burned down the great monastery of St. Sabas and the manuscript written by blessed Sophronius was sacrificed to the flames, the most wise John of Damascus, like an industrious bee, once again transmitted this tradition to his descendants, and it has been preserved thus to the present day.'[112] Simeon of Thessalonica gives us an identical version of this tradition of the Ordo. 'Our divine father Sabas wrote out the

Ordo, having received it from St. Euphemius and St. Theoktitus, and they had received it from those before them and the Confessor Khariton. But when this Ordo was destroyed, then our father Sophronius, who is among the blessed, industriously wrote it out, and then after him our divine father John of Damascus, expert in theology, restored it and copied it out.' [113] As Skaballanovich remarks, 'Of course it is possible to question the reliability of all the details of this genealogy, but for it to have arisen at all there must be a kernel of historical truth lying at its basis.' [114] Its historical probability lies primarily in the fact that in all the fragmentary evidence which has come down to us from all monastic traditions it is precisely the Palestine tradition which has from the beginning been connected especially with the 'secular' worship, and which has therefore been most open to the movement toward synthesis. The majority of Palestinian monasteries were located not far from Jerusalem, and we know how famous the Holy City was for its liturgical splendour and influence after its restoration as a centre of Christianity during the reign of Constantine. 'The Catechetical Instructions' of Cyril of Jerusalem and the descriptions of Sylvia show that Jerusalem was in fact one of the main centres in the rise of that historical–mysteriological worship which became central in the 'secular' layer of the Ordo. Sylvia refers to the participation of the monks in the solemn services of worship in Jerusalem. Later memorials indicate the existence of a special monastery of 'vessel-bearers' near Episcopia. 'It is to be noted,' Skaballanovich remarks, 'that the role of "vessel-bearers" (*spudei*) in the *Typicon* of the Holy Sepulchre of 1122 is exactly the same as that described in the *Pilgrim-age of Sylvia.*' From Cassian we know that the distinctive feature of Palestinian monasticism was the similarity of its Ordo to that of the secular churches, especially in what touched on the hours for and structure of prayer.[115] Thus it is in Palestine, in the immediate vicinity of the sacred and holy centre of the entire Christian world, indeed in its liturgical centre, that we may properly see the beginning of the synthesis in the Ordo. This conclusion is supported by the unanimous agreement of all Byzantine liturgiologists. It may also be assumed that in one of its first stages the synthesis was accepted in the Studite monastery of Constantinople. The liturgical connection between Constantinople and Jerusalem is beyond doubt. There is also a very probable dependence of the '*Spudaion* Monastery,' founded in Constantinople in the fifth century, on the Jerusalem monastery which served as its proto-type. Finally, there are grounds for believing that the 'vessel-bearers' of Constantinople were closely associated with the rise of the Studite monastery. It is more than probable therefore that the Jerusalem 'syn-thesis' was accepted at the Studite Monastery and subjected to revision there, and that it formed the basis for the independent development of the Studite Ordo.[116]

We must take into account also the fact that there was an especially strong note of mysticism in Palestinian monasticism, borne out by the violent controversies over the theology of Origen (in fact over the nature and purpose of the monastic life) in the sixth century (during the lifetime of St. Sabas the Blessed), which led to the condemnation of the Alexandrian Doctor by the fifth ecumenical council. By remaining orthodox after the falling away of Egypt and the East, Palestinian monasticism found itself at the centre of the Christological controversy, and it withstood the attack of monophysitism. It was for just this reason that monasticism in Palestine was especially sensitive to theological interpretations, and moreover open to that mystical and mysteriological concept of monasticism which took form in this period in the eastern provinces of the Empire. When taken together, these conjectures do give some real support to and offer at least a general explanation for the tradition which connects the beginning of the *Typicon*—the general 'rule of prayer' for the whole Church—with the Palestinian and indeed the most important of all Palestinian monasteries.[117]

No copy of this original Jerusalem Ordo has come down to us. But besides the already mentioned tradition concerning the liturgical work of Sabas, Sophronius and John of Damascus, later compilers of the *Typicon* also testify to the fact that copies did exist. Nikon of Montenegro (11th cent.) writes: 'The various Studite and Jerusalem *Typicons* were simplified and collated . . .' He also quotes directly from the 'Ancient Secret *Typicon* of Jerusalem' found by him 'near Spas in Laodicea,' and this *Typicon* was used by him as the basis for his own work as a compiler.[118] The author of the short 'Description of the Studite Monastery' and St. Athanasius of Athos also mention the existence of numerous written Ordos before the appearance of complete texts of the Studite and Jerusalem *Typicons*.[119] On the other hand there can be no doubt that all these Ordos which have been lost to us were variations of one common Ordo, i.e., various recensions of a 'synthesis' which was already basically complete. This is clear from the fact that the differences and disagreements between them which are mentioned by later compilers touch only on details and minor points. The common structure and rite of each individual service is beyond all question. Thus the basic synthesis of the Ordo can be regarded as complete by the ninth century.

The second period in the history of this synthesis—the era of its final 'crystallization'—begins with the 'triumph of orthodoxy' at the end of the iconoclastic crisis. This has been an epoch of conservative approach to ancient traditions, and its characteristic feature has been the striving for uniformity, for an Ordo considered no longer merely as a norm but as a 'law' worked out in every detail, and as far as possible providing answers to all 'perplexing questions.' This era has been well documented. A. A. Dimitrievsky has collected and described the texts from this period, and his remarkable work is still the major if not the only tool for any one working in the field of the history of Byzantine worship. Here the original synthesis (what we may call the early Jerusalem–Palestine Ordo) is set before us in two basic 'recensions.' These are the Jerusalem (in the narrow sense of the term) and the Studite Ordos. We are well-informed about the development and crystallization of the Jerusalem 'recension' of the synthesis, first of all by Nikon of Black Mountain, Abbot of the Monastery of St. Simeon of the Wondrous Mount, not far from Antioch.[120] In his canonical regulations and *Tacticon* he 'made a start,' in the words of Mansvetov, 'on the tremendous task which the Ordo of that period had set before liturgiologists.' [121] But it is important to emphasize that this task consisted in the comparison and collation of different variations of essentially the same Ordo, in the 'correction of its weak points and the introduction of uniformity.' It was not creative theological work, but rather the business of compilation. Nikon is very characteristic of his time in his desire for complete uniformity, in his interest in 'rubrical details.' It is also possible to trace the process of the unification and formulation of the Jerusalem Ordo in the *Typicons* described by Dimitrievsky. His earliest complete texts date from the twelfth century—and in them the final development of the Ordo (in the second, 'legal' sense of this word) is completely clear. It is different from our modern *Typicon* only in a few details. These details (e.g., the chanting of 'Since ye are baptized in Christ' at Pentecost, the liturgical similarity of the Christmas fast with Lent, etc.) are sometimes remarkable and interesting, in that they either explain the obscurities in our modern practice or bear witness to the existence of certain liturgical tendencies which have disappeared and been forgotten. But the development which can be traced through these *Typicons* no longer involves the structure of the Ordo as a whole.

As for the Studite recension, its success and widespread distribution is explained by the importance of the Studite Monastery in the capital in the post-iconoclastic epoch. Many Byzantine texts bear witness to the intensiveness of the liturgical and rubrical work begun as early as the lifetime of Theodore, and continued under his successors. The Studite tradition is especially notable for its hymnographical creativity—above all for the development of the Lenten *Triodion*. As for the Ordo in the proper sense of the word, here again stress was laid on the harmonizing of ancient Ordos, on liturgical 'uniformity.' The Studite Ordo is also the 'synthesis of a synthesis' and its difference from the Jerusalem recension is explained, first, by the unique position of the Studite Monastery itself, by the adaptation of the Ordo to specific external circumstances (e.g., the elimination of Vigils and Little Vespers—a distinctive feature of the Studite tradition noted by all historians). It should be observed here that although the sphere of influence and acceptance of the Studite Ordo was very wide (Dimitrievsky traces nine of his western manuscripts to Greek monasteries in southern Italy), and although it 'took the lead' over the Jerusalem Ordo for a long time, not one reliable copy of it has come down to us. The Ordos which we possess were written for specific monasteries (the so-called 'Wardens' Ordos'—or 'Collated Ordos'—see, for example, the remarkable *Typicon* of the patriarch Alexios the Studite, compiled for the Monastery of the Assumption in Constantinople),[122] and they reflect the 'adaptation' of the Studite Ordo to local situations. 'The pure Studite Ordo has yet to be found,' writes Dimitrievsky, 'and in the meantime, without a definite and clear knowledge of what the Studite analysis was like or what were its distinctive peculiarities, further work on the historical development of our *Typicon* is impossible.' [123] But here as in the Jerusalem recension enough is known to be certain, first, of the basic structural identity of the Studite and Jerusalem Ordos (demonstrating that both are variations of the original Byzantine synthesis), and second, of the completed state of this Ordo in the age of the texts which have come down to us. The development of the Ordo in the time since then, no matter how important or interesting it may be from various viewpoints, reflects no change either in structure or in its expression of the 'rule of prayer.' The history of the development of the Ordo as such is ended. The process that follows is a process of 'filling up' this Ordo with elements previously lacking (new hymns, memorials, etc.), and the refining of 'rubrics.' Characteristic of this process was the liturgical work of the patriarch Philotheus Coccinus (14th cent.), and the growth of the so-called 'Chapters of Mark.' [124] In the first case we have an example of the completion of the Ordo by the addition of rules obviously required by the context but missing from the text. The rubric on censing, the clarification of the rules concerning the vesting of the sacred ministers, the differentiation of festal from simple services : these are the kinds of problems dealt with in Philotheus' *Diataksis*. They clearly grow out of the view of the Ordo as a precise law, out of the whole spirit of the late Byzantine striving for complete uniformity. 'The Chapters of Mark,' which form an imposing part of the modern

Typicon, show the very characteristic concern of late Byzantine liturgiologists to define with utmost exactitude the principles for combining different cycles in one service. (Cf. the endless variations in the combining of the Feast of the Annunciation with the Paschal cycle.) But as in the case of Patriarch Philotheus the revisions touch on details only. The Ordo as a whole is regarded as complete and unchangeable.

What are the principles underlying the Ordo? This is the question which we must try to answer in the final pages of our present work. In our approach to this question we have had occasion to speak at length about certain things in the development of the Ordo which might seem to be of small value. Side by side with the true development and discovery of the Church's *lex orandi* there has been an obscuring of her tradition. We feel that this fact should be admitted and at least some attempt made to explain it, no matter how much this conclusion may run counter to the extraordinarily widespread and blind 'absolutization' of the *Typicon* in all its details which exists throughout the Orthodox Church. What is truly fixed and eternal in this Ordo which has come down to us through such a complicated process, and which includes so many various layers of material? What is its essential nature as the liturgical tradition of the Church, as the 'rule of prayer,' which, according to the Church's teaching, contains and reveals her 'rule of faith'? If we have termed the culmination of this development and building up of layer upon layer a 'synthesis' rather than a hodge-podge, in what way does this synthesis have a creative and determining significance for the future? At a moment when the world in which the Church lives can no longer be called Christian in the sense in which it was Christian from the fourth to the twentieth centuries, this is the only question which really matters. No restoration in history has ever been successful. Only if there is a lack of faith in the Church herself as the source of Life can the traditions of the past be dealt with on the principle 'Let what has been set before us remain for ever!' Tradition for the Church is not the vista of a beautiful past which can be admired in a mood of aesthetically religious nostalgia, but rather a summons and an inspiration. Only a liturgical theology, that is, a detailed study and elucidation of all the elements which form the liturgical tradition of the Church (her Sacraments, cycles, rituals and ceremonies) can provide a true answer to our question. The present work is only a very general introduction to a proposed complete course in liturgical theology. In concluding this introduction we must point to what we are convinced the Ordo shows to be the guide in the study of Orthodox worship.

L

What is absolutely essential for a correct understanding of the general spirit of the Byzantine synthesis is that it was unquestionably formed on the basis of the Church's original rule of prayer, and from this point of view must be accepted as its elaboration and revelation, no matter how well developed are the elements which are alien to this *lex orandi* and which have obscured it. Thus in spite of the strong influence of the mysteriological psychology on the one hand and the ascetical–individualistic psychology on the other, the Ordo as such has remained organically connected with the theology of time which contained its original organizing principle. This theology of time was obscured and eclipsed by 'secondary' layers in the Ordo, but it remained always as the foundation of its inner logic and the principle of its inner unity.

This connection is evident, first, in the correlation (preserved throughout all the changes) of the Eucharist with the liturgy of time or, in other words, in the special place occupied by the Eucharist in the general structure of the Ordo. The Eucharist has its own time, its καιρός, and this time is distinct from the units used to measure the liturgy of time. We have spoken of the ascetical and individualistic modification which occurred in the view of the Eucharist under the influence of monasticism, and of how, in connection with this, the Eucharist was included within the liturgy of time as one of its component offices. But this change was never fully accepted in the Ordo, and in it there is a characteristic ambiguity toward the Eucharist. The lectionary, the setting apart of a relatively small number of non-liturgical days, and a whole series of other rubrics all point to the success of one tendency in this process. Its success can be traced also in the popular acceptance of the so-called 'votive masses,' of the idea that the Eucharist can be subordinated to individual needs. On the other hand if all the rest of the prescriptions of the Ordo are taken together, if one carefully considers their inner logic and also the rite of the Liturgy itself, it can hardly be doubted that the Eucharist has preserved its basic character as the Feast of the Church, as the expression and actualization of her eschatological fullness, as an action which is combined with the liturgy of time and related to it, but precisely by virtue of its ontological difference from it. It is true that the prescriptions concerning the *kairos* of the Eucharist have become a dead letter in modern times. But what is important is that these prescriptions have in fact been preserved, and this means that for those who have been brought up on the 'Byzantine synthesis' they constitute an inviolable part of the liturgical tradition of the Church and are part of her rule of prayer. What else do these prescriptions prove, this whole complicated system of relationships between the Eucharist and time—with its hours, days and cycles—if not that the time of the Eucharist is something special, and that what it expresses in time fulfills time and gives it another standard of measurement. The fundamental meaning of these different prescriptions must be seen in the principle of the incompatibility of the Eucharist with fasting. The Eucharist is not celebrated during Lent. On the strict fast days of the eves of Christmas and Epiphany it is celebrated in the evening, just as the Liturgy of the Presanctified Gifts is celebrated in the evening. The whole complicated system for the transfer of the Christmas and Epiphany eves of fasting to Friday if they happen to fall on Saturday or Sunday expresses the same idea : Saturdays and Sundays, being Eucharistic days, are incompatible with fasting. Obviously what is preserved here in full force is the liturgical concept of fasting as a condition of expectation in the Church herself, related to the Eucharist as the Sacrament of the *Parousia* of the Lord. Even where the Eucharist is thought of as a daily service, it is not simply inserted into the system of daily offices, but preserves its special καιρός depending on the length of the fast, the degree of importance of the commemoration, etc. The meaning of all these prescriptions is clear : the Eucharist must be preceded by a fast or vigil (which is in fact the liturgical expression of fasting, as a station, or *statio, vigilia*), since in this fast or vigil, in this time of expectancy and preparation, time itself is transformed into what it has become in the Church : a time of waiting and preparation for the unending Day of the Kingdom. The entire life of the Christian and the entire earthly life of the Church become a fast in the deepest meaning of this word : they receive their significance and their secret fullness from the ἔσχατον, from the end and fulfilment of time, since everything is connected with this End, everything is judged and illuminated in relation to it. But this 'End' can become a force which transforms life and transmutes 'fasting' into 'joy and triumph' only because it is not something in the future only, the terrifying dissolution of all things, but rather something which has already come, already begun, and is being eternally 'actualized' and 'fulfilled' in the Sacrament of the Church, in the Eucharist. 'We have been fulfilled by thine everlasting life, we have joyfully tasted thine inexhaustible food, which thou has deigned to communicate to us all in the age to come . . .' That same Life will appear at the End which is already in existence, that New Aeon will begin in which we are already participating, that same Lord will appear who is now coming and is with us . . . This rhythm of fast and Eucharist which is perhaps the forgotten and unfulfilled but still obvious and basic principle of the Ordo shows

L*

that at the foundation of the Church's liturgical life there is still that same unchanging and inexhaustible experience of eschatology, the experience of the Church as new life in new time existing within this old world and its time for the express purpose of its salvation and renewal.

Thus too in the daily cycle, which is the basis of the liturgy of time, the Ordo or structure of its services can be understood only in relation to the theology of time which they contain and express. Outside it they become an inexplicable, arbitrary sequence of diverse elements connected in no way other than by a 'formal' law. The Christian theology of time is clearly expressed in Vespers and Matins, in which four themes follow one another in a definite sequence. In Vespers there is the theme of Creation as a beginning (the preparatory psalm 'Praise the Lord, O my soul'), the theme of sin and fall ('Lord I have cried . . .'), the theme of salvation and the coming into the world of the Son of God ('O Gentle Radiance'), and the theme of the End ('Lord, now lettest thou thy servant . . .'). The same themes form the order for Matins, only in the opposite order. The daily cycle is a kind of constant contemplation of the world and the time within which the Church dwells, and of those ways of evaluating the world and its time which were manifested by the *Parousia* of the Lord. The note of cosmic thanksgiving, the perception of God's glory in creation, its affirmation as something 'very good,' these insights which come at the beginning of Vespers, followed by the commemoration of the fall of this world, of the indelible mark of separation from God which accompanied it, the relationship of all things to the Light of salvation which has come into and illuminated this world and, finally, the concluding 'thy Kingdom come' of the Lord's prayer—here is the liturgical order of the daily cycle. Each day Christians pray that in and through the Church the time of this world may become the new time for the children of light, may be filled with new life for those whom she has brought to life. And so she 'refers' this day to that which constitutes her own life, to the reality of the Presence which she alone in this world knows, and which she alone is able to reveal.

The Church year, which has been torn away from the theology of time more than all the other liturgical cycles, still preserves the sign of its original and inerradicable connection with this theology in Easter and its year long cycle. No matter how many other Feast Days there are and no matter what they celebrate, they all reflect something of the light of Easter, and it is not by chance or for the sake of an artificial emphasis that the late Byzantine liturgiologists constructed the 'prefestivals' of Christmas and Epiphany—two of the most ancient and important feast days of the Christian year—on the pattern of Holy Week. Whatever is being celebrated, the celebration is fulfilled in the Eucharist, in the commemoration of that Paschal night when before His Sacrifice our Lord bequeathed the Supper of the Kingdom to the Church, in the commemoration of that morning when the new life shone in the world, when the Son of Man had completed His passage to the Father, and when in Him the New Passover had become the Life of men. Each Feast Day is related to that New Time which is celebrated by Easter. Like the Lord's Day in the week, so also Easter each year manifests and 'actuaiizes' that eternal beginning which in the old world appears as an end, but which in the Church signifies an End that has been turned into a Beginning, thereby filling the End with joyous meaning. Easter is an eschatological feast in the most exact and deepest meaning of this word, because in it we 'recall' the resurrection of Christ as our own resurrection, eternal life as our own life, the fullness of the Kingdom as already possessed. As the beginning and end of the Church year Easter links this eschatological fullness with real time in its yearly form. Life in the world becomes a 'correlative' of the eternal Easter of the New Aeon. Thus Easter reveals the essential nature of every Feast Day, and is in this sense the 'Feast of Feasts.'

Having preserved the eschatological theology of time as its foundation and principle of formulation, the Byzantine synthesis has also preserved the ecclesiological significance of the Church's 'rule of prayer.' No symbolical explanation, no mysteriological piety and no ascetical individualism could obscure completely the unchanging essential nature of worship as the Church's act of self-revelation, self-fulfilment, self-realization. It must be frankly admitted that in our modern 'liturgical piety' this essential nature has been very poorly understood. Nowhere is the need to 'unfetter' the meaning of the Ordo so apparent, nowhere is the need to rediscover the meaning of the Ordo's now dead language so urgent. The Ordo was fettered and became the private possession of the *typikonshckiki* precisely because the ecclesiological key to its understanding and acceptance had been lost and forgotten. It is only necessary to read over the 'rubrics' and prescriptions with new eyes, and to meditate on the structure of the Ordo, in order to understand that its major significance lies in its presentation of worship as the service of the new people of God. From the unchanging liturgical 'we' of all liturgical texts to the most complicated rite for an All-night Vigil, with its vesting and unvesting of the clergy, its shifting of the centre of the service from the altar to the middle of the church, its censings, processions, bows, etc., everything that is important and basic in the Ordo is a Byzantine 'transposition' of the original meaning of worship as the corporate act and 'fulfilment' of the Church. From the standpoint of 'eternal' value and inner consistency certain details of this transposition can be called into question; one can distinguish between what is local (and often accepted as 'universal') and what is universal (and often accepted as 'local'); but it is impossible to deny that in the overall design of the Ordo, in its essential and eternal logic, it was, is and always will be the Ordo of the *Church's* worship, a living and vital revelation of her doctrine about herself, of her own self-understanding and self-definition.

Finally, the ultimate and permanent value of the Ordo, a value which determines the whole complex path of its Byzantine development, is the Church's 'rule of faith' which is revealed and imprinted within it. The theology of time and ecclesiology which in some way define the very essence of the Church's cult have been preserved in the Ordo in spite of the various pressures exerted upon it, and the revelation in and through the Ordo of the Church's dogmatic teaching must be regarded as a genuine product of Byzantine Christianity. The Byzantine period of history still awaits a proper evaluation in the mind of the Church. It can hardly be doubted that the development of dogmatic thought went hand in hand with a weakening of ecclesiological consciousness. The 'Christian world' on the one hand and the 'desert' on the other obscured the reality of the Church, which had come to be understood more as the source of a beneficient sanction, as the dispenser of grace, than as the people of God and the new Israel, a chosen people, a royal priesthood. This eclipse of ecclesiological consciousness was reflected in liturgical piety, in the forms and the view of the cult. But what constitutes the permanent value of this period is that in Byzantine worship the Councils of Nicaea, Constantinople, Ephesus and Chalcedon were not simply 'transposed' from the language of philosophy into the language of sacred liturgical poetry; they were revealed, fathomed, understood, manifested in all their significance.

On this note we may suspend rather than terminate our analysis of the problem of the Ordo. The view presented here of the theological problem of the Ordo and its development can find its application and 'justification' only in a liturgical theology in the true meaning of this term, i.e., in a theological apprehension of worship itself. The present work is offered simply as an introduction. Its goal has been to define the perspective and to mark out basic guide lines. If we are right in our view that what actually determines the whole liturgical and devotional life of the Church is the Ordo, that by its very nature it contains the theological meaning of this life and therefore ought to be subjected to theological investigation; if, furthermore, we are right in

THE BYZANTINE SYNTHESIS

saying that such a study of the Ordo and of the cult which it regulates is impossible without at least some preliminary understanding of its historical formulation; and if, finally, we are right in asserting that the absence of both these conditions (extending now over many centuries) only underlines the urgency of the problem of the Ordo in our own time, then this introduction will perhaps have served some good purpose.

FOOTNOTES TO CHAPTER FOUR

[1] Skaballanovich, op. cit., p. 318.

[2] J. M. Hanssens, *Nature et Genèse de l'Office*, p. 58.

[3] Baumstark, op. cit., pp. 118ff.; cf. L. Petit, article 'Antiphones' in *Dict. Arch. Lit. chrét.*, I, 2461–88.

[4] cf. J. A. Jungmann, 'Beitraege zur Geschichte der Gebetsliturgie,' in *Zeitschr. f. Kathol. Theol.*, 72, 1950, pp. 223–6.

[5] cf. Baumstark, op. cit., pp. 60ff.; Skaballanovich, op. cit., pp. 88ff.

[6] Baumstark, op. cit., pp. 69ff.

[7] E. Wellecz, *A History of Byzantine Music and Hymnography,* Oxford University Press, 1949, p. 26; also Pitra, op. cit., pp. 38ff.

[8] Wellecz, op. cit., p. 29.

[9] Baumstark, op. cit., pp. 37ff.

[10] Wellecz, op. cit., pp. 33–5.

[11] ibid., pp. 33, 273.

[12] cf. F. E. Warren, *Liturgy of the Ante-Nicene Church,* London, S.P.C.K., pp. 374ff.

[13] Dugmore, op. cit., p. 57.

[14] Skaballanovich, op. cit., pp. 89ff.

[15] Thus, during Lent when the celebration of the Eucharist is not permitted on weekdays, Saturday always preserves its liturgical character.

[16] Skaballanovich, op. cit., pp. 120ff., 264ff.

[17] cf. Paul Cotton, *From Sabbath to Sunday: a Study in Early Christianity,* Bethlehem Pa., 1933.

[18] cf. the texts of Irenaeus of Lyons (P.G. 8, 1012), Origen (P.G. 12, 749); 'Origen's picture of the Sabbath . . . is strangely reminiscent of the best rabbinic teaching on the subject' (Dugmore, op. cit., p. 31); in the West there was no fast on Saturday before the third century.

[19] Quoted by H. M. Hyatt, *The Church of Abyssinia,* p. 292.

[20] *Didache,* 8; Clement of Alex., *Stromat.,* 7, 12; Origen, *In Levit.* 10; *Didascalia,* 5, 13; *Can. Hyppolit.,* 157.

[21] cf. H. Lietzmann, *Hist. de l'Eglise ancienne,* Vol. II, Paris, Pagot, 1937, p. 132.

[22] cf. A. Jaubert, *La Date de la Cène,* Paris, Gabalda, 1957.

[23] Warren, op. cit., pp. 101ff.

[24] Basil the Great, *Epis.* 93, P.G. 32, 484–5.

[25] Socrates, *Hist. Eccles.,* 5, 22.

[26] *De Orat.,* 19.

[27] Skaballanovich, op. cit., p. 122.

[28] *Testament,* 1, 22.

[29] On the development of the pre-Easter fast cf. Baumstark, op. cit., pp. 203ff.; A. Chavasse, 'La Structure du Carême et les lectures des messes quadragésimales dans la liturgie romaine' in *Maison-Dieu,* 31, 1952, pp. 76–119; McArthur, op. cit., pp. 114ff.; J. Daniélou, 'Le symbolisme des Quarante Jours,' in *Maison-Dieu,* 31, 1952.

[30] *Didache,* 7.

INTRODUCTION TO LITURGICAL THEOLOGY

[31] Justin Martyr, *1st Apol.*, 61.
[32] Quoted in Skaballanovich, p. 124.
[33] cf. J. Daniélou, 'Les Quatre-Temps de Septembre et la fête des Tabernacles' in *Maison-Dieu*, 46, 1956, pp. 114–36; criticism in A. Jaubert, op. cit., p. 114.
[34] P. Carrington, *The Primitive Christian Calendar*, Cambridge, 1940, p. 44; E. C. Selwyn, 'The Feast of Tabernacles, Epiphany and Baptism' in *Journal of Theology*, 1911, pp. 225–36.
[35] Daniélou, 'Les Quatre-Temps,' p. 117.
[36] Carrington, op. cit., pp. 23–31; cf. criticism of this theory by W. D. Davies, 'Reflections on Archbp. Carrington's *The Primitive Christian Calendar*' in *The Background of the New Testament and its Eschatology*, Cambridge, 1956, pp. 124–53.
[37] Jaubert, op. cit., pp. 92ff.
[38] ibid., pp. 105ff.
[39] Daniélou, 'Les Quatre-Temps,' p. 124.
[40] ibid., p. 127.
[41] A. A. Dimitrievsky, *Opisanie liturgicheskhikh rukopisey khranyashchikhsya v bibliotekakh pravoslavnago vostoka* (A Description of Liturgical Manuscripts Preserved in the Libraries of the Orthodox East), Vol. I, 'Tipik' (Typicon), Kiev, 1895; also N. F. Krasnoseltsev, *Tipik Sv. Sofii v Konstantinople 9-go veka* (The Typicon of St. Sophia in Constantinople in the Ninth Century), Odessa, 1892.
[42] *Pisania Sv. Otsov i uchiteley Tserkvi otnosyashchikhsya k istolkovaniu pravoslavnago bogosluzheniya* (The Writings of the Fathers and Teachers of the Church Pertaining to the Interpretation of Orthodox worship), Vol. 2, St. Petersburg, 1856, pp. 402ff., 155, 628ff.
[43] A. Baumstark, 'Das Typikon der Patmoshandschrift 266 und die altkonstantinopolitanische Gottesdienstordnung' in *Jahrbuch Liturgiewissenschaft*, Vol. VI, 98–111.
[44] *Pisania Sv. Otsov*, p. 470.
[45] I. Mansvetov, 'O pesnennom posledovanii' ('On the Sung Service') in *Pribavlenie k tvoreniam Sv. Otsov* (Supplement to the works of the Holy Fathers), 1880, pp. 752–97.
[46] ibid., p. 752.
[47] cf. Wellecz, op. cit., pp. 119ff.
[48] cf. M. Setton, *The Christian Attitude Towards the Emperor in the Fourth Century*, New York, 1951; Dix, op. cit., pp. 397ff; J. A. Jungmann, *Missarum Solemnia*, Vol. I, Paris, Aubier, 1951, pp. 67ff.; H. Leclercq, 'Adoration' in *Dict. Arch. Lit. chrét.*, I, 539–46; E. Bishop, 'Ritual Splendour' in R. H. Connolly, *The Liturgical Homilies of Narsai*, Cambridge, 1909, pp. 88–91.
[49] A. Alfoeldi, 'Die Ausgestaltung der monarchischen Zeremoniells am roemischen Kaiserhof,' *Mitteilungen der Deutsc. archaeolog. Inst. Rom.*, 49, 1934, pp. 1–118; Wellecz, op. cit., pp. 86ff.; H. J. W. Tillyard, 'The Acclamations of Emperors in Byzantine Ritual,' in *The Annual of the British School in Athens*, 18, 1911–12, pp. 239–60.
[50] Wellecz, op. cit., pp. 32, 119ff.
[51] Pitra, op. cit., p. 25.
[52] A. Baumstark, 'Festbrevier und Kirchenjahr der Syrischen Jacobiten,' *Geschichte und Kultur der Altertums*, 3, 1910; P. Maas, 'Das Kontakion,' *Byz. Zeitschr.*, 1910, pp. 290ff.
[53] cf. C. Emereau, *St. Ephrem le Syrien*, Paris, 1919, pp. 97ff.; also E. Wellecz, 'Melito's Homily on the Passion: An investigation into the sources of Byzantine Hymnology,' in *Journal Theological Studies*, 44, 1943, pp. 41ff.
[54] Wellecz, *Byz. Hymnography*, p. 129.
[55] *The Heavenly Hierarchy*, 2, 4.
[56] *Pisania Sv. Otsov*, p. 472.

[57] ibid., pp. 404–5.
[58] ibid., p. 405.
[59] Pitra, op. cit., p. 45.
[60] Besides the names of Wellecz and Pitra, see also: P. Maas, 'Fruhbyzantinische Kirchenpoesie,' in *Kleine Texte*, 52/53; A. Baumstark, 'Te Deum und eine Gruppe griechischer Abendhymnen,' *Orient chrétien*, 34, pp. 1–26; J. Jeannin, 'Octoechos,' *Dict. Arch. Lit. chrét.*, XII, 1889; E. Mioni, *Romano il Melode*, Turino, 1937 (cf. bibliography in this book).
[61] *Pisania Sv. Otsov*, p. 485.
[62] O. Casel, 'Art und Sinn der aeltesten Christlichen Osterfeier,' *Jahrbuch f. Liturgiewiss.*, 14, 1938, 8, 58.
[63] J. Daniélou, *Origines Chrétiennes* (mimeographed lectures), p. 73.
[64] *Sermon on Epiphany*, P.G. 36, 349.
[65] P. de Ghellink, *Pour l'histoire du mot sacramentum*, Louvain, 1924, p. 17.
[66] Baumstark, *Liturgie Comparée*, p. 171.
[67] Botte, *Les Origines*, pp. 78–9.
[68] Baumstark, *Liturgie*, p. 200.
[69] McArthur, op. cit., pp. 77ff., 141ff; J. W. Tyrer, *Historical Survey of Holy Week*, London, S.P.C.K., 1932, pp. 31ff.
[70] cf. J. B. Ferreres, *Ephemerides theol. Lovaniensis*, 5, pp. 623ff.; A. Baumstark, *Oriens Christianus*, 3, 11, 1936, p. 113.
[71] cf. M. Jugie, 'La première fête mariale en Orient et en Occident: l'Avent primitif,' *Echos d'Orient*, 22, pp. 153–81; Baumstark, *Liturgie*, pp. 199ff.; B. Botte, 'La première fête mariale de la liturgie romaine,' *Ephem. liturg.*, 1933, pp. 425–30; 1935, pp. 61–264.
[72] Baumstark, *Liturgie*, pp. 202ff.; E. Flicoteaux, 'Notre Dame dans l'année liturgique,' *Maison-Dieu*, 38, 1954, pp. 95–121.
[73] F. Cabrol, 'Assumption,' *Dict. Arch. Lit. chrét.*, 1; Baumstark, *Liturgie*, p. 202.
[74] P. de Puniet, 'La Fête de la Nativité de la Vierge,' in *Vie et Arts Liturgiques*, 1926, pp. 481–9.
[75] H. Leclercq, 'Présentation de Marie,' *Dict. Arch. Lit. chrét.*, 14, 2, 1729–31; E. Bouvy, 'Présentation de la Vierge,' *Bessarione*, 1897, pp. 552–62; S. Vailhé, 'La Fête de la Présentation,' *Echos d'Orient*, 5, 1901, pp. 221–4.
[76] Baumstark, *Liturgie*, p. 196.
[77] ibid., p. 195.
[78] H. Delehaye, *Synaxarium Ecclesiae Constantinopolitanae e codice Sirmondiano nunc Berolensi . . . Propylaeum ad Acta Sanctorum Novembris*, Brussels, Bollandistes, 1902; P. Peeters, *Le Tréfonds Oriental de l'Hagiographie Byzantine*, Brussels, Bollandistes, 1950; R. Aigrain, *L'Hagiographie*, Paris, Bloud et Gay, 1953.
[79] Baumstark, *Liturgie*, p. 192.
[80] H. Delehaye, *Sanctus: Essai sur le culte des Saints dans l'Antiquité*, Brussels, Bollandistes, 1927, pp. 2–73.
[81] cf. Grabar, *Martyrium*, I, pp. 28ff.
[82] Delehaye, *Les Origines*, pp. 40ff.
[83] Grabar, op. cit., p. 349.
[84] Delehaye, *Les Origines*, pp. 461ff.; and his *Les Légendes Hagiographiques*, second edition, Paris, pp. 222–32.
[85] Delehaye, *Les Origines*, p. 463.
[86] ibid., p. 139.
[87] Sermon 285:5, P.L. 38, 1295.
[88] Quoted in Delehaye, *Les Origines*, pp. 137–8.
[89] R. Aigrain, *L'Hagiographie*, pp. 121–2; cf. H. Delehaye, *Les passions des martyrs et les genres littéraires*, Brussels, Bollandistes, 1921.
[90] cf. Grabar, *Martyrium*, II, pp. 343ff.
[91] Skaballanovich, *Typikon*, p. 231.

[92] Quoted in Skaballanovich, pp. 239ff.
[93] Skaballanovich, *Typikon,* p. 243.
[94] Cassian, *Instit.,* 2, 5.
[95] ibid., 2, 7.
[96] Quoted in Skaballanovich, p. 243.
[97] For details see Skaballanovich, pp. 202ff.
[98] *Orientalia Christiana Periodica,* 13, 1–2 (Miscellanea Guillaume de Jerphanion I), pp. 282–98.
[99] cf. J. Pargoire, *L'Eglise Byzantine de 527 à 847,* Paris, Gabalda, 1923, p. 339.
[100] *Epis. to Magnesians,* 9.
[101] *Contra Celsum,* 8, 22–3.
[102] cf. Pitra, *L'Hymnographie,* pp. 43ff.
[103] ibid., p. 43.
[104] Skaballanovich, p. 418.
[105] cf. A. P. Dobroklonski, *Prep. Feodor, Ispovednik i Igumen Studisky* (St. Theodore, Confessor and Abbot of Studion), Vol. I, Odessa, 1913.
[106] Mansi, *Ampliss. Concil. Collectio,* 8, 1007–18.
[107] Skaballanovich, p. 258.
[108] *In Matt.* 68, 70.
[109] Skaballanovich, p. 221.
[110] ibid., p. 261; cf. Pargoire, op. cit., pp. 210ff.
[111] Mansvetov, op. cit., p. 61.
[112] Quoted by Skaballanovich, p. 248.
[113] *On Divine Prayer,* Chaps. 302–3.
[114] Skaballanovich, p. 249.
[115] ibid., p. 250.
[116] ibid., pp. 258ff.
[117] cf. A. Ehrhard, 'Das Griechische Kloster Mar-Saba,' *Palaestina Rom. Quartalsch.,* 7, 1893, pp. 32–79.
[118] Skaballanovich, p. 411.
[119] Mansvetov, pp. 61–2.
[120] cf. Mansvetov, pp. 187ff.
[121] ibid., p. 192.
[122] cf. Mansvetov, pp. 103ff.
[123] Dimitrievsky, op. cit., p. 143.
[124] cf. Mansvetov, pp. 216ff.